# GENDER VIOLENCE IN RUSSIA

# GENDER VIOLENCE IN RUSSIA

*The Politics of Feminist Intervention*

JANET ELISE JOHNSON

Indiana University Press   Bloomington and Indianapolis

This book is a publication of

Indiana University Press
601 North Morton Street
Bloomington, IN 47404-3797 USA

http://iupress.indiana.edu

*Telephone orders*   800-842-6796
*Fax orders*   812-855-7931
*Orders by e-mail*   iuporder@indiana.edu

The paper used in this publication meets the minimum requirements of American National Standard for Information Sciences— Permanence of Paper for Printed Library Materials, ANSI Z39.48-1984.

Manufactured in the United States of America
Interior design and composition by BW&A Books, Inc.

*Library of Congress Cataloging-in-Publication Data*
Johnson, Janet Elise.
Gender violence in Russia : the politics of feminist intervention /
Janet Elise Johnson.
p. cm.
Includes bibliographical references and index.
ISBN 978-0-253-32593-8 (cloth : alk. paper) —
ISBN 978-0-253-22074-5 (pbk. : alk. paper)
1. Women—Violence against—Russia (Federation). 2. Family violence—
Russia (Federation). 3. Sex crimes—Russia (Federation). I. Title.
HV6250.4.W65J658 2009
362.83—dc22
2008037050

1 2 3 4 5 14 13 12 11 10 09

*To all who stand in opposition to gender violence*

# CONTENTS

# PREFACE: CAN INTERVENTION HELP WOMEN?

In 2006, at the height of President Putin's campaign to dominate nongovernmental organizations (NGOs), the European Union sponsored a conference on Russian civil society. On the surface, the event seemed woman-friendly, perhaps even feminist. Held in Finland—celebrating its first century of women suffrage and having a critical mass of women parliamentarians—the conference began with greetings from Finland's female president. On that first day, there were several high-profile speeches by women about women. On the second day, there were workshops on women's organizations, women's political participation, and the question of whether intervention can help women live free from gender violence. It was at this latter workshop that I had been invited to present the findings in this book. Overall, women speakers constituted half the total speakers and half the attendees.

This EU conference illustrates just how much women's organizing and gender violence had become important issues for international organizations by the middle of the first decade of the new millennium. While violence against women had been first highlighted in Russia by North American feminist activists, it was now an official European focus and was articulated in a transnational language of women's human rights. A transnational consensus that gender violence is a problem worth substantial attention—what I shorthand in this book as a global feminist consensus—had emerged by the mid 1990s. The conference also suggests why the issue of gender violence in Russia requires the lens of foreign intervention. Although there was interest among late Soviet feminists in these issues and many Russian activists have now made the issue their own, international donors, transnational feminists, human rights activists, and even the George W. Bush administration had concentrated attention on gender violence in the 1990s and early 2000s.

The EU conference's focus on women's organizing and gender violence also offers a window into the promise of foreign intervention for Russian women. Transnational activism and funding for women's organizations generated a women's crisis center movement. Funding for awareness raising, for training of law enforcement, and for legislative reform—often with the support of local activists—helped to raise the issues of domestic violence and trafficking in women to the Russian policy agenda. By the first few years of the new millennium, new laws had been passed, and the Russian government appeared poised to take more responsibility to address violence against women. Considering the weakness of Russia's civil society and the history of mostly ignoring the problem, this moment was remarkable, suggesting the potential for the gradual and deep changes required for meaningful reform of the Russian response to gender violence.

Peering deeper into this EU conference, however, uncovers a more insidious reality. The most prominent participants, such as Marc Franco, the head of the European Commission's delegation to Russia, and Sergei Markov, an official from Putin's appointed Public Chamber, were men. In this period of EU expansion into the former Soviet bloc, the high-stakes political game surrounding EU-Russian relations remains male. Moreover, their language revealed how superficial women's inclusion really was. For example, the male director of the European Union–Russia Center in Belgium explained the new reluctance of Europeans to send funds to Russian NGOs by suggesting that one "can't just give money to a beautiful blonde Tanya on a train." Like other metaphors deployed at the conference that were gendered but portrayed as universally applicable, this one depicted the donors as heterosexual men interested in exoticized Russian women, leaving no role for the dedicated women activists I examine here.

Explicit sexism was also present in the more casual social gatherings surrounding the conference. Later the first evening, at an unofficial gathering of mostly Russian women activists, one of Putin's *siloviki*—a special forces veteran—came up behind me, put his arm around my shoulders, and asked if this was "sexual harassment." As is common in the Russian press, this was a joke made about American women and their sexual unavailability. Following an animated conversation about the ultranationalist and openly misogynist Russian parliamentarian Vladimir Zhirinovsky by the women in the gathering, this *silovik* proposed a toast for us to find a "man who takes a long time to climax, that brings such relief to a woman, that it will take your minds off this Zhirinovsky." I had heard similarly sexist comments at a 2002 conference on women's organizing in St. Petersburg. It seems that the more that women's personhood was asserted, the more that women's bodies and sexuality were invoked and their voice and rights marginalized.

The implicit marginalization of women from the higher-level political dealings and the explicit sexism expressed through these comments about Tanyas and orgasms at this transnational conference illustrates the obstacles that have always faced activists combating gender violence. Even ostensibly woman-friendly Nordic governments have remained resistant to the more radical claims of women's rights to bodily integrity and sexual autonomy. After the attacks on the World Trade Center and the Pentagon in 2001, many states have paradoxically been even more reluctant to circumscribe masculinity and violence even as they assert more concern about gender violence. In the United States, the Bush administration abused the rhetoric of women's rights in the service of increasing male power, for example, by justifying the war in Afghanistan as protecting women. In Russia, activism against gender violence had met a nationalist and sexist brick wall. At the end of Putin's two terms in office, as an underexamined impact of his preference for *siloviki* loyalists, there was a renewed sense of male dominance and new acceptance of locker room talk in public places. By the end of the first decade of the new millennium, the opportunity for real reform of gender violence policy seems to have vanished.

## The Argument

The central question of this book came from the more hopeful moment, asking whether foreign intervention in the name of women works. Looking at the period of intense foreign intervention, the book considers what happens when Westerners bring attention to an issue ignored by a state such as Russia. Although we are still far from knowing what policies and practices are most effective at eradicating violence, we can ask whether interventions at least achieve the objectives that transnational feminists seemed to have agreed upon: to foster women's mobilization and activism, to cultivate a new public awareness of violence against women, and to shift policy and practice toward recognizing violence against women as a human rights violation. To address these questions, I compare various types of intervention into Russian gender violence politics and policymaking from the early 1990s to the middle of the first decade of the new millennium.

The findings suggest the possibility for some success. Regrettably, the least coercive interventions—the alliance between transnational feminists and human rights advocates to monitor, blame, and shame the authorities for their dismal response to gender violence—are insufficient, at best leading to superficial changes. But, given already-existing local interest in the issues, the Russian case suggests that the addition of significant and sustained financial assistance can lead to greater awareness of gender violence and more responsiveness. On the other hand, the most aggressive interventions—by strong states using "sticks," not just "carrots"—may trigger rapid policy reform but prioritize the concerns of the strong state, not of global or local feminists. Most significantly, the study suggests that achieving global feminist objectives is more likely when there is more of a consensus on "best practices" and when transnational feminists and local activists are included in the intervention process. In terms of theorizing feminist change in non-Western contexts, the book advances the argument that, in the aftermath of the Cold War and the global feminist consensus, study of gender politics must blend the traditional political science fields of comparative politics and international relations to elucidate the nexus between the global and the local.

## My Stance

In this book's discussion of intervention into gender violence politics in Russia, I do not mean to discount the enormous efforts made by local activists. On the contrary, considering Russian resistance to feminism and its underdeveloped economic and democratic infrastructures, their accomplishments are astounding, even if not the broad-based, "sisterly" movements that Western feminist observers had hoped to see. Building upon the Soviet legacy of "social responsibility" (*obshchestvennaia otvetstvennost'*), Russian activists seized the new opportunities afforded by liberalization to organize, study, and serve. They have drawn upon local traditions and contemporary experiences to legitimate their work.

Instead, my goal is to approach empirically the many questions raised by Third (and Second) World women about the impact of Western attention to non-Western contexts. Western feminism can make universal claims of women's oppression based on the experiences of some middle-class white women living in the West, erasing the huge global inequalities fostered by the West's foreign and trade policies and stinking of missionary zeal (e.g. Mohanty 1991; Drakulic 1993). Supporting universal human rights carries the weight of an imperialist legacy, as the strongest proponents are the former colonial powers of Europe and North America and their targets are former colonies (Merry 2006a, 226). Advancing the idea that gender violence should be seen as a violation of human rights also brings with it certain modernist assumptions about individualism, autonomy, choice, secularism, bodily integrity, and equality (220–21). I place these questions of power—not just between the West and the target countries, but between states and domestic women's organizations and women and men—as central. Like other recent and important studies that examine women's crisis centers in Russia (Henderson 2003; Sundstrom 2006; Hemment 2007), this book is not a "cautionary claim," but a pragmatic assessment of the complex results of interventions when transnational and local activists take advantage of internationally available financial and normative resources (Funk 2006). Whereas those studies probe the impact of foreign assistance in promoting civil society and democracy (Henderson and Sundstrom), reflecting on questions of cultural imperialism and local agency (Hemment), here the focus is explicitly feminist, specifically concerned with the impact of intervention on women's lives and on the problem of gender violence.

My U.S. standpoint is different than one might expect. I came to Russia undoubtedly as a beneficiary of the U.S. violence-against-women movement and a feminist theorist, but not as a feminist activist. It was my fieldwork in Russia and among Russian feminists, viewed through my own experiences, that brought me to studying such violence. My belief about women's rights to bodily integrity as a basic right in the social contract between the state and its citizens might sound American, but these ideas are now entrenched in international law and repeated by Russian and transnational feminists. Although there is much focus on the United States and the rest of the West in this study, this was driven by their impact as I observed it in Russia. Instead of the assessment being from the vantage point of the West, my analysis reflects calls from Third World feminists to study the global in their local (Naples 2002, 7)—in other words, the view of the West from Russia as seen by a Westerner. Russian activists helped me see both how powerful the U.S. movement and how stingy the U.S. government response have been. For example, with their commitments to what they call "economic violence"—such as a man's preventing an intimate partner from finding a job, depriving her of economic resources, forcing her to turn over her salary, and so on—these Russian activists heightened my awareness of the limitations of criminalizing domestic violence in truly reforming the social order.

My straddling of U.S. and Russian feminism creates terminological difficulties. While many U.S. feminists are committed to the term "violence against women" to refer to a variety of forms of violence, this book more often uses "gender violence" as an ethnographic nod to the terminology used among global women's activists. Similarly, I, like most activists from Europe and Eurasia, use the term "domestic violence" rather than woman battery or torture. In both cases, choosing to use a term that makes sense contextually leaves me with terminology that may domesticate the violence and minimize the male power, a sacrifice made in hopes of fostering communication and terminological consistency with Russian/ transnational activists. Finally, because some of the Russian activists I study engage the question of whether prostitution should be treated as "sex work" in their thinking about trafficking in women, I wade uncomfortably into the tumultuous waters of a transnational feminist debate over prostitution. Despite this book's claim of pragmatism in judging empirically which interventions are most successful, discussing trafficking in women, not unlike the abortion debate in the United States, requires language that seems to reveal a person's perspective. For many antiprostitution feminists, any discussion of sex as work is incriminating. But for most Russian activists, even those allied with Western antiprostitution feminists, this debate is not applicable, but instead a Western imposition.

### My Methods

Feminist social science, especially in places such as Russia where such research is new, requires eclectic methods. In exploring the impact of intervention on gender violence mobilization, awareness, and state responsiveness, my method is grounded in what social scientists refer to as "participant observation." I follow other scholars of gender violence politics in this approach because it combines systematic observation of the "daily life" of activists with an investment in relationships and the cause (Elman 1996, ix; also Dobash and Dobash 1992). Since 1994, I have periodically lived in or traveled to Russia to engage with Russian feminism, sometimes literally participating in and observing activists' daily lives when local and transnational activists invited me to stay in their homes. Since 1997, my research has focused on violence against women, and in addition to participant observation, my methodology has included unstructured interviews with other intermediaries: policymakers, legislators, funding officers, academics, and foreign embassy staff. More recently, employing "deterritorialized ethnography" (Merry 2006a), I began to observe other important global contexts, such as the 2006 EU conference discussed above and the postcommunist women's caucus at the United Nations' 2005 Commission on the Status of Women in New York (a.k.a. Beijing+10). Events designed as encounters between the "local" and the "global" are moments where exchange, reinterpretation, resistance, and appropriation are brought into relief. The promise of this kind of intense observation is that it can connect theory with people and elicit accounts of feminist activism and gender politics that are often left out of dominant interpretations about Russia and the United States/West.

This fieldwork is complemented by systematic textual analysis. I studied the language used in interactions as Russian activists struggled to create Russian terms for global feminist concepts. I collected and examined primary source materials created and/or distributed by local and transnational activists, academics, policymakers, human rights monitors, and law enforcement authorities, such as bulletins, fliers, model or actual legislation, books, reports, posters, stickers, and websites. I employ a simplified content analysis of Russian newspapers to monitor media coverage balanced by discourse analysis of dominant ways of articulating gender violence (see appendix 2 for more details on measurement and method). Based on all this evidence, I use process-tracing to capture the unfolding of the process of foreign intervention and gender violence politics, from the early 1990s until 2007.

The study constitutes a sample of the range of activities and articulated frames of violence against women in the urban centers of Russia. My research was centered in Moscow, the capital and by far the most populous and most wealthy city in Russia as well as the city through which most foreign intervention flowed. In Moscow, I found many of the elites, domestic and international, involved in the politics of violence against women. Research outside of Moscow, in cities such as St. Petersburg, Orel, Kaluga, Saratov, Barnaul, Kazan, and Arkhangelsk, revealed additional complications and dynamics. Although my fieldwork research was limited to the more Western areas of Russia, it is undisputed that the West, especially United States, has had great impact, even in the Russian Far East. I regret that undertaking this global-local study in a large, difficult, and quickly changing country has meant that I cannot fully engage questions of ethnic, religious, sexuality, urban-rural, and class differences among women within Russia. A future project, I hope.

## The Rest of the Book

Chapter 1 puts these questions into the context of feminist and political science theories and clarifies the study design and key concepts. Chapter 2 discusses the construction of a global normative consensus on violence against women and contrasts this consensus with Russia's historical approach to gender violence. It also provides more background on gender in Russia and the impact of the Soviet collapse. Chapter 3 details the emergence of a women's crisis center movement in Russia and the impact of foreign intervention on this mobilization. Chapters 4 through 6 examine the effect on activism, awareness-raising, and reform of this new Russian women's crisis center movement as the activists worked with dif-

ferent types of intervention into three different gender violence issues: sexual assault, domestic violence, and trafficking in women. Chapter 7 situates this Russian case study within other interventions into gender violence politics elsewhere
and considers alternative explanations. This conclusion elaborates the implications
for the political science fields of comparative politics and international relations
and makes suggestions for practical applications for those concerned with helping women globally.

For most Russian words, I have followed the Library of Congress system for
transliteration. Exceptions are the proper names common in the U.S. press (such
as Yeltsin instead of El'tsin) and those Russian activists and women's organizations that represent themselves otherwise in English (such as Moscow-based
Syostri [Sisters] instead of Sestry). The translations from Russian, unless specifically noted, are mine with some assistance from research assistant Gulnara
Zaynullina.

# ACKNOWLEDGMENTS

To finish a project of this size requires both professional and personal support. I have had both in abundance, and I am truly grateful.

For their patient descriptions and explanations, I thank the activists and scholars active in Russia, especially Nataliia Abubikirova, Elisabeth Duban, Gabrielle Fitchett-Akimova, Venera Ibragimova, Irina Khaldeeva, Zoia Khotkina, Marina Malysheva, Mariia Mokhova, Al'bina Pashina, Marina Pisklakova, Larisa Ponarina, Dianne Post, Elena Potapova, Marina Regentova, Nataliia Sereda, Guzel' Sharapova, and Elena Tiuriukanova. I am grateful to the Moscow Center for Gender Studies for their cultivation of excellent gender-related research and their willingness to share it with all the Western feminists, like me, who show up at their library. I thank R. Amy Elman and Valerie Sperling for their thorough review of the manuscript. I am deeply indebted to Jean Robinson, whose support and insight guided me through my graduate training and who has now become a co-editor, a co-author, and a friend.

I also thank the many colleagues whose comments and questions kindled insights in the book or encouraged me to keep writing, especially Laura Brunell, Jillian Cavanaugh, Sheila Croucher, Karen Dawisha, Dorothy McBride, Kelly Moore, Carol Nechemias, Aino Saarinen, S. Laurel Weldon, and Sharon Zukin. I thank Nanette Funk, Sonia Jaffe Robbins, and Ann Snitow for their nourishing monthly workshop of activist-scholars speaking on gender in postcommunist Europe and Eurasia, sponsored by New York University's Center for European Studies and the Network of East-West Women. I thank my students, particularly those at Brooklyn College who keep me on my intellectual toes with their unexpected questions grounded in complex and transnational lives. I thank Rebecca Tolen and Carol Kennedy for their careful editing at different stages in the process.

During this project, I have benefited from the institutional support of Indiana University, Miami University, and Brooklyn College, City University of New York, especially the uncommon political science department. A fellowship from the Ethyl Wolfe Institute for the Humanities at Brooklyn College gave me a year to draft the book, and a Whiting Teaching Fellowship provided some financial resources. Financial support for field research came from the City University of New York PSC-CUNY Research Award Program, Brooklyn College's Tow Faculty Travel Fellowship, the International Research & Exchanges Board, the National Security Education Program, and the Russian and East European Institute at Indiana University.

I express deep gratitude to my partner in life, John Mark Summers, whom I met just as I was starting this project. Our mutual support for each other, through many endeavors, has taught me a new way of being. I appreciate the encouragement and assistance of my multitalented and globally knowledgeable friends, especially Belinda Cooper, Roberta Krauvette, Sara VanGunst, and Sarah Webb. I thank my parents who taught me to see injustice.

JANET ELISE JOHNSON
*Brooklyn, New York, 2008*

# ABBREVIATIONS

| | |
|---|---|
| ABA-CEELI | American Bar Association Central and Eurasian Law Initiative |
| CEDAW | Convention on the Elimination of All Forms of Discrimination Against Women |
| CIDA | Canadian International Development Agency |
| CrC | criminal code |
| CrPC | criminal procedural code |
| G/TIP | U.S. State Department Office to Monitor and Combat Trafficking in Persons |
| GAATW | Global Alliance Against Trafficking in Women |
| ILO | International Labor Organization |
| INL | U.S. State Department's Bureau of International Narcotics and Law Enforcement Affairs |
| IOM | International Organization for Migration |
| IREX | International Research and Exchanges Board |
| MAHR | Minnesota Advocates for Human Rights |
| MCGS | Moscow Center for Gender Studies |
| NCRB | Network for Crisis Centres for Women in the Barents Region |
| NEWW | Network of East-West Women |
| OSCE | Organization for Security and Cooperation in Europe |
| OSI | Open Society Institute |
| RAROLC | Russian American Rule of Law Consortium |
| RF | Russian Federation |
| RSFSR | Russian Soviet Federated Socialist Republic |
| TFNs | transnational feminist networks |
| TIP | trafficking in persons, as in the U.S. State Department Trafficking in Persons reports |
| TraCCC | Transnational Crime and Corruption Center at American University in Washington, D.C. |
| UNIFEM | United Nations Development Fund for Women |
| USAID | United States Agency for International Development |
| WAVE | Women Against Violence Europe |

# GENDER VIOLENCE IN RUSSIA

# CHAPTER ONE

## Introduction: Foreign Intervention and Gender Violence

WHEN THE RUSSIAN BORDERS opened in the early 1990s, the international community responded with an unprecedented torrent of attention to issues such as rape, sexual harassment, domestic violence, and later, trafficking in women. Small grants and then larger grants funded Russian academics to research and then to create crisis centers and other nongovernmental organizations (NGOs) to help women living with such violence. Every kind of donor—from small feminist groups and charitable foundations to international development agencies—seemed interested in helping Russians address violence against women. Young Western feminists arrived on exchange programs, bringing the experience of shelter movements and rape crisis centers in their backpacks; transnational feminists arrived as part of new global networks. Passionate lawyers and judges, many with long-standing interest in Russia or gender violence, hopped on transcontinental planes, hoping to advance human rights and the rule of law. States and the evolving European Union sent diplomats to important international meetings to speak about gender violence and law enforcement experts to train their Russian counterparts. There was so much interest that many activists in Russia assumed that the problem of gender violence had been solved in the West—why else would foreigners pay so much attention to violence against women in other places?

The bulk of the intervention came from the United States, the leading donor to Russia since the Soviet collapse. By 2006, more than $10 million had been distributed from donors—such as the U.S. Agency for International Development, the U.S. State Department, and the New York–based Ford Foundation—to small organizations for whom the grants were often substantial. Millions of U.S. dollars paid for public awareness campaigns and law enforcement and judicial trainings. The United States–based Human Rights Watch and the Minnesota Advocates for Human Rights—along with Amnesty International, the United Nations, and the International Organization for Migration—documented the Russian government's failures to provide even minimal assistance or protection to women experiencing violence. Other interventions were more unexpected, such as when the United States passed antitrafficking legislation that took the remarkable step of requiring other countries to meet U.S.-mandated standards or to suffer the termination of non-humanitarian assistance. When the United States delayed action, allies of a U.S.-Russian antitrafficking organization recruited U.S. evangelical Christians to lobby their conservative Congress members to promote change in Russia.

These foreign interventions have had significant impact on Russian gender violence politics. From a feminist perspective, some of it seems good. So-called democracy assistance provided the necessary financial resources for an NGO-based women's crisis center movement that included, by 2004, some two hundred new organizations in two-thirds of Russia's regions, most offering hotline counseling, some providing shelter, and many advocating for change in society. Awareness campaigns spread new consciousness of violence in the family and sometimes even evoked sympathy and outrage. Training of state personnel and foreign lobbying led to some significant reforms on domestic violence in Russian regions and to national legislation on trafficking in persons. By 2006, even the ministry in charge of Russian police seemed changed when it initiated a widespread campaign telling people to call local precincts if they are experiencing "violence in the family," a new term for Russian people and a new responsibility for Russian authorities.

These changes are remarkable given the typical accusations directed at women who suffered gendered violence: "Why did you [insert: talk to him, bring him back to your apartment, agree to go to dinner with him, wear that outfit, drink with him, flick your hair, marry him, agree to go abroad . . . or otherwise provoke him]?" The changes are also astonishing given the general rollback in state social services, the overall consequences for women's political power and economic status of the shift from socialism, and the authorities' previous widespread denial of the existence, prevalence, and severity of all types of violence against women by police. Antitrafficking legislation was surprising given that many Russian officials financially benefit from trafficking and prostitution.

On the other hand, donors' funding whims have hamstrung committed and effective organizations and programs and increased fragmentation in the women's movement in Russia. Global controversies over how best to understand trafficking in women have forced Russian activists to take sides and have institutionalized personality and resource conflicts. The U.S. preemption of the issue of trafficking in women—because of U.S. domestic politics—excluded many of those committed to feminist ideas and led to an outcome that many found frustrating and perhaps even damaging to the cause. Reform on all forms of gender violence has been incomplete. It is not clear that the lives of most women in Russia are better than before the interventions.

Understanding why there was so much attention to violence against women in Russia requires recognizing the dramatic shifts in the transnational women's movement and other international politics. These interventions were a result not of the West's great success at addressing its own gender violence—far from it— but of the development, by the mid-1990s, of what I call, for this analysis, a new *global feminist consensus* on violence against women. After more than a decade of disagreement between the feminists from the Global North (industrialized democracies such as the United States, Canada, Western Europe) and the Global South (developing countries in South America, Africa, Southeast Asia), U.N. gatherings in the 1980s initiated a new way of networking across these divides. United by a new understanding linking gender justice with human rights, global feminists' central idea was the broad concept of "violence against women," which summed up a myriad of issues of interest to those from both regions. Driven by new "norms of inclusivity" and a respect for autonomous self-organizing (Weldon 2006), feminists created transnational feminist networks constituted by organizations from around the world (Moghadam 2005). This new global feminist consensus also created the possibility of alliances with the international donors and human rights advocates just as they were beginning to direct attention to Central and Eastern Europe and Eurasia following the demise of the Soviet Union (Moghadam 2005; Keck and Sikkink 1998, ch. 5). Simultaneously, many Western feminists, especially American feminists, faced backlash at home and fantasized that they could have more impact abroad.

This global feminist consensus has transformed the politics of gender violence around the world. By the late 1990s in Russia, almost all activists employed the language of women's human rights, and even those activists who criticize the more aggressive forms of intervention see the Russian movement as "integrating" into the global "war against violence against women."[1] In regions as different from postcommunist Eurasia as Latin America and Asia, global influences similar to those impacting Russia have become important in shaping local activism and national debates (Hester 2005; Luciano, Esim, and Dubbury 2005; Merry 2006a). Transnational pressures and ideas concerning gender violence have penetrated into Western European democracies (Kantola 2006; Zippel 2006). Even in the Middle East (Al-Ali 2003), a region often particularly resistant to intervention regarding gender, the availability of international funding and U.N. interest has begun to be important, at least in raising of the issue of gender violence. In most places—perhaps the United States is the exception—the politics of gender violence is no longer primarily a national affair.

This book explores this new phenomenon of foreign intervention into states' gender violence politics, tracing global ideas and funds, transnational activists, and more conventional agents of international diplomacy as they engaged Russia's activists, policymakers, and state officials in law enforcement and social services. It examines the intervention-heavy period of the early 1990s up through the middle of the next decade, when many interveners had lost interest. By 2006, Russian president Putin had also reined in organized civil society and consolidated a much more authoritarian regime buoyed by surging oil prices. Through an examination of the actual impacts of intervention, I centralize concerns about the possibility of a new era of imperialism in the name of women's rights. In sum, this book addresses the essential question for transnational feminist activists today: Does intervention justified by global norms of women's human rights work? More briefly, can foreign intervention help women? If yes, which kind and under what circumstances? The question of foreign intervention into gender violence also raises crucial theoretical puzzles for social scientists concerned with gender politics, especially those within the political science fields of comparative politics and international relations.

## THEORIZING INTERVENTION AND FEMINIST REFORM
### Comparative and International Models

Over the last two decades, social scientists steeped in both feminist theory and social science rigor have begun the comparative study of gender violence politics. The first studies understood the emergence of activisms against gender violence and the passage of policy reforms, such as new domestic violence laws and new protections for rape victims, as national processes (e.g., Dobash and Dobash 1992; Elman 1996; Mazur 2002, ch. 9; Weldon 2002). Amy Elman (1996), for example, argues that, in comparison to the centralized corporatist Swedish state, the decentralized American state both fostered an autonomous women's movement and created more opportunities for gender violence policy reform. Similarly, S. Laurel Weldon (2002), in a study of thirty-six industrialized democracies, argues that national governments are most responsive to demands for policy change when there is a "strong, autonomous [national] women's movement that draws on and reinforces state institutions designed to promote the status of women" (Weldon 2002, 5). Even studies that looked at developing contexts, such as India (Bush 1992) and elsewhere in the Global South (Heise et al. 1994), saw gender violence reform as primarily a result of interactions between domestic women's movements and the state.

These studies coincide with the emergence of a new subfield in political science, feminist comparative policy theory, summarized in Amy Mazur's (2002) *Theorizing Feminist Policy* and employed in the multibook project by the Research Network on Gender Politics and the State (e.g., Stetson 2002; Outshoorn 2004). Theorists using this approach systematically study the impact of women's movements and women's policy agencies on the policymaking of various gender-related issues. This work comes from a tradition among feminist social scientists to point to the importance of the ideological and institutional context as structural impediments or opportunities as well as suggesting the kinds of strategic alliances between activists, politicians, and civil servants that were more likely to be effective. They were applying and elaborating mainstream social science theories about structure and building on feminist frameworks such as the "triangle of empowerment"— "the interplay between . . . the women's movement, feminist politicians and feminist civil servants (femocrats)" (Vargas and Wieringa 1998, 3).

Useful in what they are beginning to tease out about national feminist policymaking in established democracies, these studies are less helpful in the post–global feminist consensus era when the global has become preeminent over the national and local. As feminist comparative policy theory does not intend to cover non-Western democracies, these studies assume strong states, in terms of both policy effectiveness and sovereignty. Although international influence is one among a number of exogenous determinants that could shape the formulation of policy, in practice these studies have focused overwhelmingly on domestic determinants.[2] Weldon's wider study up to 1994 showed that the transnational women's movement did not seem to have had an impact independent of local women's organizing (Weldon 2002, 206). Feminist comparative policy studies also assume the existence of—or at least the legacy of—a broad-based women's movement that emerged in the 1960s and 1970s. In contrast, Russia, like many countries, has had less state strength, has been more influenced by outside forces, and is characterized by more recent and weaker women's mobilization.

On the other hand, international relations theorists following the paradigm-shifting publication of Margaret Keck and Kathryn Sikkink's (1998) *Activists beyond Borders: Transnational Advocacy Networks in International Politics* highlight the international dimensions of these kinds of politics. These constructivists explain how human rights issues such as gender violence get onto the international agenda. Through what they call "the boomerang," local organizations can circumvent a recalcitrant state by finding international allies to pressure intergovernmental organizations such as the United Nations to establish new norms. Their insight has led to an explosion of new studies, some of which cross the divide between the political science fields of international relations and comparative politics, but most leave underexplored the question of how those international institutions, norms, and intervening states impact domestic policy. The literature's primary approach to this latter question is the theory of the *norms cascade,* the acceptance of new global norms as indicated by rapid treaty ratification and adoption of new law and practices—an approach that begs the political questions about how norms get institutionalized nationally, regionally, and locally. Other international relations approaches, such as the sanctions literature (e.g., Pape 1997), similarly (and unsurprisingly) underplay the domestic politics involved in responding to foreign pressures.

The case of Russia—as many other polities—poses the question of how we study the nexus of the international and the domestic when foreign intervention justified by global feminism, in collaboration with local women's NGOs, is the primary engine of domestic reform. Like legal anthropologist Sally Engle Merry (2006a) in *Human Rights and Gender Violence: Translating International Law into Local Justice,* I argue that to understand gender politics in those places we must examine in detail the "interface between global and local activism" (3). As in the interdisciplinary studies of the impact of democracy assistance on civil society in postcommunist Europe and Eurasia (Wedel 2001; Mendelson and Glenn 2002; Henderson 2003; Kuenhast and Nechemias 2004; Sundstrom 2006; Hemment 2007), we must consider the consequences, intended and unintended, of foreign aid on social mobilization. Considering the balance of power following the end of the Cold War, the second Bush administration's preemptive warfare, and the potential of a united Europe, we must also consider the local impact of interventions by strong states or the European Union. Along with my colleagues who have been recently studying gender violence politics (Kantola 2006; Zippel 2006), I put forward a model that gets beyond the artificial division in political science between comparative political analysis and international relations.

## Global-Local Structural Framework

To do this, I employ a structural approach to policy analysis in which the policy process is understood "as being fundamentally shaped by social structures that systematically disadvantage some groups and advantage others" (Weldon 2002, 6). By social structure, I refer to "a mode of social organizations, a set of relationships that position people relative to others" constituted by norms, rules, and social, political, and economic institutions (179). A structural approach allows for complex interactions between social movements and institutions, much more so than the concept of *political opportunity structure* promoted in social movement theory (e.g., Tarrow 1994). For example, even a very small, NGO-based social movement does not just arise in response to the structure, but also can impact state institutions to craft new ways of interacting with the state. This framework of policy analysis also allows for agency within the structures of social relations. Individuals and groups often struggle within a multiplicity of constraints and limits, sometimes undermining them through sustained collective campaigns, other times through everyday life choices (Weldon 2002, 183; also Sandoval 2000; Johnson and Robinson 2007).

For this book, the key social structure is gender. Gender is more than just a concept of differences created by culture and society linked to physiological sex; it is a composite of norms, formal and informal rules, and institutions that privilege the masculine over the feminine. Gender pervades individual consciousness and behavior, society, the polity, and the economy, with deep historical roots, but varies across time and place. A structural gender policy analysis requires "analyzing social and political institutions and social movements in terms of whether they undermine or reinforce women's subordinate position. . . . Gender analy-

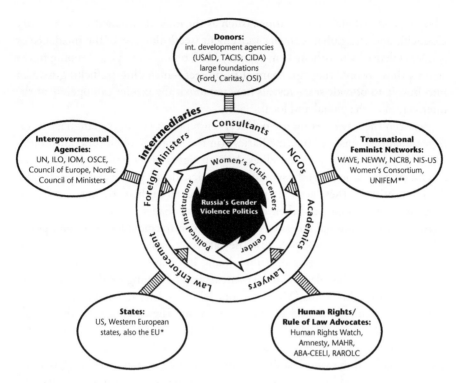

FIGURE 1.1. Global-local structural framework (and the key entities involved in Russia's gender violence politics).

The figure contains the following labels:

**Donors:** int. development agencies (USAID, TACIS, CIDA) large foundations (Ford, Caritas, OSI)

**Intergovernmental Agencies:** UN, ILO, IOM, OSCE, Council of Europe, Nordic Council of Ministers

**Transnational Feminist Networks:** WAVE, NEWW, NCRB, NIS-US Women's Consortium, UNIFEM**

**States:** US, Western European states, also the EU*

**Human Rights/ Rule of Law Advocates:** Human Rights Watch, Amnesty, MAHR, ABA-CEELI, RAROLC

Intermediaries · Consultants · NGOs · Academics · Lawyers · Law Enforcement · Political Institutions · Foreign Ministers

Women's Crisis Centers · Gender · Russia's Gender Violence Politics

* In this process, the EU has functioned more as a state, marshaling amalgamated diplomatic pressure, than an intergovernmental agency.
** Although a part of the UN, UNIFEM has functioned more like a transnational feminist network, providing funding and a platform for organizations working against gender violence in Russia (see also Moghadam 2005, 98–99).

sis should critically examine how policies are embedded in and reflect power relations, and not just differences, between the groups designated as 'men' and 'women'" (Weldon 2002, 182).

Because gender politics in Russia is shaped by foreign intervention, this domestic gender analysis must be embedded in the global context, creating a two-level "game" (Putnam 1988). Conceptualizing this international realm is a contentious issue for international relations theorists, who argue over which actors are significant and how integrated and/or stratified the realm is. This study does not insert itself into these debates, but sees the global realm as similar to the concept of the domestic social structure, as a kind of global social structure in which norms, states, and international organizations can (but do not necessarily) influence domestic political processes (see figure 1.1). Gender is one of these global structures as gender operates within the various parts of the global realm. Gender can be constituted, reified, or undermined at the global level through gendered global norms (such as the norm articulating who is responsible to protect whom), gendered global institutions (such as the male-dominated U.N. Security Council), and the global women's movement (see Enloe 1993). The incidence of gender violence by mostly male in-country U.N. officials and peacekeeping forces against those people they are charged to protect—including trafficking women into Bosnia to provide sex—reveals how paradoxically gender can operate at the intersection of the global and local.

Between these two realms are political "entrepreneurs" (in the language of international relations) or "intermediaries" (in the language of cultural anthropology), such as national political elites, human rights or feminist activist leaders, service providers, legal professionals, academics, development consultants, and foreign ministers. These activists are entrepreneurial in their sharing of information, their networking, and their drive to attract broader publics and create new channels of institutional access based on their commitment to norms and policy reform (Keck and Sikkink 1998, 14). They are intermediaries in that they negotiate between the local, regional, national, and international, such as by translating global rights principles into local contexts and reframing local grievances into global human rights terms (Merry 2006b, 39). They vary in their commitments to these different arenas and to global feminism. They are also simultaneously powerful and vulnerable, working "in a field of conflict and contradiction, able to manipulate others who have less knowledge than they do but still subject to exploitation by those who installed them" (40). They operate within global, national, regional, and local structures "whose commitment to women's rights [and alleviation of gender violence] is at best ambivalent" (48).

As a result, the nexus between the global and the local can create unintended consequences. For example, foreign donors' commitments to their "shareholders" can create incentive structures, institutions, and interests in the target country that impede their stated goals (Henderson 2002; 2003). In this environment, both funders and NGOs are encouraged to chase short-term projects with tangible outcomes over the long-term, more complex work. Dependency on foreign grants—as well as other types of foreign intervention such as transnational feminist networking—can lead to patron-client relationships between the global and the local rather than ties with the local population. On the other hand, when such projects have been more inclusive of locals, foreign assistance has fostered mobilization, dialogue, and new networks of women (True 2003, ch. 6).

As a framework for analysis, the book's approach is to make all these structures subject to observation. Components of the global-local social structures matter when they combine to impact an issue as observed through close study, and their impact is not simply quantified but elaborated. In sum, this kind of structural gender analysis asks how norms, rules, and institutions, at multiple levels, impact the policy process, including how the global-local structure constructs and reinforces gender operating in society. The analysis also examines how transnational and local activists take advantage of these various structures to promote change.

## *Neoimperialist Concerns, Empirical Obstacles*

Investigating this study's central question—whether foreign intervention can help women—requires creating standards of measurement, a move complicated by the colonial history of justifying imperialist projects under the guise of "helping" women. This concern is especially acute when the United States claims to be "in the forefront of advancing women's causes around the world,"[3] yet leaves unexamined its long history of resisting global initiatives aimed at improving women's status or of creating policies that restrict others' response to gender injustice. These include the U.S. opposition to the creation within the United Nations of a robust commission on the status of women (Hawkesworth 2006, 88–90), the refusal to ratify the Convention on the Elimination of All Forms of Discrimination Against Women, and the initiation of the 1984 "global gag rule" banning foreign NGOs from receiving U.S. funds if they (using other moneys) also perform or discuss abortion.

Even in this new global feminist consensus era in which many struggled to be more inclusive and responsive to local concerns, Western feminists arrived in Central and Eastern Europe "trailing their own increasing marginality and conceptual confusion at home" (Snitow 1999, 36). This baggage multiplied "the likelihood of wasted effort, misunderstanding, and even . . . damaging uses of the categories of gender." And, there have been some troubling results, such as when Western feminist ideas, "accompanied as they often are with glamour or with foundation money," drown out local activist interests (37). Also problematic is that much of global feminism had become unmoored from its radical critique as Left ideologies were destabilized following socialism's collapse. For the case of violence against women, the global feminist discourse can downplay the role of the government's management of the economy and the broader issues of poverty that shape women's experience of violence, especially domestic violence and trafficking. In this context, intervention may foster the aims of neoliberalism, either by serving the role of former state social services or by justifying the privatization of such former state functions (Funk 2006, 269–70).

At the same time, these concerns about neoimperialism should not keep social scientists from asking the tough questions about how policies and practices can help women. Gender in this analysis is not only a tool in service of abstract scholarly inquiry, but a challenge to existing power structures. The feminism that gave us gender analysis is an ideology that calls for remedying gender injustice. Further, the imperialistic critiques can oversimplify and overgeneralize, missing the differences in types of interventions, agents of intervention, or responses by local NGOs (Funk 2006, 275). By focusing on the intentions of Western governments, they can fail to notice the actual consequences. I, like Nanette Funk (2006, 265–66), take the position that foreign intervention, even with "some imperial aims[,] can, in certain cases, be compatible with . . . the demands of justice." This approach was driven by the observations that it was Russian feminists who sought and appropriated global feminist and human rights discourses in ways similar to activists in very different contexts and that it is those leaders resistant to responding to gender violence who most often invoke the imperialist claim about women's human rights (Merry 2006b). I intentionally use the word "help" to invoke the imperialist concerns and to centralize the aspiration to eliminate gender injustice.

Additional problems with creating standards for measurement of what it means to help women are empirical. The end goal for most feminists concerned with the problem is to eliminate gender violence. Measuring the achievement of this goal would involve looking at the relationships between various responses and the rates of gender violence as well as the systematic analysis of victims' reports about their experiences in shelters and with the criminal justice system. This kind of assessment of the effectiveness of state policy and practice is only beginning to become possible in established democracies and remains practically impossible in post-communist societies (Weldon 2002). Even looking at comparative rates of gender violence can be misleading. Since gender violence has been ignored by authorities, lower statistics can indicate either that there is less violence (i.e., the policies are working) or that the victims of violence assess that there is no use in reporting the violence, suggesting that violence is high (i.e., the polices are not working) (Elman 1996, vii). Finally, real reform is a slow process. If all the initiatives imagined by the most astute activists were implemented today in the best polity, ending gender violence would take at least one generation if not more.

## *Meeting Global Feminist Objectives*

In light of these concerns and obstacles—as in most studies examining gender violence in comparative perspective (e.g., Elman 1996; Weldon 2002; Kantola 2006; Zippel 2006)—this study relies on assessing responsiveness of the state and society rather than effectiveness. In other words, the study investigates the degree to which certain initiatives are taken up rather than assessing the complex relationship between initiatives, the services provided and received, and the incidence of gender violence. Despite the limitations in this approach, increasing responsiveness represents a de facto enhancement of women's status, as increased state response "to assuage physical and sexual abuse of women . . . can, in effect, delegitimize male force and violence against women" (Elman 1996, 3).

To address the concerns raised about neoimperialism, I use as standards of responsiveness the broad, multifaceted initiatives imagined by global feminists. I further specify in the following chapters what global feminists see as best practices for addressing different forms of gender violence. Here, I summarize the global feminist goals as increased mobilization, awareness, and responsiveness. Underneath is the desire, as articulated in the United Nations' Millennium Development Goals, to "promote gender equality and empower women" in order to help women live fuller, richer lives.

## Feminist Mobilization

The new global feminism is about promoting women's mobilization at the local level. The consensus that overcame the deep divisions between feminists from the North and South required *norms of inclusivity:* a commitment to including different types of women, to creating separate organizations for disadvantaged groups, and to sustaining consensus even with dissent (Weldon 2006, 55). Activists working across divides also developed strategies such as "transversalism," where each group gets an opportunity to talk openly about their values and experiences and then listens to the other group do the same, and "deliberative disagreements," in which actors hold different views but commit to finding a mutually acceptable solution (Saarinen 2004). These new norms and strategies created the possibility to get beyond the universalistic (and thus divisive) global sisterhood model promoted by Northern feminists to a new global feminism. As such, any foreign intervention justified as global feminism would have to encourage the mobilization of women in the target country.

In this study, interventions are seen as successful to the degree to which they promote feminist mobilization in the target country of Russia. This is a question not simply of speed or even size, but of the quality of mobilization. Are Russian women's groups, with foreign interventions, more or less capable of transforming gender by interacting with society and the state? The quality of mobilization and their capacity for activism is partially a question of resources, including money, but also access, influence, reputation, and expertise, some of which foreign intervention may augment (McCarthy and Zald 1975; Sperling, Ferree, and Risman 2001).[4] Another important aspect is the degree to which organizations can coordinate their action, for example, how networked the various movement organizations are, an important way of keeping organizations involved in the movement (Tarrow 1994; Staggenborg 1989). Yet, the assessment of Russian mobilization must be put within the context of recent feminist mobilization worldwide that, in most places, looks more like formal NGOs than grassroots protests (Henderson 2003).

Although many women's groups, in the Global North, South, and East, reject the term "feminism" for various reasons (Basu 1995), for analytical simplicity, I use the term "feminist" here to refer to organizing as women to challenge gender injustice, whether or not groups themselves embrace the label. In other words, I adopt a concept of *de facto feminism,* in which I consider as feminist all women's groups and networks who seek social or political change to lessen sex/gender hierarchies (Moghadam 2005, 79). At the same time, I recognize that there are multiple feminisms locally and globally. Global feminist intervention is "simultaneously an encounter between two (or more) specific and concrete types of local feminism and also about constructing something that is new, different, and self-consciously more globally framed than either was initially" (Sperling, Ferree, and Risman 2001).

## Feminist Awareness

Despite these limitations on the ground, global feminists, as a transnational social movement, have always sought more than just policy reform; they aim to transform the organization of social and political life. In the language of social structure, the global feminist movement aims to transform the global and local social structures of gender. This objective is encapsulated in the idea of raising awareness. In contrast to the consciousness-raising of Western feminist groups in the 1970s, raising awareness is typically an external process in which women's groups use the mass media or public events to distribute information about violence against women. One of the most successful global campaigns is the annual 16 Days of Activism against Gender Violence, from November 25, the International Day Against Violence Against Women, to December 10, the International Human Rights Day.[5] The hope is that these kinds of campaigns might also prevent some forms of gender violence, such as trafficking in women.

For this study, interventions are assessed as effective when they help transform public awareness of gender violence. Does intervention cultivate local activism and awareness campaigning? Does the intervention introduce—or assist local women's organizations in introducing—new terminology for gender violence based on global feminist ideas and terms? Does the intervention promote—or help local women's organizations promote—global feminist understanding of gender violence, such as seeing violence against women as a violation of women's human rights? As I elaborate in chapter 4, raising awareness represents the "meaning work" of politics, that is, "discursive politics" (Fraser 1990). The assumption is that policy reform will likely follow shifts in the meanings of violence against women. This study uses insights from various schools of thought on discursive politics, including the anthropological discussion "appropriation," "translation," and making of global norms "into the vernacular" (Merry 2006a).

## Responsiveness in Policy and Practice

Finally, global feminism calls for states to shift their formal policy and everyday practice. An essential part of linking gender violence with human rights is to hold states accountable for punishing and penalizing perpetrators of violence against women as well as for providing social assistance to victims so that they can escape and recover from violence. States' commitment is revealed in public policy, state procedures, and institutions that make gender violence a crime, require official attention to it, create social policy to alleviate the consequences or the conditions leading to it, or establish credible initiatives to prevent gender violence in the future. These formal changes must also matter for the practice of police, prosecutors, lawyers, judges, social workers, and healthcare providers. This second step is incredibly important for most countries, such as Russia, with little history of the rule of law—where legislation can have little meaning.

For this global feminist objective, intervention is seen as effectual when interventions promote reform of both policy and practice. Do interventions support local activists' lobbying for reform? Can and do interventions allow external actors to bypass locals and directly advance positive reforms? Does intervention lead states to address gender violence as a violation of women's human rights? Or does intervention compel other states to promote only the illusion that they respond to gender violence?

For all three global feminist objectives—mobilization, awareness, and responsiveness—I assess the interventions as successful, from the perspective of global feminists, when a substantial part of the sought changes have been achieved, when the interventions occurred prior to the changes, and when no more credible explanation exists for these changes (Pape 1997, 97).

### Comparing Foreign Interventions

The global feminist consensus on violence against women created new opportunities for all sorts of foreign interventions beyond what global feminists might have imagined. The new global feminist consensus itself, articulated in key international documents, shifts the global social structure by formalizing new global norms against gender violence. These norms can then be appropriated and translated by local activists, giving them some international cachet and perhaps new and powerful ways to articulate their demands locally (Merry 2006a). These norms were also sponsored by the new organizing force of the global feminist movement, transnational feminist networks (Moghadam 2005), the feminist form of what Keck and Sikkink (1998) called "transnational advocacy networks." Framing gender violence as human rights violations also brought alliances with human rights advocates, who in the late 1980s began to take responsibility for addressing violence against women in their activities. These advocates expanded their typical tactics, such as monitoring human rights abuses through extensive reports highlighting victim testimonies and then using these reports to "blame and shame" states for failure to meet international human rights standards. In addition to perhaps encouraging a state to shift its policy and practice, these interventions can promote women's mobilization by legitimating their activities (Tarrow 2001).

Additionally, the global feminist consensus led to alliances with donors to provide assistance to women's groups around the world. At first, the donors were those traditionally committed to feminist causes, giving fairly small and limited numbers of grants. Later, as part of their assistance designed to foster postcommunist civil society, states' international development agencies started funding organizations that addressed gender violence. This infusion of funds can provide women's organizations with the necessary funds for survival, for new campaigns, and for the expansion in the number of organizations. Other funds can pay for training of law enforcement and other legal personnel, providing a direct avenue to shift state practice.

Finally, in some cases, states and intergovernmental agencies have taken on some global feminist objectives in their traditional diplomacy or even warfare. Foreign ministers from such states can persuade other states' foreign ministers

**TABLE 1.1.** *Intervention Continuum*

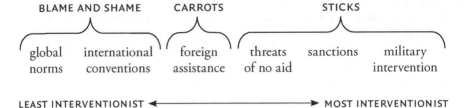

that it is in their interest to adopt certain policies. States can also employ state-craft, including economic sanctions, or they can wrap their military interventions with the justifications of protecting women; one of the United States' justifications for military intervention in Afghanistan was to help the women in burkas. All these interventions—cloaked in the ideas of global feminism but not necessarily global feminist—can be placed on an intervention continuum (see table 1.1), from the least interventionist, the establishment of global norms, to the most coercive, military intervention.

These types of intervention also vary in the degree to which the process of designing and implementing the intervention includes those committed to global feminism. Drawing upon distinctions made by the subfield of feminist comparative policy theory (see Stetson 2002; Outshoorn 2004), I define *descriptive representation* as the inclusion of such global feminists in the intervention process and *substantive representation* as the meeting of a substantial part of global feminist objectives.[6] Combining these leads to a two-by-two matrix of ideal-type interventions in which intervention can have either (preemption or cooptation), both (alliance), or none (see table 1.2).

### Gender Violence

The concept of violence against women succeeded in uniting women's activists around the world because of its breadth, covering issues from sexual and domestic violence to dowry murders and female genital mutilation and beyond. In the interventions into Russian gender violence politics, the issues that received the most attention were rape, sexual harassment, domestic violence, and, later, the trafficking in women for sex. These are problems that appear to be widespread, impacting in one form or another perhaps one-third of all women globally over their lifetimes, mostly perpetrated by someone known to them (UNIFEM 2003). Although the very definitions of these problems are up for debate and the Russian government collects no credible statistics, these problems appear perhaps even more severe in Russia than the global average (Johnson 2005). For example, one extensive survey found that half of married women respondents reported at least one incident of physical violence (e.g., striking, pushing, shaking, arm-twisting) from their present husbands (Gorshkova and Shurygina 2003).

**TABLE 1.2.** *Global Feminist Interventions*

| | NO DESCRIPTIVE REPRESENTATION | DESCRIPTIVE REPRESENTATION |
|---|---|---|
| no substantive representation | **no global feminism:** movement achieves no access to intervener and the intervener meets none of their intervention objectives | **cooptation "global feminism":** intervener brings feminists into the intervention process, but no desired intervention |
| substantive representation | **preemption "global feminism":** intervener satisfies some global feminist intervention objectives, but does not include feminists in the intervention process | **global feminist alliances:** intervener accepts feminists into the process and effects intervention in line with global feminist objectives |

*Source:* Adapted from Research Network on Gender Politics and the State project (see Stetson 2002; Outshoorn 2004).

By looking at different types of gender violence, I can also compare the impact of different types of foreign intervention into Russia's gender violence politics. The foreign intervention into rape and sexual harassment, more similar issues in the Russian context than in the United States, was predominantly by transnational feminist networks allied with human rights organizations. The intervention into domestic violence added foreign assistance facilitated by alliances with international donors. The United States and other Western powers intervened on the issue of trafficking in women through diplomatic pressure and threats of economic sanctions. This study focuses only on violence against adult women, regrettably leaving out important questions about intervention and violence against girls and boys.

### A Case Study

Although I compare within the case, this is a case study of Russia. This choice reflects my commitment to "thick description" (Geertz 1973) and the sense that often the social science that matters most are those studies that tell good stories, paying attention to historical circumstances and particularities (Tilly 1984). As this is a story whose lead roles are played by the former superpower rivals, it illuminates the still unsure post–Cold War world order, in two political environments, where, on the surface, gender concerns are not cast as important.

The study examines a crucial period in Russia, from the tremendous democratic opportunity at the break-up of the Soviet Union in 1991 up through President Putin's consolidation of a semi-authoritarian regime. In 2005, Putin created a Public Chamber, a controlled forum of only those NGOs he saw as legitimate, to substitute for the articulation of citizen demands of a free civil society. In 2006, he signed into law regulation of NGOs, limiting foreign funding and allowing NGOs to be closed down if they threaten the country's "sovereignty, independence, territorial integrity, national unity and originality, cultural heritage and national interests." These limitations on civil society, perhaps not as bad in practice as they might seem to many Americans, came after Putin had circumscribed the mass media (with state ownership of television channels and with a policy of not protecting journalists), institutionalized more regional control (through making governors appointed by the president), and quelled political opposition (by imprisoning his greatest electoral threat through what appears to be arbitrary rule enforcement).

In some ways, Russia is a "critical case," a case where existing theory would suggest global feminism is least likely to take root. As I elaborate in chapter 2, at the end of Soviet communism, there were few existing women's organizations, a widespread rejection of feminism, and a resurgence of nationalism that would make intervention likely to backfire. In the concluding chapter, I look at the particularities of Russia and situate it within other cases in order to explore what this Russian story suggests about other global feminist foreign interventions.

# CHAPTER TWO

# The Global Feminist Challenge, Communism, and Postcommunism

THE CONSENSUS AMONG GLOBAL feminists constructed by the early 1990s issued a challenge to governments around the world. In contrast to this vision of women's rights as human rights, violence against women had most often been treated as a woman's individual misfortune that states had no responsibility to address. As the Cold War ended, human rights critiques could even be leveled—with new effectiveness—at the former Soviet superpower, which had previously exempted itself from such standards (not unlike the United States). How did this global feminist challenge differ from the Soviet and post-Soviet regulation of gender violence? How have the political, cultural, and economic changes of the postcommunist transformation complicated the possibilities for global feminist success?

The analysis of the historical and national conditions shows that the new global feminist norms about gender violence were unlikely to take root in Russia. The communist regime sometimes regulated gender violence as part of its tight control of intimate life, a control rejected with Soviet collapse. It also established some political institutions designed to help women, institutionalizing a weak kind of de facto feminism into the state and leaving no real room for autonomous feminist activism. Postcommunism adds a tendency toward the privatization of issues that were previously part of the state's purview and toward gender neotraditionalism—a reflection of and reaction to the communist ideals, pre-Soviet traditions, and global fantasies. These have legitimated the privatization of gender violence, a response that illustrates the opposite of global feminist arguments about gender violence as a violation of women's human rights. As there was a simultaneous rejection of the most feminist aspects of communism, an embrace of nationalism, and the emergence of only a small women's movement, there were few avenues for resistance in Russia in the 1990s.

Thus, this chapter details the global and local structures, including culture, that constitute the environment for foreign intervention in Russia. In contrast to the political culture approach—although I suggest interplay between culture and politics—I do not rely on an assumption of a stable, uniform culture. I do not see "policy preferences . . . [as simply] a result of a culture that prefers those policies" (Weldon 2002, 36). This study also does not use the common way of approximating culture as dominant religion that those who study postcommunism often employ (e.g., Fish 1998). I also do not resort to simplistic notions of culture that some feminists use to abbreviate their critiques, such as through condemning "violence against women as a product of traditional cultural practices" (even while simultaneously affirming the "cultural heritage is something to treasure") (Merry 2006a, 11). As I have argued elsewhere, the reason for the extent of violence against women in Russia and the lack of state response is not that Russia is so patriarchal (nor the opposite, because Russia is so matriarchal) (Johnson 2007b). Instead, this chapter portrays culture as "consist[ing] of repertoires of ideas and practices that are not homogeneous but continually changing because of contradictions among them or because new ideas and institutions are adopted by members. . . . Cultural discourses legitimate or challenge authority and justify relations of power" (Merry 2006a, 11). Although culture may congeal into political institutions, both are open to new ideas, even from across borders.

## CONSTRUCTING GLOBAL FEMINISM

### From Global Sisterhood to Global Feminism

Like many other social movements, feminism has long been transnational, including the transnational woman suffrage movement in the nineteenth and early twentieth centuries (Keck and Sikkink 1998). Yet, even though the United Nations had declared a commitment to equality in the U.N. Charter, the idea for an international conference on women and the following U.N. Decade for Women was historic (Fraser 1987). Mainstream women's organizations with consultative status to the United Nations, most of which eschewed the feminist label, had created the U.N.'s Commission on the Status of Women. Outside the United Nations, women's organizing—extending to radical feminism—was gathering strength around the world in the 1960s and 1970s. The first conference held in Mexico City in 1975—and the following conferences in Copenhagen in 1980 and Nairobi in 1985—meant a new venue for transnational feminism where voices for all kinds of women's groups, from many places, could meet, in both the formal meeting and the parallel NGO forum.

Unfortunately, the high hopes of many women for the emergence of a "global sisterhood" were dashed by "deep divisions" and "resentment" (Basu 1995, 3). For many from the Global South, the universalistic agenda of Northern feminists erased important differences among women, veiled global inequality, and silenced their concerns. For some, drawing from postcolonial critiques, feminism became a new kind of imperialism within a global context of increasing economic and political divides between industrialized democracies and the developing world (Mohanty 1991). Although some issues were shared, there was no agreement on "how to define these issues, how and whether activists ought to pursue policy change, and how discussions ought to be organized" (Weldon 2006). The gatherings were also disrupted by broader international conflicts, such as the Cold War and the Israeli-Palestinian dispute.

By the mid 1980s, as the Cold War was ending, women's activists at the United Nations responded to these concerns and disputes. The new approach was symbolized in the decision to hold the third conference in Africa and to include more women from the developing world than from the industrialized world. Charting a course between the centripetal force of universalism and the centrifugal forces of recognizing important divisions based on race, class, gender, nationality, level of development, and the like, the movement developed *norms of inclusivity* (Weldon 2006). "Such norms include a commitment to descriptive representation [including different categories of individuals in the movement], the facilitation of separate organizations for disadvantaged social groups, and a commitment to building consensus *with* institutionalized dissent" (55). The movement simultaneously became more united and "more dispersed, decentered, and divided" (Basu 1995, 18). This re-imagining of global feminism, while still confronted with global structural inequalities, created a new "politics of solidarity" (Saarinen 2004) that enabled policy influence domestically and globally. The result was a fresh kind of global feminism that sought to be more culturally sensitive than earlier approaches by creating unity based on common interests, not common identity (Moghadam 2005).

Although also about economic justice, this new global feminism was expedited by the creation and popularization of the composite concept of "violence against women" (Keck and Sikkink 1998; Moghadam 2005; Weldon 2006). Although different groups of feminists, from the North and South, had raised various gender violence issues—such as rape, domestic violence, female genital mutilation, torture of political prisoners, and dowry deaths—until the mid 1970s these had been separate campaigns (Keck and Sikkink 1998, 171). Framing all these issues as violence against women created solidarity between movements—all forms were constituted equal, none exoticized—but also allowed for "autonomous self organization" (Weldon 2006). In other words, there were interconnected global and local campaigns simultaneously. The new global feminist consensus does not reflect perfect congruence in understanding the root of the problem or even in policy recommendations. In contrast to the earlier sisterhood attempts, the consensus allows for these disagreements, albeit imperfectly, as part of a tactical alliance to speak to the mostly nonfeminist world.

## Violence against Women as a Violation of Women's Human Rights

Linking women's organizing worldwide to the United Nations meant, for many activists, a new language, culture, and tradition, often bewildering to outsiders. At the United Nations, activism is centered on "working sessions" to produce consensual documents through an almost interminable process of negotiating word choice (Merry 2006a, ch. 2). Ostensibly about such questions as whether to add qualifying language (e.g., "as soon as possible") to documents obligating state commitments, these debates are also about the ways in which different states understand and commit to women's equality. This "wordsmithing" was situated within other U.N. traditions. Importantly, in the 1970s, resistance was divided into three distinct international movements: national liberation, human rights, and women's rights (Fraser 1987, 6). Within this context, women's issues were framed as about equality and discrimination, such as in the first and only women's convention, the Convention on the Elimination of All Forms of Discrimination Against Women (CEDAW), which was passed in 1979 but had been drafted a decade earlier (Keck and Sikkink 1998).

Violence against women was different from the typical women's issues raised at the United Nations because the concept's central assertion was women's right to bodily integrity. In this way, violence against women could be connected to human rights (Keck and Sikkink 1998, 721). Despite the inclusion of slavery and racial discrimination, which "also occur in the private sphere at the hands of private actors" (Bunch 1995, 14), when it came to including women, human rights had been argued to be only "state-sanctioned or -condoned oppression." The U.N. venue and the new solidarity among transnational feminists facilitated a critique of international human rights law as "gendered" because of its "artificial distinction between the 'public' and 'private' spheres" (Peters and Wolper 1995, 2, 7). Gender violence, they argued, should not be excluded just because it was often committed by private actors in intimate and domestic contexts; states should be held accountable for preventing or at least addressing such violence. Organizing in the Global South against torture and rape of political prisoners further illuminated the link between gender violence and human rights (Friedman 1995, 22). By the 1990s, both human rights and women's rights activists were declaring that "women's rights are human rights," a shift in thinking so significant that it is now almost impossible to talk about women's issues in any other way at the United Nations.

This new way of thinking and organizing allowed violence against women to move onto the intergovernmental agenda. While CEDAW made no mention of the concept of "violence against women," women's human rights activists scored a big coup when the governments at the 1993 Vienna World Conference on Human Rights agreed to include violence against women in the Vienna Declaration and Programme for Action (see appendix 1). The same year, the United Nations passed the (nonbinding) U.N. Declaration on the Elimination of Violence against Women, elaborating forms of gender violence, including rape, sexual harassment, domestic violence, and trafficking in women. In 1995, at the next major U.N. women's conference, the Beijing governmental conference and parallel Huairou NGO forum, violence against women was central, and the Beijing Platform for Action (1995) established violence against women, including trafficking in women, as one of the twelve areas of central concern. Violence against women had become important for both women's rights and human rights activists, bringing unprecedented attention to this so-called women's issue and related activism.

Aligning violence against women with human rights also extended the U.N.'s modes of intervention (Merry 2006a, 48–50). The creation of international documents creates global norms—the U.N.'s policy—and the new salience of gender violence gave more power to these norms. In addition, the United Nations has complaint mechanisms in which NGOs can send representatives to lobby government representatives, including through the Commission on the Status of Women, CEDAW (as of 2000), and the Commission on Human Rights. Endowed with the power to investigate complaints, the High Commission on Human Rights can also appoint an expert—or special rapporteur—to travel to particular countries to follow up on charges of human rights abuses. In 1994, as mandated by the Vienna Declaration, the commission appointed a special rapporteur on violence against women, Radhika Coomaraswamy, whose personal strengths brought even more attention to gender violence. In 2004, the commission appointed a special rapporteur on trafficking in persons, especially women and children.

Finally, the United Nations can regulate treaty compliance, such as the compliance to CEDAW, through periodic hearings on country reports to the treaty committee. In contrast to the commissions, the treaty committees are constituted not by government representatives, but by experts who are not supposed to represent their respective governments. Although violence against women was not originally a part of CEDAW, the CEDAW Committee's General Recommendations 12 (1989) and 19 (1992) requested that gender violence be included in countries' reports.

Unfortunately, none of these U.N. mechanisms has been very powerful at enforcing human rights, not to mention women's rights. The Commission on Human Rights has been highly troubled, undermined by members such as Sudan, Libya, and Zimbabwe, which not only are gross human rights violators, but used membership as a way of protecting themselves from condemnation. In 2006, in an attempt at reform, the commission was replaced with a new body, the Human Rights Council, but its first few years suggested little improvement. In 2007, a proposal was even circulated to eliminate most of the rapporteurs. The Commission on the Status of Women has been weakened by the predominance of conservative governments in the world. In this context, CEDAW hearings may be the most effective U.N. mechanism for monitoring women's rights because they are still under the radar.[1]

## Enlisting Human Rights Advocates among Others

The new link between violence against women and human rights also enlisted human rights monitors already active on other issues, such as Human Rights Watch and Amnesty International. Despite early assertions that rights could not be denied based on sex (e.g., in the U.N.'s Universal Declaration of Human Rights), most human rights advocates had considered women's rights as "special interests" even while considering violations that impacted a smaller part of the population—such as ethnic minorities—as "general interests" (Bunch 1995, 12–15). As gender violence activists succeeded in altering the U.N.'s terrain, the major international human rights organizations also began to shift their understanding.

In postcommunist Europe and Eurasia, the human rights advocate that has focused the most attention on violence against women as a violation of women's human rights is the Minnesota Advocates for Human Rights (MAHR). By 1993, MAHR had established a Women's Program that "works to improve the lives of women by using international human rights standards to advocate for women's rights in the United States and around the world."[2] Using conventional human rights tactics, conducting field research working with local women's organizations, MAHR published a series of reports documenting state failures to respond to domestic violence, mostly in postcommunist Europe and Eurasia. In 2000, MAHR joined up with the U.N.'s Development Fund for Women (UNIFEM) and the Open Society's Women's Program to establish a Stop Violence Against Women campaign centered around a website in English and Russian.[3]

MAHR's work and their Stop Violence Against Women campaign illustrates the new global feminist approach to gender violence. The homepage proclaims that MAHR sees "violence against women as one of the most pervasive human rights abuses worldwide."[4] The campaign focuses on domestic violence, sexual violence, sexual harassment, and trafficking in women, framing each as a human rights issue. The campaign website, which has a collection of country pages summarizing current legislation and developments and links to important international documents on gender violence and human rights, reflects MAHR's commitment to monitoring states using human rights standards. The website also demonstrates MAHR's goal of raising awareness of women's rights through providing information and encouraging educational programs. Imagined as a resource for activists from Central and Eastern Europe and the former Soviet Union, the campaign represents MAHR's dedication to working with local women's activists, who they assume will be organized into NGOs, independent and voluntary associations of individuals working together to provide social services and advocate for change. As part of their commitment to this local organizing and to reform of policy and practice, the website includes a summary of what are seen as "best practices" and training materials. In contrast to some human rights advocates, MAHR also brings a new kind of (global feminist) reflexivity. For example, in 2004, they turned their tools back on the United States, releasing a report on the local response to domestic violence against refugee and immigrant women in the Minneapolis–St. Paul area of Minnesota.

The global feminist re-imagining of violence against women as a violation of women's human rights also had consequences beyond the human rights community. For example, by 2000, the new attention brought the inclusion of gender-based violence as a health problem by the World Health Organization. Although such language was not included in the original document establishing the U.N.'s Millennium Development Goals, global feminists succeeded in getting condemnation of violence against women in the 2005 conference document. By the late 1990s, violence against women had been incorporated almost everywhere: by the leading intergovernmental agencies (e.g., the United Nations, the International Organization for Migration, and the Organization for Security and Cooperation in Europe), by Western governments' international development agencies, and by virtually all large foundations open to funding initiatives focused on women. The potential for influence, especially for re-imagining issues pertaining to women, was so great that feminist observers began to see gender violence activism as potentially a new form of imperialism (e.g. Hemment 2004a; 2007).

## THE SOVIET LEGACY

As these changes were underway among transnational women's activists and around the global conception of the issue of gender violence, Russia was also undergoing a huge transformation. For some seven decades in the twentieth century, Russia had been the leading republic in the Soviet Union. This multiethnic empire was marked by the Communist Party that controlled policymaking and a command economy, in which government planners, not the market, dictated what to produce and how to produce. This Soviet system also produced a particular approach to gender violence, promoting women's status, and gender.

### Haphazard Policy and Practice

In contrast to this global feminist call for the systematic response to violence against women as a violation of women's human rights, the Soviet response to various forms of gender violence was haphazard. For instance, before 1991, domestic violence was intermittently regulated under the rubric of "hooliganism" (Sperling 1990, 19). Not explicitly about violence between intimate partners, hooliganism was a crime: "the flagrant violation of public order expressed by a clear disrespect for society" that accompanies violence against a person and her or his property (e.g., Art. 206 1960 Russian Soviet Federated Socialist Republic Criminal Code, hereafter RSFSR CrC). As many Russians were forced to live in shared state-owned apartments, the public included a lot of homes and relationships. According to some estimates, domestic violence constituted up to 40 percent of crimes charged under hooliganism (Shelley 1987). Periodically, there were other avenues, such as through official state or party organs that would reprimand members for violating "socialist morality" (Attwood 1997, 102). Some women even received assistance from women's magazines, which could shame offenders. Socialist commitments to women's employment, equal pay, daycare, and universal healthcare—although not fully met—also lessened women's economic dependence on their husbands, creating exit options that many women in places with limited welfare states, such as the United States, do not have.

Paradoxically, Soviet police also often ignored violence between intimate partners as outside their jurisdiction. If extreme, such violence might be seen as a "family scandal" but not as an injustice, and the goal of police intervention was reconciliation. This was the case even though the rates of spousal homicide were particularly high. In the 1980s, women in Russia were almost three times more likely to be murdered by their current or former intimate partner than women in the United States, where the rates were also comparatively high (Gondolf and Shestakov 1997). The Soviet housing system, regulated through a system of residential permits (*propiski*) instead of property ownership, and chronically short of apartments, created additional problems. Divorced women were frequently obligated to live in the same apartment with their abusive ex-husbands, who retained a residential permit. The residential permit system meant that women could even be forced to share a communal apartment with violent men with whom they had no current or previous personal relationship (Attwood 1997, 102).

Similarly, Soviet authorities erratically attended to other forms of gender violence. Some high-profile rapes, especially gang rapes, received substantial attention and resulted in serious punishment, while others, such as marital or acquaintance rapes, were mostly ignored despite the absence of any explicit wife exemption for rape in the criminal codes (Johnson 2004).[5] Quid pro quo sexual harassment, in which an employer required sex in exchange for employment, was criminalized as "sexual compulsion" (*ponuzhdenie*) in 1923, decades before it became an issue in the West, but was never prosecuted (Juviler 1977, 245; Suchland 2005).[6] Various Communist Party and labor boards sometimes allowed women to lodge complaints about the "rude," "base," and "disparaging treatment" they received from the men in their workplaces, giving some recourse for the hostile environment form of sexual harassment (Granik 1997). The Soviet government also took a stand against trafficking in women with the ratification of the 1949 U.N. Convention for the Suppression of the Traffic in Persons and of the Exploitation of the Prostitution of Others, but added the proviso that "in the Soviet Union the social conditions which spawned prostitution have been removed" (Tiuriukanova 2006, 11).

In essence, in contrast to the concerted and woman-focused global feminist approach, gender violence was sometimes regulated as a by-product of other concerns during the Soviet period. The system was totalitarian in that it left little of life outside state or Communist Party control. Sometimes such violence was regulated as part of the state's coercive involvement in intimate and family life. Sometimes violence was regulated as part of anti-alcohol campaigns, because alcoholism was portrayed as the root of wife battery. And yet other times, such as in serial rape-murders, gender violence was regulated as it might be in more democratic societies, because mass public attention to these extraordinary, horrific crimes help maintain a sense of community, making sense of right and wrong, innocence and guilt (Johnson 2004).

Nevertheless, there was no consensus that gender violence was a distinct and structural problem that impacted women collectively, nor much cultural critique (Zabelina 1995). No statistics were collected on the extent of gender violence (Israelian and Zabelina 1995, 19); there was not even an agreed-upon term designating gender violence. Soviet ideology highlighted class violence, not gendered violence, never countering myths about women's culpability in their own violation, leading "several generations of people [to] not think about violence as violations of their rights" (Zabelina 2002, 6). The Soviet discipline of *victimologiia* even focused on women's provocation—a vague collection of behaviors seen as non-womanly—as explaining violence against women. Despite some radical ideas and initiatives in the early years of the regime, Soviet leaders did little to challenge general skepticism about most forms of violence against women.

## *Parafeminism*

This communist approach to gender violence was predicated on a traditional gender ideology about women's and men's roles in the home and intimate life. Soviet promises of equality were not realized in everyday life. Women faced a double burden, having to work outside the home as good Soviet citizens while also expected to shoulder the bulk of responsibilities for the home and childrearing. In an economy rife with shortages, procuring goods through long lines at multiple stores and through social networks meant a triple burden. Stalinist control of family life—through laws that complicated divorce, registered children born outside state-sanctioned marriage as fatherless, prohibited homosexuality, and limited abortion to women who had more than one child—clarified the Soviet stance on women's responsibility to live within and to promote marriage and motherhood.[7] Even as these laws were relaxed by later leaders, this underlying gender ideology remained dominant.

An essential part of the reason is that gender, as I am using it in this study, remained unexamined by Soviet authorities (Johnson and Robinson 2007). For Soviet leaders and scholars, equality of women and men did not mean the erasure of what were presumed to be natural psychological and social differences (Attwood 1997). Teachers and parents were urged to instill traditional norms, including weakness in women and strength in men. That these characteristics were understood to be natural meant that the impact of such gender socialization on encouraging gender violence could be ignored. This kind of doublethink legitimated extensive social policies, but these Soviet policies were seen only as a form of social protectionism for women's "natural" maternal function. Limits on the jobs women could hold (regardless of whether they were or planned to be mothers) and extensive maternity leaves (as wonderful as they might seem to harried American mothers) reinforced gendered assumptions about women's and men's domestic responsibilities and solidified women's status as second-class workers. These policies resulted from the practical problems of how to accommodate women (who were assumed to have maternal and wifely functions), who were much needed in the labor force (Buckley 1985, 26). The law against sexual compulsion, for example, was a reaction to the problems resulting from women's mass entry into the workforce during Lenin's New Economic Policy and was predicated on sexual difference (Juviler 1977, 245; Suchland 2005).

Within this limited understanding, the Soviet commitment to women did extend to the establishment of institutions designed to help women. Revolutionary socialist feminists created a Women's Department (*Zhenotdel*) within the Communist Party, perhaps the first official women's institution in the world, yet the primary goal was to recruit women into the party (Lapidus 1977). The founders' more radical hopes that the department would transform the status of women and their role in families were marginalized and contributed to its abolishment by the 1930s. Founded during the Khrushchev regime and lasting even longer were the women's councils (*zhensoviety*), which were designed to help women "harmonize" work and home life, but not by recruiting men as full participants in the home (Racioppi and See 1995). For all these institutions, the goals were driven not by the women participants, but by the party or government with whom they were associated. At the same time, this communist neocorporatism meant almost no non-party, non-state spaces for challenging gender.

These kinds of women's institutions contrast with the "state feminism" that researchers have found in some industrialized democracies (Stetson and Mazur 1995; Stetson 2002). Like the women's policy agencies found in some Western European governments, communist women's institutions claimed to be promoting women's rights and women's equality (Robinson 1995). They even represent, in some ways, challenges to sex hierarchies in the sense of helping women overcome problems of consumption and reproduction to be better workers. Yet, "they did not accept . . . that the system of oppression operated within the private as well as the public sphere . . . [or understand] the need to change the structure of consumption and reproduction" (207–208). Women's policy agencies constitute state feminism when they are "effective in promoting women as a group and undermining patterns of gender-based inequities in society" (Stetson and Mazur 1995, 2); the communist women's institutions represent the "state's usurpation of a parafeminist agenda" (Robinson 1995, 205).

In other words, this Soviet legacy highlights the need to draw some distinctions within de facto feminism, that is, actions seeking social or political change to lessen sex/gender hierarchies. Feminisms tend to share three core components: concerted response to problems that women tend to face, an opposition to sex

**TABLE 2.1.** *Range of de Facto Feminisms*

| | COMPONENTS | | |
|---|---|---|---|
| | 1. Concerted response to problems women tend to face | 2. Opposition to sex hierarchies | 3. Appreciation that gender is constructed |
| pseudofeminism | X | | |
| parafeminism | X | X | |
| comprehensive feminism | X | X | X |

hierarchies, and the appreciation that gender, if not also sex, is constructed (and thus changeable) (see table 2.1).[8] Marxism-Leninism, framed through Engels's "woman question," recognized the systemic problems facing women in the bourgeois family and held that bringing women into the workforce and then socialism would solve these problems. In communist practice, that meant institutions, policies, and organizations to address problems faced by women as they entered into the workforce and other initiatives such as quotas to include women in public and political life (such that it was). Thus, the Soviet response met the first two components, but the failure to recognize the social construction of gender meant that the critique did not meet the third. The challenge was only to the sex hierarchy, not the gender hierarchy. Other responses discussed in this book satisfy only the first component, constituting what I call pseudofeminism. While others theorists may label these responses as antifeminist for their acceptance of sex/gender hierarchies, I have chosen the term pseudofeminist to highlight the falseness of their post–global feminist consensus claims—often couched in global feminist language—to be helping women.

## PRIVATIZING GENDER VIOLENCE

As Soviet rule waned in the late 1980s, even this haphazard parafeminist approach to women and gender violence became suspect. Mikhail Gorbachev's policy of glasnost meant not just more freedom of speech, but less authority to intervene in people's lives. His reforms also unintentionally eroded the legitimacy of communist institutions, including many that had helped women, eventually leading to the dissolution of the Soviet system in 1991. This last Soviet leader restructured the economy, allowing more market-like mechanisms and the establishment of cooperatives, and inadvertently strengthened the underground economy. Following the collapse, the new Russian leader Boris Yeltsin (1991–99) expanded these reforms. His more chaotic rule was followed by the presidency of Vladimir Putin, who claimed a mandate to reinstate order even at the expense of fledgling democratic and market mechanisms. The following section, divided by issue, details the post-Soviet changes in law enforcement response and the legal thinking on gender violence as well as provides some background on the extent of the problems. This is the postcommunist baseline.

## Rape and Sexual Harassment

Russia's transformation meant a significant alteration in the response to sexual violence. Whereas earlier Soviet police might take action when a woman was raped by those known to her, by the 1990s, police began routinely rejecting all sorts of sexual violence statements without any investigation (Human Rights Watch 1997, 21–24). If they accepted the initial complaint, they often obstructed the process at every point, for example by refusing to give referrals to forensic doctors or delaying the referrals and not informing the rape victims of the consequence of showering before their examination (Johnson 2004). Women reported being turned away or simply choosing not to report sexual violence because they did not believe the police would help them (Israelian and Zabelina 1995, 23–24). Arrest rates for rape had begun to fall in Russia in the mid-1980s (Nalla and Newman 1994). Other women persisted. For example, a fifteen-year-old gang rape victim said that after she told her story twenty times, the police finally accepted her statement. According to Human Rights Watch (1997), victims of sexual violence usually had to tell their stories at least four times to different police officers. Even when women overcame police reluctance, they met a similar coldness from prosecutors; the majority of cases that were closed during the preliminary investigation stage were rape cases (30). Other times the criminal justice system assisted alleged rapists who would blackmail, threaten, or bribe women to drop the charges. The results were disastrous for women's rights. For example, a Saratov lawyer-activist reported that she had not had a single case where a woman wanted to go through with prosecution for sexual violence.[9]

Although part of the problem may be attributed to the dysfunctional and weak state,[10] most police and prosecutors were explicit that their actions were based on their beliefs about women's culpability. Most police detectives believed that young men were often victims of false allegations made so that the alleged rape victims could extort them, that 70 percent of the men who are convicted of rape in Russia are "essentially not guilty."[11] In other cases, women are held responsible for "provoking" their own rape, such as by drinking with men in their car or apartment (Human Rights Watch 1997, 19–20), confusing what global feminists might consider bad judgment for legal responsibility. At the same time, police and prosecutors tended to continue to employ coercive measures in response to some types of rapes—particularly vicious gang rapes and serial murders—even forcing innocent men to confess (Khodyreva 1996; Johnson 2004). In sum, law enforcement had moved more types of sexual violence from "real rapes" (Estrich 1987) into the category of rapes that they did not see as real.

Their justifications reflect late Soviet and early post-Soviet legal thinking about sexual violence.[12] An analysis of the two leading legal specialists on rape who were writing in the early 1990s illustrates the role of the idea of a particular concept of morality (Attwood 1997, 104–106). While earlier Soviet theorists might have referred to the "woman question" and the public order as justifications, these theorists hinged their argument on the idea that a civilized or moral society "strictly protects the honor and dignity of woman as a symbol of its own honor" (Iu. M. Antonian and A. A. Tkachenko, cited in Attwood 1997, 104). With convoluted logic, they turned their "moral" critique onto the women, holding that rapes have increased during the liberalization of communism because of the immoral behavior of young women who, influenced by the West, now drink and have sex with many men. Building on earlier theories of provocation (and *viktimnost'*), they cast drinking and drunkenness by women as particularly contributory. Illustrating the continued reliance on essentialist notions of sex differences, these theorists also placed blame for the problem of rape on the "the demise of traditional masculinity and femininity" (Attwood 1997, 106). In contrast to global feminist concerns with consent and coercion, they suggested that police should prevent dubious people from gathering in courtyards and on the streets.

As a result, in contrast to all other forms of violent crime, which rose steeply, official statistics on rape and attempted rape suggested an implausible drop of approximately one-half throughout the 1990s. Officially, the number of male rapists (of women) decreased from 13,902 in 1991 to only 6,688 in 2000, with only a slight upsurge from 1992 rates in 1993 and 1994.[13] This suggests a decrease in the rape rate from 9.5 per 100,000 persons in 1991 to 4.9 in 2000, which is especially unbelievable when compared to the mean European rate of around 6.4.[14] This decrease follows some thirty years of sharp increase, interrupted only by a marked decrease just as Gorbachev lessened control of society in the mid 1980s (Kon 1995, 211; D'iachenko and Koloskova 1995). Even police officials begrudgingly recognize that these official rates do not reflect reality. Illustrating the particular Russian morality-based thinking, a spokesman for the Ministry of Internal Affairs defensively explained that this decrease is a result of women not reporting rape "because their moral standards have been corrupted by sex on television."[15]

There are only limited studies indicating the actual rate of rape in Russia. Activists have argued that actual rates are ten times the official statistics, finding that somewhere between 5 percent and 12 percent of those who call their hotlines also report their rapes to the police. Experts suggest perhaps only 3 percent of victims report rape (Zabelina 2002, 10). A 1993 sociological study in St. Petersburg found that one in four women admitted they had been raped (Kon 1995, 213). The fact that one in two registered rapes is a gang rape and the stories women tell of sex without consent suggest that rape is very common (212). Studies suggest that younger women are predominant targets (perhaps 40 percent of all victims) and that almost all rapes are accompanied by other physical violence or threats of murder (D'iachenko in Zabelina 2002, 9–10). By the 1990s, being raped was a constant fear for most women. For example, a 1994 survey found that only 5 percent of Muscovite women did not fear rape (Zabelina 1995, 20).[16]

The state response to sexual harassment was even worse. Without effective local Communist Party or labor boards, as the system was transformed, the only recourse left to women was the criminal justice system, whose reluctance to respond to most rape complaints apparently extended to all sexual harassment cases. Up through the early 1990s, there were apparently no criminal cases opened.[17] Women were unlikely to even file a complaint. For example, one leading St. Petersburg activist had many women coming to her after being harassed—typically they had been promised benefits for sexual services, refused, and then lost their jobs—but none had filed complaints.[18]

Yet, the problem of sexual harassment was more common than previously as economic liberalization created more workplaces outside the state. By the mid 1990s, job advertisements often specified young and attractive women employees "without inhibitions" (*bez komplekhov*). In response, women seeking jobs in newspapers explicitly stated that they want no expectations of sexual services (Khotkina 1996, 15). One study in St. Petersburg found that approximately one in three women had experienced this kind of sexual harassment (Kletsin 1998). Inappropriate comments—or what American feminists call a hostile environment—are so common to be seen as normal.

### Domestic Violence

By the 1990s, police were also ignoring cases of domestic violence (Human Rights Watch 1995; Human Rights Watch 1997; Johnson 2001). Entering the home and prosecuting domestic violence under the pretense of "hooliganism" became less justifiable, and more people lived in private (as in privately owned or noncommunal) apartments. Despite the fact that there were many criminal articles, such as those regarding assault, that would still apply,[19] more than under Soviet rule, police were reluctant to act in response to domestic violence calls or to initiate a criminal inquiry. The 1995 Human Rights Watch report cited as typical cases in which women said that even though they had complained to the police for months or years, the police never spoke to the abuser, never wrote out a formal complaint, or never initiated a case. The Russian Association of Crisis Centers for Women reported that 70 percent of women calling hotlines claim that the police refused to help them. In one case, a woman repeatedly went to the police, who offered the suggestion to sleep with the former partner currently stalking her. Growing tired of her persistence, they offered her the phone number of a hit man.

Once again, this negligence was not simply a result of corruption or low morale of the police. The police and officials at the Ministry of Internal Affairs recognized and justified their failure to respond to woman battery, claiming that it is not their responsibility. Surprisingly, given the widespread neglect of the laws they were charged to enforce, police claimed that the Russian Constitution established a right to privacy that proscribes their involvement in domestic violence.[20] In other cases, they justified their disregard for domestic violence using Soviet-period criminal procedure in new ways. They insisted that domestic violence, regardless of the severity, only constituted the type of crime that was privately prosecutable, a particular category of crime for which a victim must investigate and bring charges herself (Human Rights Watch 1995, 21; Human Rights 1997).[21] Judges, socialized in a system with virtually no urban private property, suddenly began to enforce abusive men's rights to their apartment regardless of the consequences for their partners (Human Rights Watch 1997, 48).[22]

Although couched in the new (gender neutral) language of protecting rights, their response reflected the current legal thinking on domestic violence. While communist theorists had explained domestic violence as a problem of a bourgeois family, Gorbachev's reforms signaled the need for new explanations. One important new theorist instead blamed the inclusion of women into the workforce, which both took them away from their homes and created financial independence (G. G. Moshak in Attwood 1997). Domestic violence was a result of this disruption of the "natural" order of things, leading husbands to see "physical punishment as morally acceptable." Extending arguments about women's "provocation," the suggestion is that women could lessen their chances of experiencing violence if they returned to their "natural" roles as selfless mothers with restrained behaviors (not smoking or drinking) and gave in to their husbands. Another contemporary theorist, after interviewing men who had murdered their wives, argued that such violence was a result of men's dissatisfaction with women's emancipation (D. A. Shestakov in Attwood 1997, 107–108). He pointed to the general unhappiness of such families, found by sociologists, in which women are insufficiently feminine (by earning more money or being too authoritarian). This thinking meant that domestic violence, even femicide, was represented as "an extreme but not unjustified response to the erosion of traditional patriarchal gender roles." Police, prosecutors, and judges made these theories concrete when they refused to intervene because, they asserted, women provoked their violence by a wide variety of behaviors such as earning too much money, wearing the wrong clothes, being unfaithful, taunting the abuser, nagging, and complaining about bad behavior. (When the batterer is drunk, almost anything can be considered provocation.)[23]

At the same time as the communist justifications for criminal justice system intervention were being eroded, the state welfare system that had provided at least some indirect assistance to women was collapsing. Problems dated back some two decades before Gorbachev, leading to the necessity of bribes for medical services, but by the early 1990s, the social service system was in chronic disrepair. Experts on domestic violence estimated that the social service system could meet only 7 percent of demand due to lack of funding and staff. Other communist institutions that helped shame perpetrators completely vanished, while the restrictive residential permit system remained (although the rich could now buy apartments).

In this context, the incidence of domestic violence has risen sharply. Official data from the 1990s reveal that men commit almost 90 percent of the most vicious interpersonal violence, what the Russians call grave harm, hooliganism, and murder (Johnson 2005). These data also show an overall rise, throughout the period, in male-perpetrated interpersonal violence, peaking in 1994–95. Since divorce rates have risen and families have been generally seen to be in crisis (Lyon 2003, ch. 2), this increase suggests that domestic violence in particular has probably increased. By the late 1990s, despite the prevalence of images of Russian mafia violence on Western media, the Russian Ministry of Internal Affairs admitted that some 80 percent of violent crimes take place in the home (e.g., U.S. Department of State 1997). Of the violent offenses between spouses conducted in the home, the ministry found that wives are the victims in four of five cases (Zabelina et al. 2007, 10).

There have also been several surveys conducted by activists and researchers that suggest the extent of the problem. According to a small 1996 survey in Moscow, one-fourth of wives and one-third of divorced women experienced physical abuse in their relationships; in the more rural regions of Pskov and Saratov the proportions were even higher (Vannoy et al. 1999). A larger survey conducted in 2001 and 2002 of men and women found that while the most extreme physical and sexual assaults were fairly rare (in 2–4% of relationships), respondents reported that emotionally abusive behaviors—such as cruel joking (36%) and scolding and rebuking (58%)—were common to many relationships (Zabelina 2002, 57). A follow-up survey conducted in 2006 suggests that these latter problems have increased (Zabelina et al. 2007, 81). Another survey found that half of the women respondents reported at least one incident of physical violence (e.g., striking, pushing, shaking, arm-twisting) from their present husbands (41% had been struck at least once, 26% more than once, 3% at least once a month; over 13% had been struck while pregnant, breastfeeding, sick, in distress, or in a similarly vulnerable state) (Gorshkova and Shurygina 2003). Some 57 percent of surveyed Russians estimate that women are the primary victims of violence in the family (36% thought children were and only 3% pointed to men; Zabelina et al. 2007, 30). In the Northern Caucuses, resistance to Russian rule and the post-Soviet Chechen wars have reinvigorated violent traditions, including bride abduction, forced marriages, blood feuds, and honor killings (Open Society Institute 2007, 17).

Since the mid 1990s, Russian activists, researchers, and more recently, even the government assert that some 12,000–15,000 women die every year from femicide in Russia (for example, see Zabelina 1995; Russian Federation 1999; Amnesty International 2005), but unfortunately, credible data is not available (Johnson 2005). As part of its negligence, the Russian government does not keep track of the relationship between the murdered and murder victim. As late as 2007, the state had not released any documented and detailed indicators of the extent of the problem (Open Society Institute 2007, 49). In general, violent mortality rates in Russia are three times the world average (Bobylev and Alexandrova 2005, 66).

Officially, the problems associated with trafficking in women—the exploitation of prostitution or coercive labor—did not exist until Gorbachev's perestroika. Prostitution was neither legal nor criminalized, but penalized with a small fine.[24] As coercion declined, prostitution was brought to the public consciousness by the 1986 publication of Yevgeny Dodolev's *Interdevochka* (a book later made into a popular film), which glorified the lives of prostitutes working the hotels housing the businessmen flocking into Russia (Kon 1995, 223). Many young women, while perhaps uncomfortable with the morality, came to see hard-currency prostitution as the only avenue to the glamorous life available in the West, a source of important dollars as the Russian ruble's value dropped precipitously. A 1989 survey found that high school women saw such work as a prestigious profession. But the reality for most prostitutes was much grimmer, working for rubles from poor Russian men, perhaps at railroad and subway stations; as the Soviet economy disintegrated, many women saw no other options for making money. As the markets became legal, prostitution burst out into the open, advertised as massage or escort services in newspapers, especially English-language ones. By the early 2000s, some 15,000 women were prostitutes in Moscow, four out of five of these were street prostitutes (Mukhin 2002, 55–57). According to the preeminent Russian sexologist (Kon 1995, 226), the selling of Russian women abroad began in the 1980s for pornography, but then expanded in the 1990s as the borders opened and organized crime and corruption became rampant.

Labor markets, on the other hand, were allowed to exist during Soviet rule; people, in general, could choose their jobs. But until Soviet collapse, the freedom of movement was limited by the registration permit system and the closed borders. Starting in the early 1990s, Russia became a major hub for labor immigration, both into and out of Russia, to the tune of some five million workers entering Russia per year and some million leaving Russia to work abroad (Tiuriukanova 2006, 33). The failures of the official Soviet economy also led to the growth of a substantial underground economy, constituting some one-quarter to one-half of GDP in Russia (compared to 5–10% in developed countries), where labor exploitation is more common (55). These exploitative sectors include construction, commerce, catering, car repair, tourism, entertainment, and construction. Women are relegated to the most unskilled and uncontrollable sectors, such as market trading, entertainment, and domestic services. For example, in the large Moscow market Luzhniki, immigrant women work for a hierarchy of bosses who sometimes keep them in debt bondage and sometimes require sexual services.[25] In her review of the existing studies of trafficking for the United Nations and the International Organization for Migration, trafficking expert Elena Tiuriukanova (2006, 35) found that "[t]rafficking for labour exploitation is the most common type of human trafficking in the Russian Federation," although women were more likely to be sexually exploited.

By the new millennium, the region of Central and Eastern Europe and Eurasia became the second largest source (after Southeast Asia) for the trafficking of women globally. Some estimates are that some 175,000 women are trafficked per year, of which one-fifth to one-third are estimated to come from Russia (see Tiuriukanova 2006, 13). According to one Russian expert, "Russian (*rossiiskii*) women are engaged in prostitution in more than 50 countries . . . [i]n several of which . . . the import of women from Russia and from the other Soviet Republics is so great that prostitutes there are called 'Natashas'" (Erokhina 2002).

The main routes are through the Baltics or through Poland or the Czech Republic to Northern and Western Europe or the United States, the main destinations for trafficked women (Tiuriukanova 2006, 23–24). Other women are trafficked through the Caucasus (such as Georgia) into Turkey, Greece, and the Mediterranean region. Others are sent through Egypt and into Israel or other Middle Eastern countries such as the United Arab Emirates. And still others are sent to or through China to Japan or South Korea. Trafficking for labor exploitation has been discovered in Germany, Turkey, and Portugal. At the same time, Russia is also a destination for trafficking from the poor formerly Soviet states, such as Tajikistan, Uzbekistan, Kyrgyzstan, Georgia, Armenia, Moldova, and Ukraine. For some women, Russia is a transit country through which they are trafficked from other post-Soviet states to the Gulf states.[26]

Officials are more directly and actively culpable for the problem of trafficking than for other forms of gender violence. Border or immigration officials forge signatures, exact bribes, and accept fraudulent migration documents (Tiuriukanova 2006, 58–59). Employers and organized criminals collude with law enforcement authorities, sometimes even "returning" trafficked women who have come to them for help to their captors. ECPAT International (End Child Prostitution, Child Pornography and Trafficking of Children for Sexual Purposes) estimates that pimps in Moscow spend 4.5 million U.S. dollars a month in bribes to law enforcement and public officials. Other authorities are lax in monitoring companies that illegally sell registration and migration permits, while police routinely demand bribes for improper or missing documents. Activist-scholars found that there are no government organs that help control prostitution, even teenage prostitution (Zabelina 2002, 10).

As with other forms of gender violence, the official response at least partially reflects the legal thinking on the problem. Without a critique of gender as socially constructed, criminologists view prostitution as mostly an individualistic problem of sex-crazed women (Kon 1995). While Soviet theorists might also raise concern about bourgeois conditions of poverty leading to prostitution (at least in other places), post-Soviet thinking focused on physiological proclivities (of women). This logic was extended to sex trafficking, especially for those women who they assumed went abroad thinking of the possibility of working in the sex industry. These women, the legal thinking goes, should have known better (Duban 2006, 49). They are held accountable regardless of the violations of their rights that follow, creating a classification, much like for rape, where only a very small number of cases are seen as real trafficking. Labor trafficking, in the 1990s, was barely on the radar of legal thinkers.

In sum, in contrast to the global feminist appeal for gender violence to be seen as a problem of public concern, the disintegration of the Soviet system in the early 1990s meant the privatization of much gender violence, even more so than under communism. The creation of a private sphere outside state penetration—in the market, civil society, and personal and family life—was desired by reformers from Russia and the West as the antidote to totalitarianism. But, as in Western liberal democracies, this new private sphere reflected men's interests more than women's interests (Watson 1993). While men (even when violent) gained protection from state intervention into their domestic and sexual relationships with women, women lost previous avenues for holding men accountable and for attending to some of the medical and psychological consequences of violence. As markets expanded, women's bodies were commodified—advertised and sold domestically and internationally—mostly benefiting the male buyers and the pimps and traffickers as well as the organized crime syndicates and law enforcement officers who provided "protection" to these businesses.

## TRANSFORMING COMMUNISM

### Gendered Transformation

This privatization of gender violence in the 1990s was part of a larger gendered process across postcommunist societies in Central and Eastern Europe and Eurasia (hereafter the "region"). Although moving the system toward a liberal democracy where markets prevail was portrayed as a gender-neutral process—with the rhetoric of gender-neutral citizens and consumers—the consequences were not neutral because the roots of gender inequality remained within both society and the new forms of political and economic systems (Pateman 1988; Watson 1993). This gendered transformation complicates a campaign against gender violence.

One of the biggest problems in Russia has been the feminization of poverty; not only were most of the new poor adults women, but political decisions created an economy in which women's contributions are systematically undervalued. The massive changes led to massive upheavals as the GDP per capita dropped precipitously in the early 1990s, surpassing Soviet levels only in the new millennium (Varbanova 2006, 14). In a country where women are more likely to live in single-parent households than anywhere else in the region, the problem is particularly acute for single mothers and their children (19). In 2000, more than one in three children in such households were living in poverty (in contrast to approximately one in four in two-parent households). State subsidies for childcare, maternity leave, and parental sick leave have been cut or permitted to devalue, exacerbating the problem.

In the early years of the transition, women seemed to be suffering in the new labor market much more than men. In societies marked by their high rates of women's economic activity, women were the first to be laid off and the last hired, a problem dismissed by the Yeltsin administration (Bridger 1999; Einhorn 1993). Now, with more time and better data, the story is more complicated. For example, although there was a precipitous decline in women's economic activity (either in the labor force or unemployed) from 1989 to 2004, the decline was more extreme for men (–12.7% as compared to –16.3%) (Varbanova 2006, 14). Similarly, men's unemployment rates have remained slightly higher than women's (32), but women are much more often classified as economically inactive (22). This difference itself has a lot to do with gender roles: when asked, unemployed women may be more likely to describe themselves as a homemaker (thus economically inactive) than are unemployed men, who are more likely to describe themselves as actively seeking work (i.e., officially unemployed). Women are also often pushed into extended parental leave (because there is no daycare) or into retiring earlier.

Other statistics more clearly point to women's stratification in the labor market. For example, women are much more likely to be unemployed long term, causing their skills to become obsolete and their chances of reemployment to decrease (Varbanova 2006, 33, 34). The gap between women's and men's monthly wages is the largest in the region, at 36 percent in 2003, larger than it was under Soviet rule and most problematic for women twenty to forty years of age (50). There is also significant segregation of women into sectors of the economy that tend to earn less as well as vertical segregation, meaning that the higher status the position is within the sector, the fewer women (Bobylev and Alexandrova 2005). Women are more often found in government jobs or the informal economy, where they make tradeoffs on income or safety.[27] Other problems include the increased discrepancy between job specifications and the professional qualifications of women and the prevalence of sexist job advertisements (including appearance requirements for jobs such as clothing salespeople), which appeared first in the early 1990s and continue to today. As a result, most women do not have the economic resources, time, or energy for activism as they struggle to take care of themselves, often their children, and even sometimes their husbands.

These changes in the labor market were accompanied by the commodification of images of women's bodies and sexuality. The early 1990s witnessed a huge and jarring deluge of pornography (Goscilo 1996). The porn was everywhere, even pinned to the omnipresent kiosks where everyone was buying their food. On the one hand, these reflected the sexual revolution that accompanied the dramatic political and economic changes. Sex in the Soviet Union had been taboo, but burst into the public agenda during Gorbachev's glasnost, revealing dramatic changes in sexual morality that had begun in the 1960s and '70s (Kon 1995). The new freedoms included sexual freedoms. They included liberalization of policies toward homosexual individuals who had been hospitalized (and sometimes convinced that they were transsexuals), imprisoned, tortured, and sometimes executed (Essig 1999). For many women, these changes were liberating, freeing them from ubiquitous cultural icons of asexual women and lessening the double standards about women's sexuality. In 2004, the new freedoms even led to the production and popularity of a Russian *Sex and the City*, titled, *The Balzac Age, or All Men Are Bastards*. The dramatic changes have even led to public (albeit fabricated and for men more than women) lesbianism, such as by the young women in the pop group t.A.T.u.

On the other hand, the sexual freedoms represent the expansion of sexual rights for heterosexual men even at the cost of others. Most negative, from the perspective of most global feminists, was the proliferation of images of violence against women in the media (Attwood 1996). As in the West, many of the pornographic images eroticized women's subordination, portraying women happily and passively submitting to violence, bondage, and even murder. These images link sex and violence and sexualized women while constructing a violent masculinity. Although the amount of pornography has since decreased, the marketing of women and women's images has become at least as common as it is in the United States. At the very least, this commodification and sexualization of women highlights their differences from the ideal gender-neutral (male) citizen just as citizenship is becoming more meaningful.

More clearly troubling from the perspective of global feminists is the reaction to these changes, what the prominent sexologist Igor Kon (2005) has labeled a "moral panic." Driven by the new Russian Communist Party and the Russian Orthodox Church, with support from pro-life advocates, the new "antisexual crusade . . . targets . . . sex education, women's reproductive rights, and free access to sexuality-related information. The campaign is openly nationalistic, xenophobic, homophobic, . . . anti-Semitic," and sometimes even violent (III).

Another complicating factor is what the Russians call the demographic crisis; the Russian population is declining precipitously because of decreasing fertility among women and increasing mortality among men. In 1995, the life expectancy of men had dropped from 64 in 1990 to 58, the lowest in the region. While women's life expectancy has fluctuated only between 72 and 74 years, the men's life expectancy reached 60 again only in 2003 (Varbanova 2006, 15). For some, men's disastrous life expectancy has been taken to be a simplistic indicator of men's inequality vis-à-vis women, but women too face the consequences of these problems, which are driven mostly by increased smoking and alcohol consumption, often spiking after the men become unemployed. Women are left before and after their partners' early death to deal with increased violence and decreased contributions to the household. Further, it is (ethnically Russian) women who are predominantly blamed for their decisions to have fewer children (even as they reflect rational decisions in the context of the huge upheaval). In 2006, President Putin introduced monetary incentives for Russian women to have more children. Public officials' and society's preoccupation with this problem never includes discussions of the solving of it through allowing more non-Russian immigrants from the former Soviet republics because the crisis is seen as one of the ethnic Russian (*russkii*) nation.

The problems facing women are particularly acute because there are so few women with political power, despite a few notable exceptions such as Irina Khaka-mada or Ella Pamfilova and the surprising and short-lived success of the Women of Russia political movement in the early 1990s (Buckley 1999; Nechemias 2000). The Soviet system had kept up the appearance of gender equality with a one-third quota for the Supreme Soviet as well as local soviets (but not for the legislative and executive bodies with the real power). In the first contested elections in 1990, the proportion of women in the lower house dropped to 5.4 percent. In subsequent elections for the new lower house, the Duma, women have constituted 13.5 percent (1993–95), 10.2 percent (1995–99), and 7.7 percent (1999–2003) despite the fact that women constitute some 53–54 percent of the population and tend to vote more than men (Duban 2006, 55). In the 2003–2007 Duma, women constituted 9.8 percent of all deputies, putting Russia near the bottom of countries around the world.[28] Only four of the twenty-nine legislative committees were chaired by women (Duban 2006, 56). In local legislatures, women account for only 10 percent of representatives. This underrepresentation of women has contributed to a very limited impact of women deputies on government policies—only when an issue or the context is nonpartisan and when they articulate their stances from a neotraditional gender ideology (Shevchenko 2007).

## Gender Neotraditionalism

Underpinning this gendered process was a neotraditional gender ideology, a belief that physiology dictates that men are to be the strong providers and protectors and women the beautiful loving caretakers. A powerful force in the new Russia, this gender neotraditionalism has been part and parcel of the nationalism that came later to Russia than to other Soviet republics, but was essential to the push for the democratization of Russia. As elsewhere (Yuval-Davis 1991), gender is an organizing strategy for nationalism. In Russia, this neotraditional gender ideology draws upon pre- and anti-Soviet beliefs and practices advocating women's roles as mothers and homemakers, not unlike (nor unconnected to) the nineteenth-century "cult of domesticity" exalted in the West (Lyon 2003). It also references earlier Russian Orthodox articulations of women's roles, such as the sixteenth-century text the *Domostroi,* about how the home is to be run by an obedient wife for the worship of God incarnate in the husband.[29] Although these ideas about family life were more fantasy than reality (Lyon 2007), a reprint of the *Domostroi* was one of the most purchased books in the early 1990s. These beliefs about gender also drew from more recent global sources, such as from fantasies of 1950s American traditional gender roles (Zvinkliene 1999). The gender ideology is traditional—embracing the privatization and domestication of women's lives (Attwood 1996)—and also new in that it responds to the impact of communism and exists in a new more interconnected world, where gender ideologies can more easily cross borders (Johnson and Robinson 2007).

The neotraditional ideology was most persuasive in the 1990s in its call for women to give up their jobs and return to the home (Vannoy et al. 1999). This call was particularly compelling to women, if they had a choice, exhausted as they were by their double and triple burdens. The promotion of women by gender neotraditionalism to a new, exalted status, at least in theory, was also attractive. It brought stereotypes of "idealized women," who masterfully resist the state in their "bedrooms and kitchens," and "little men," who always need women's help (Lissyutkina 1999, 171). These ideas were also powerful because Soviet intrusion led the family—including gender roles—to be seen as a haven from the state. Unfortunately, the economic reality of Russia in the 1990s meant no room for such sacrifice. Most women had to work to support themselves and their family.

The dominance of this gender neotraditionalism creates the possibility for unapologetic public sexism, for example, from the ultranationalist politician Vladimir Zhirinovsky. In an article in the communist *Pravda*,[30] he explained the criticism of Russia by the U.S. secretary of state Condoleezza Rice as a result of her being a "a single woman who has no children. She loses her reason because of her late single status. Nature takes it all. . . . Condoleezza Rice needs a company of soldiers. She needs to be taken to barracks where she would be satisfied." Although taken as a maverick, Zhirinovsky has been elected to the parliament every election since 1993, and he often articulates beliefs held by many others in the society. These beliefs have been illustrated in the public chastisement of women seeking political positions for a wide variety of behaviors based on gender. In one region, a male deputy asked if women entering politics were "preparing to breast-feed the electorate" (Duban 2006, 57–58). Other candidates were publicly slandered for being "loose." One party campaigned against a woman running for St. Petersburg governor with the slogan "Being Governor Is Not a Woman's Business." Summarizing Russian gender neotraditionalism, President Vladimir Putin has asserted that "[w]omen should have one unquestionable privilege—the right to be protected by men."[31]

The dominance of gender neotraditionalism has also meant widespread resistance to feminism and the concept of gender. Under communism, feminism was seen as inherently anti-male, an extreme problem in a society where men are seen as often helpless like children (Lissyutkina 1999). Even the idea of the social construction of gender has been resisted by most women, who believe in essential roles of women and men (Vannoy et al. 1999).

At the same time, some women's groups, like some women parliamentarians, have been successful by playing upon these neotraditional ideas. The most effective has been the Committee of Soldiers' Mothers, a popular and longstanding women's organization that has inserted itself into military politics (Caiazza 2002). Another group, the Committee of Beslan Mothers, which emerged following Russia's botched response to the Chechen terrorist siege of a school, has become one of the few outspoken critics of the Putin administration. Acting in the prescribed role as mothers allows them to pretend that they are not political and to seem less threatening.

Within this dominance of gender neotraditionalism, there has been only limited feminist resistance. The Soviet leadership had reacted strongly against dissident feminism, for example, by expelling Tatiana Mamonova in 1980 for her feminist publications. When Gorbachev's reform spurred the development of some independent and critical organizations, women's organizations were slow to emerge (Nechemias 1991). The watershed event of what was to become the movement was a gathering of some two hundred women from forty-eight different Soviet women's groups in Dubna, Russia, in 1991, for what is now called the First Independent Women's Forum (Sperling 1999; Kay 2000).[32] This gathering and a second one a year later were astute and radical in their critique not just of the Soviet regime, but of the economic and political reforms and the exclusion of women from the process of democratization.

Following the first gathering, the movement grew in size. In 1991, there were fifty women's organizations officially registered; two hundred in 1992; three hundred in 1994, and six hundred in 1998 (Sperling 1999, 18–19). There were many more operating unofficially, having not jumped through the considerable bureaucratic hoops necessary for registration with the Russian Ministry of Justice— perhaps two thousand in 1998 (Abubikirova, Klimenkova, Kotchkina, Regentova, and Troinova 1998, 9). They represented a diversity of activities, from lobbying, holding conferences and seminars, publishing feminist magazines, and conducting research to conducting self-help groups or providing social services for unemployed women, single mothers, and artists (Sperling 1999, 19). These forums also helped the various organizations coordinate themselves, creating a connected movement from what had been disparate organizations. Some of these organizations embraced feminism; most were de facto feminists in their challenge to the status of women, both in their actions and in simply organizing, which challenged "gender climate" in Russia, where women were encouraged to be politically silent (Kay 2000).

Despite the admirable efforts of many activists, however, the women's movement remains small and fairly powerless. Many of the organizations lasted only a short time; some seemed only to be clever ways for charismatic, English-speaking Russians to support themselves during tough times (see Henderson 2000, 65–82, 2003: Richter 2002; McMahon 2001, 45–68; Sundstrom 2002, 207–29). Almost none of the long-lasting organizations have large constituencies. Finally, although Russia is officially a federalist state, power has been remarkably centralized, especially since Putin's rise to power, leaving few avenues for even more powerful NGOs.

Similarly, there are some small pockets of a kind of feminism within the state. In 1993, President Yeltsin created the Commission for Women, Family, and Demography under the office of the president. Headed at one time by an activist, the commission was disbanded in 2000. There was also a Department on the Affairs of Women, Family, and Youth within the Ministry of Social Development, but a series of reorganizations moved the department around until 2004, when the department was dissolved, as was a Permanent Roundtable of Women's NGOs (Duban 2006, 34).[33] In 2005, a replacement Coordinating Council on Gender Issues was formed within the new Ministry of Health and Social Development and charged with gender analysis. There are also bodies within both houses of the Federal Assembly to address women's issues. Within the upper house, the Federation Council, is an Expert Council on Equal Rights and Opportunities of Men and Women, and within the lower house, the Duma, is the Committee on Women, Family, and Youth. In 1997, the Commission on Improving the Status of Women was created to coordinate between the state institutions and NGOs and to monitor for CEDAW, but it appears to have been disbanded in 2004 (Open Society Institute 2007). The new Public Chamber designed by Putin—officially to coordinate between the state and society—includes one feminist, Elena Ershova, the head of the Consortium of Women's NGOs.

Not only do these organizations come and go depending on political whims, they tend to be within larger weak institutions, not the power ministries. Much as with the Soviet institutions, these post-Soviet entities are also not the kind of women's policy agencies that promote a comprehensive state feminism. They are predominantly focused on social protection, not advancing women's rights (Duban 2006, 37). Like their Soviet predecessors, they are parafeminist in their dependence on social norms about women and men.

## ASSESSING THE LIKELIHOOD
## OF GLOBAL FEMINIST SUCCESS

In sum, despite the Soviet commitments to women's emancipation, the new Russia was not a hospitable environment for global feminist activism. While global feminists became united in their shared interest in combating violence against women, the Soviet haphazard and parafeminist response to gender violence gave way, in the 1990s, to the privatization of gender violence, in which the state took even less responsibility to respond to the problem and justified its new position with revised victim-blaming theories. The huge changes in society from the move away from communism left women disempowered as workers and citizens and their imagined bodies sexualized and commodified for heterosexual men, while their actual bodies were busy laboring to support and care for themselves and their families. Neotraditional ideologies about women's and men's roles held sway, providing what may be the only respite and source of (limited) authority for women. The women's movement and state women's policy agencies, the combination of which political scientists have found to be key to feminist policy reform (Keck and Sikkink 1998; Mazur 2002; Weldon 2002), were fairly weak and only more powerful when they drew upon gender neotraditionalism. Global feminists hoping to foster activism, shape awareness that gender violence constitutes a violation of women's human rights, and implement progressive reform faced tremendous obstacles in Russia.

# CHAPTER THREE

# The Women's Crisis Center Movement: Funding and De-funding Feminism

E VEN AS THE NEW Russia was inhospitable to global feminism, liberalization and then the collapse of the Soviet regime opened Russia to a variety of global interventions designed to foster women's mobilization, the first objective of global feminism. Some feminist foreigners and foreign women's advocacy groups came at the invitation of local groups hoping to join already existing global campaigns; other activists invited themselves, but found locals who shared their interests. Transnational feminists in alliance with development agencies and large charitable foundations also secured for women's mobilization some of the West's optimistic infusion of financial assistance into the region. By 2002, some funding was even also coming from foreign and justice ministries, such as from the U.S. State Department Office to Monitor and Combat Trafficking in Persons. Do these various interventions—transnational feminist networking, alliance with donors, and state preemption—foster feminist mobilization against gender violence? Do different types of intervention have different consequences?

The analysis of these various interventions into women's mobilization in the new Russia shows that, although transnational feminist networking can help establish and shape feminist mobilization, greater financial assistance is required to expand beyond a few organizations into a small social movement. What began as only a handful of organizations in prominent Russian cities in the early 1990s became, with monetary support, a small women's crisis center movement, in 2004 consisting of two hundred organizations engaged in a combination of service provision and advocacy. Yet, more invasive intervention—from antitrafficking initiatives undertaken by strong states—undermined feminist mobilization. The new millennium brought de-funding of many of the older and more feminist organizations, a relative windfall for the least feminist, and increased ill feeling between them.

In terms of the global feminist goal of fostering mobilization, intervention is more effective when there is an alliance between feminists and donors rather than when the state preempts activists by accepting (some of) their ideas, but excludes them from the process. Foreign intervention justified by global feminist ideas works better when global feminists are actually involved in the process of assisting women's mobilization. Global feminist involvement is much more likely to keep the focus on feminist mobilization and more likely to encourage global-local partnerships. At the same time, even at its best, global feminist intervention does not counter the forces pushing NGO-based mobilization rather than grassroots oppositional movements.

## THE NEW FEMINIST INTERVENTIONISM

In Russia and beyond, the consensus on global feminism legitimated three new types of interventions to foster the mobilization of activists into groups and social movements working against gender violence: transnational feminist networking, the funding of women's rights advocacy through feminist alliances with donors, and states' preemption of global feminism in initiatives against trafficking.

### Transnational Feminist Networking

The consensus among many feminists on the composite concept of violence against women signaled new opportunities, perhaps even an obligation, for feminists from the Global North and West to attend to women and women's organizing in other places. They believed that "all women face gender violence," albeit different forms, and the solidarity created by the new consensus, especially following on the heels of some bitter North-South disagreements, led many activists to believe that they ought to help out. Armed with the new norms of inclusivity (Weldon 2006), Northern transnational feminists imagined that they could now get involved without being patronizing. Instead of coming in as experts analyzing the local gender problems, they could help foster local women's organizing, to promote the development of local gender expertise.

These transnational feminists' interests were also flamed by the fall of the Berlin Wall (Funk 2007). Eastern European women, while different from Western women, were less unfamiliar than women in many other places. Some Western feminists had genealogical ties to the region. Others whose feminism was grounded in Marxist critiques wanted to understand firsthand, without ideological blinders, what had been the actual experiences and daily life of women in state socialism. Many, including me, wanted to have a direct look at the world historical transformations underway, particularly from the position of women in that society (Funk 1993). The elimination of the once substantial obstacles to travel to the region also created a new frontier for Western feminists. Often unable to act effectively in their home countries, they were hopeful of being able to support women's activity elsewhere and to play a role in preventing the entrenchment of Westernized gender injustice. Some, as Croatian writer Slavenka Drakulic (1993) alleged, may have gone solely to advance their own careers.

To reflect the new consensus, global feminists sought new organizational forms. Similar to the transnational advocacy networks becoming popular for other human rights issues, they created *transnational feminist networks* (TFNs) (Keck and Sikkink 1998; Moghadam 2005). These feminist forms of transnational advocacy networks are "structures organized above the national level that unite women from three or more countries around a common agenda, such as women's rights, reproductive health, violence against women, peace and antimilitarism, or feminist economics" (Moghadam 2005, 4).

In contrast to social movements that—traditionally understood—mobilize masses and take up confrontational tactics, these networks "mobilize smaller numbers of individual activists who use more specialized resources of expertise and access to elites" (Sperling, Ferree, and Risman 2001, 1157). They organize through communication technology and informational gatherings to exchange information and ideas rather than host mass demonstrations or dramatic confrontations with authorities. According to Valentine Moghadam (2005), TFNs are most notable for the following activities since the beginning of the 1990s:

- "TFNs create, activate, or join global networks to mobilize pressure outside states," such as by participating in the yearly World Social Forum (13).
- "TFNs participate in multilateral and intergovernmental political arenas," such as the U.N.'s Committee on the Status of Women (14).
- "TFNs act and agitate within states to enhance public awareness and participation" (14).
- "Whether working at the state, regional, or global levels, TFNs have framed issues and introduced new concepts" that U.N. agencies, development agencies, and donor organizations have adopted (17).

TFN activists imagined and attempted new kinds of "sister to sister" or "joint-venture" projects (Sperling, Ferree, and Risman 2001, 1160). This "transnational organizing is not a unidirectional process," but a global-local intersection where resources, ideas, and benefits can flow both "in" and "out" (Sperling, Ferree, and Risman 2001, 1155).

In terms of promoting mobilization, TFNs can provide what social movement theorists call *repertoires for action,* models of activism that activists can transplant to help them structure mobilization (Merry 2006a). Across varying contexts, activists tend to appropriate and replicate the same repertoire: the "social service approach inspired by feminists and social workers, largely middle-tier professionals and academics" (138), developing shelters, hotlines, support groups, legal aid, and batterer treatment programs. By 1997, the crisis center—an amalgam of this approach—had become "the international standard," a "kind of [transnational feminist] do-it-yourself NGO kit" (Hemment 2007, 101, 95). This *transplantation* is most effective if activists translate these initiatives, that is, adjust "the rhetoric and structure of these programs or interventions to local circumstances" (135) but not so much that they lose the challenge to the sex/gender hierarchy (Ferree 2003). Sometimes crisis centers become so professionalized, so well integrated into the state, and so well aligned with cultural norms and traditions that they lose their radical critique of the gender injustice (Matthews 1994).

Even as transnational feminists struggled to be more inclusive, the term "network"—implying equality of organizations—was more a hope than a reality. Reflecting the unequal access to financial resources, most TFNs are based in the Global North with member organizations in the Global South. Even well-intentioned transnational feminists who continually reflect on their involvement may find themselves in a particular script where they provide expertise to "thankful recipients" (Rivkin-Fish 2004). This script is especially compelling in contexts where most interactions have historically been hierarchical and because intervention can bring resources to foreign transnational feminists and their organizations, raising their international profile and fostering their own organizational growth (Sperling, Ferree, and Risman 2001, 1159–60).

## Funding Women's Rights Advocacy through Feminist Alliances with Donors

Whereas scarce financial resources can limit this kind of transnational feminist advocacy, the global feminist alliance with human rights organizations, state and non-state development agencies, and large charitable foundations created the opportunity to expand and to distribute much greater amounts of money to local women's organizations. Around the world, instead of being marginalized to receiving only funds earmarked for feminism, women's organizations working against gender violence could now receive funds through programs dedicated to development and human rights, a second type of intervention.

In the postcommunist region, the largest program was so-called democracy assistance. The collapse of Soviet power, for many Western observers and policy-makers, represented democracy's victory. These beliefs led international donors to herald a new commitment to funding a global civil society, which they understood as the essential fabric of democracy mediating between the state and family. Estimates for this "democracy industry" are only rough approximations, especially for assistance targeted only to civil society rather than other democracy reforms such as structuring government agencies, but the amounts are unprecedented. By the turn of the millennium, state funding for civil society, mostly from development initiatives, totaled $7 billion, while several more billions had been distributed by Western (primarily U.S.) foundations (Kaldor, Anheier, and

Glasius 2003). Between 1990 and 2002, Russia apparently received some $860 million in democracy assistance from the U.S. and some €800 million from the European Union, perhaps 10 percent of which went to NGOs (Sundstrom 2006, 12–13).

The ability to fund women's organizing as never before, though, involved tradeoffs for feminist mobilization, tradeoffs that had become evident in earlier development projects in the Global South. As a result of the availability of larger grants and the demands of development agencies for specialized knowledge about women, many women's organizations, especially in liberalizing regimes, reconstituted themselves as formal nongovernmental organizations (NGOs) and were increasingly drawn into the role of technical experts on policy's impact on women and gender (Alvarez 1999). At first such organizations could maintain or build linkages to broader-based women's groups and continue the essential feminist activities of advocacy and empowerment. But as such interventions went on, women's NGOs were increasingly being professionalized or "*NGO-ized*." Feminist activists gradually became gender experts, and states, within a new global environment of neoliberal social and economic policies, gradually began to use women's organizations to provide services that they had given up.

Nonfeminist observers of postcommunist Europe and Eurasia soon found similar problems, as well as others, across civil society as a result of democracy assistance. The once radical democratic movements were "tamed," de-radicalized into NGOs, often fairly attached to the new states and doing little to deepen democracy (Kaldor 2003, ch. 4; Mendelson and Glenn 2002). This trend was illustrated in the particularly postcommunist phenomenon of "flex organizing," chameleon-like organizing in which actors shift their organizations between public and private spheres as a tactic to maneuver between constraints of both spheres (Wedel 2001). Such *flex organizations* or *hybrids* pose a danger to post-Soviet civil society because they blur the boundaries between public and private that are understood to be essential to a flourishing, autonomous civil society. Anticipating Putin's moves, observers warned that, with the Soviet history of the party-state co-opting all social organizations, the post-Soviet state may also seek to control the activities and access to the state of NGOs.

The problems of the postcommunist Russian women's movement were common to the region's postcommunist civil society. Groups were suspicious of each other, reluctant to share information, and predominantly staffed by elites and their circle, becoming sites for the distribution of Western perks and reinforcing existing hierarchies. In Russia, the result was a weak civil society: Russian citizens were comparatively reluctant to participate in voluntary organizations. By the mid-1990s, the average Russian had 0.65 organizational memberships per person, one of the lowest averages in the world, and the kind of participation by far the most prevalent among Russians was labor union membership (Howard 2003, 65–66, 69). Americans, in contrast, have an average of 3.59 organizational memberships; post-authoritarian Brazilians 2.13.

Feminist observers pointed out that civil society, which across the region remained so much weaker than the male-dominated formal politics or big business, had been feminized, that is, characterized by an overrepresentation of women and associated with reconstructed ideas of femininity (True 2003; Kuenhast and Nechemias 2004; Salmenniemi 2005). The hierarchy between these arenas has reproduced neotraditional gendered assumptions and inequality. Although women have been brought out of the family, they remain relegated to the least public and the weakest sphere, based on assumptions about their affinity for social issues and their greater morality, which, according to these assumptions, should keep them from the less "moral" sphere of power politics (Tohidi 2004). More than just reinscribing this gender ideology, this segregation also represents economic stratification as women, especially those well-educated, had less economic opportunities following communism's collapse, leaving civil society as often their only real option. But as formal politics became more important in postcommunist contexts, this feminization helped civic activism become the "housework" of politics (Sperling, Ferree, and Risman 2001).

Part of the blame must be attached to domestic factors, such as the communist legacy of compulsory participation, the widespread disappointment with changes since the Soviet collapse (Howard 2003), and the false Soviet claim of "women's emancipation." But more blame must be laid on foreign donors because the postcommunist NGOs "often serve the interests of foreign donors more than those of the local population" (Mendelson and Glenn 2002, 3). The global context into which public organizations emerged is structured such that foreign donors are required to be accountable to their home constituents (taxpayers if public or stockholders if private) more than to the societies they profess to serve (Henderson 2003). This leads to a focus on short-term rather than long-term interests. In this context, NGOs, on a grant-seeking treadmill, have responded rationally, pursuing short-term and easily quantifiable projects, undermining the long-term goal of creating sustainable civil society (Hemment 2004a). Some women's NGOs in the region learned to do a kind of doublespeak, using the feminist "gender talk" required by Western funders when talking to them and employing more traditional gender discourse when working with their constituency (Ishkanian 2004). This "de-coupling" of activist statements from their public actions becomes problematic when their actions reinforce non-democratic commitments (Sundstrom 2006, xv, 171–73)

These problems of postcommunist civil society and of women organizing globally make measuring feminist mobilization quite challenging. Counting women's NGOs gives no measure of their strength, longevity, or commitment to feminist advocacy (Weldon 2002, 223–24). And comprehensive fieldwork, in a country spread out in eleven time zones, including remote areas in the circumpolar North and Siberia, would require teams of intrepid researchers over a decade. My method is to combine parts of both approaches, using fieldwork to make conservative estimates and then systematically comparing credible third-party lists of organizations involved in various national or international projects to formulate generous estimates (see appendix 2 for details). My in-depth knowledge of Russian activism allows me to assess organizations' challenge to the sex/gender hierarchy, based on their activities. Though it is unrealistic to expect the development of a mass-based social movement given the Russian and global contexts, successful feminist mobilization requires extending advocacy beyond a limited number of elite NGOs to other types of women's organizations, even perhaps to those that have a more maternalist justification for their advocacy. Since the proliferation of women's organizing during the late Soviet period was centered around mothers' rights, powerful post-Soviet women's organizing requires newer women's NGOs to build coalition with these older, more maternalist organizations (Hrycak 2002).

## States' Preemption of Antitrafficking Initiatives

By the late 1990s, a third avenue for global feminist intervention became available when foreign ministries, after many years of feminist advocacy, grew concerned with the trafficking in persons, especially women and children. For many U.S. and European governments, the issue emerged as a practical problem as the number of prostitutes/sex workers from Southeast Asia and postcommunist Europe increased dramatically, as did the involvement of organized crime. With the 2004 EU enlargement, the European Union became more concerned about porous borders, especially in new postcommunist members, and the longer borders with Russia. This *realpolitik* concern led them to begin to fund organizations working against trafficking in Europe and Eurasia. The cross-Atlantic interest created the political will to push the United Nations to debate and pass a protocol on "Trafficking in Persons, Especially Women and Children" in 2000.

U.S. interest became particularly strong after 2000. Following mounting pressure from both the political left and right, the U.S. Congress passed and President Clinton signed the Trafficking Victims Protection Act in 2000.[1] This and subsequent legislation appropriated substantial funding to support antitrafficking initiatives abroad, contributing the overwhelming majority of funds to combat trafficking in Russia (Abubikirova 2002). Some of this money was dispersed through the usual development channels, such as the U.S. Agency for International Development (USAID) or the State Department's Bureau of Educational and Cultural Affairs (ECA), a long-time funder of international exchanges. As such, the funding risked the same problems as the alliance with development donors.

Under the Bush administration, the legislation meant a new State Department Office to Monitor and Combat Trafficking in Persons, a new and distinct mechanism for intervention. This office was led not by human rights or feminist activists, but by others with different agendas (see chapter 6). Although the United States is perhaps the most extreme case, this was also true of other states' (and the EU's) foreign ministries and the justice ministries that were also brought into the intervention. In contrast to human rights organizations, development agencies, and large charitable foundations that have become more responsive to feminist concerns and inclusive of feminist activists, these so-called power ministries have been particularly resistant to feminist critiques, even to women leaders. In other words, while working with the former entities could be construed as an alliance, foreign ministries tended to preempt global feminist concerns, taking them over with little feminist input.[2] More so than for the first two types, this intervention also risked neoimperialism. These power ministries, with access to all sorts of means of coercion, had no credible commitment to norms of inclusivity.

## TRANSPLANTING GLOBAL FEMINISM, 1993–1997

Over the last decade and a half, foreigners, most often led by Americans, have attempted each of these interventions in Russia, and all have had impact on feminist mobilization. Following the lead of Russian activists-scholars (Brygalina and Temkina 2004; Pashina 2004),[3] I contend that the women's crisis movement developed in four basic stages (see table 3.1): (1) the founding of the movement, (2) the institutionalization of the crisis center as the movement organization, (3) the proliferation of crisis centers, and (4) transformation.

### Founding the First Organizations

Though some had been informally helping women since the late 1980s, Russian activists founded the first women's organizations dedicated to addressing violence against women between 1993 and 1995 in Moscow and St. Petersburg, Russia's two major cities. Moscow-based ANNA (an acronym for the No to Violence Association) began informally in 1993 as a one-person hotline, held a training for new hotline counselors in 1994, and in 1995 was officially registered with the Russian government (see map 1). Almost simultaneously, other activists founded a second Moscow crisis center, Syostri (Sisters), but whereas ANNA focused more on domestic violence, Syostri focused on sexual assault. The St. Petersburg Crisis Center began providing some services in 1991, officially opened in 1994, and began a regular hotline in 1995 (Liapounova and Drachova 2004). Although these centers' primary activity was the hotline and other crisis counseling, all centers also began broader feminist advocacy projects, including research and enlistment of journalists to write on gender violence.

Interest quickly expanded to the regional capitals in Western Russia and even beyond (Pashina 2004). For example, in 1994, in Saratov, a one-million-person city on the Volga, activists established the Interregional Association of Women Lawyers to facilitate lawyers in providing legal aid to victims of sexual violence as part of their legal practice.[4] Even though they required a fee—there was no tradition of pro bono work in Russia—the lawyers were providing a new service for victims, who play a substantial role in Russian criminal trials. This Saratov association also established a hotline, created a support group for young women, and

**TABLE 3.1.**

*Development of the Women's Crisis Center Movement in Russia, 1993–2004*

| TIME PERIOD | ESTIMATES OF NUMBERS OF WOMEN'S CRISIS CENTERS* | | DESCRIPTION OF THE PERIOD | INTERVENTION |
|---|---|---|---|---|
| | Conservative | Generous | | |
| 1993–1994 | 7 | 10 | founding organizations | global feminist ideas, transnational feminist networking |
| 1995–1997 | 8 | 24 | institutionalization of the crisis center model (services + advocacy - shelter) | |
| 1998–2001 | 40 | 120 | proliferation of crisis centers, NGO-ization | funding women's rights advocacy through feminist alliances with donors |
| 2002–2004 | 47 | 121 (229 if include antitrafficking orgs) | transformation: more fragmentation, tenuous survival for feminist organizations | antitrafficking initiatives, European partnerships |

*Note:* *The lower number includes only those organizations that both are robust and more closely resemble the crisis center model. The generous estimate includes other organizations that work against gender violence. For the sake of simplicity, I call them all crisis centers.

produced a television program on violence against women as part of the global feminist campaign, the 16 Days against Gender Violence.

In October 1994, ANNA leaders founded an informal network, the Russian Association of Crisis Centers for Women (RACCW), to link the new organizations in order to coordinate campaigns to raise public awareness of the issue and to advocate for legislative reform (Henderson 2001).[5] Founding members were located in Moscow, the region surrounding Moscow, St. Petersburg, Nizhny Tagil, Ekaterinburg, and distant Kamchatka.[6] Within just a few short years of founding, there were seven to ten women's crisis centers in Russia.

MAP 1. Cities with robust gender violence activism and the women's organizations highlighted in this study. Map created by Olga Kirsanova.

## Institutionalization of the Crisis Center Model

In the three following years, the already existing crisis centers expanded their services and began larger campaigns to raise national attention regarding the issue of violence against women. By 1997, ANNA had conducted a pilot research project, had launched a (relatively unsuccessful) "Men's Solidarity project" loosely modeled on U.S. batterer treatment programs, and had brought and won their first family violence legal case. By 1998, Syostri had received almost twenty thousand calls and was holding workshops and seminars for young people on the problems of sexual violence.[7] These included programs targeted specifically for women, such as assertiveness training and self-defense programs. Activists also founded new crisis centers in Moscow and St. Petersburg as well as in Western Siberia and the Far North.

This period is marked by the institutionalization of the women's crisis center (*krizisnyi tsentr*), which quickly replaced other kinds of organizations as the repertoire for action against gender violence. For instance, in Saratov, the Interregional Association of Women Lawyers, founded within something akin to a Western law practice, was replaced by the Saratov Crisis Center that was modeled on ANNA.[8] The Russian version of the crisis center is an organization led by a few individuals (typically professionals receiving some compensation), a hotline staffed by volunteer counselors for several hours a day several days of the week, often some in-person counseling or support groups, and usually some sort of broader advocacy work. Volunteers would listen to callers' concerns and try to help callers see new options. Often, because of the virtual collapse of the welfare system and social conditions, there is very little that they can do except try to empower the victim to feel entitled to a better life. When they can pay or cajole a lawyer to help out, crisis centers can provide some legal assistance. Historically, crisis centers have rarely helped women pursue legal action against their attackers because of victims' wishes and the legal obstacles. More often, they provide support to a woman wanting to exit an abusive relationship or to move out of an apartment that, because of financial exigencies and housing law, she is forced to share with her abuser, even if divorced.

The strength of the model was its inexpensiveness; for the crisis center to open, all that was required was a phone line in a small office (preferably with access to a toilet and to water for tea) and some volunteers. The weakness was that the crisis centers could provide only minimal assistance because, for the most part, they could not provide even temporary shelter for women wishing to escape abusive relationships. Though many activists wanted to found shelters—including the optimistically named new center in Murmansk, Priiut (Shelter)—financial realities and oppressive post-Soviet regulations made providing long-term shelter impossible (Shtyleva 2003). To overcome these obstacles, activists in St. Petersburg sought and found government support for a short-term shelter, but this meant significant compromises about who could stay and for how long.[9] Cultural proscriptions about leaving a husband because of abuse, especially when he was the father of one's children, also meant that women tended to use the shelters as a temporary respite and then return to their abusive mates. The crisis centers' inability to provide long-term shelter is an especially big problem in the new Russia, where affordable housing is scarce.

By the end of this period, there were at least eight robust crisis centers; seven of these were providing free legal assistance to women living with violence.[10] Three other centers had joined the RACCW network,[11] and, according to a directory researched in 1997–98, there were twenty-four organizations that worked in the sphere of "prevention and elimination of violence against women" within the Russian Federation (Abubikirova, Klimenkova, Kotchkina, Regentova, and Troinova 1998, 9).

## Global Feminism, Transnational Feminists

Though some local activism fizzled and some "parachute feminist" projects failed to thrive, the surviving centers grew with global feminist ideas and transnational feminist networking. The first centers in Moscow and St. Petersburg were created by gender studies centers already engaging in global feminism. New TFNs, such as the sister-to-sister feminist organization Network of East-West Women

(NEWW), founded in 1991, helped facilitate their participation in global feminism through exchanges and the creation of bi-regional network. The joint venture Consortium of Women's Nongovernment Associations (formerly NIS-US Women's Consortium), founded to build a network between American and post-Soviet women's organizations, provided start-up resources.[12] The creation of the consortium also brought transnational feminist and human rights entrepreneur Martina Vandenberg, who had an interest in violence against women, as the American coordinator. Vandenberg would become an important advocate for the crisis centers, both establishing more of them and writing about their work in English-language Russian and American newspapers. Other transnational feminists helped found specific women's crisis centers, such as British-American scholar-activist Julie Hemment working in Tver (Hemment 2007, ch. 4).

The movement's activists and scholars acknowledge the importance of global feminism and transnational feminist networking. For example, Albina Pashina, scholar-founder of the third Moscow-based women's crisis center, Yaroslavna, in her chronicle of the founding of the women's movement (2004), argues that gender violence activism emerged from Western feminism and global women's meetings, leading to the raising of the issue at the 1991 watershed event of the Russian women's movement, the Independent Women's Forum (Pashina 2004). She further asserts that the "main figures behind the . . . [expansion] to the regions were the representatives of the Western feminist movements. They initiated trips for the already functioning crisis centres' leaders to small peripheral towns arranging training sessions for local activists there" (25).

External feminist influence also helped imagine the crisis center as the movement's model. Russian activists unabashedly appropriated their ideas about the proper response to violence against women mostly from North American institutions.[13] Many crisis center leaders met with Western counterparts or even traveled to observe North American or European shelters. One activist involved in the founding a St. Petersburg crisis center and then a municipal shelter explained that she decided to head the initiative to organize the shelter because she "had been to America and knew that a shelter needed to be founded."[14] To foster the appropriation of the model, Russian activists (literally) translated a Western feminist text, *How to Start a Crisis Center for Women (Kak sozdat' krizisnyi tsentr dlia zhenshchin)* (Israelian and Zabelina 1995).

Russian activists then adapted the internationally available model to the Russian context. As the post-Soviet context made Western-style shelters unlikely, activists founded independent crisis centers and some government-supported (albeit short-term) shelters. Whereas early North American activists prided themselves on providing sister-to-sister advice rather than professional psychological services, most Russian crisis centers began to rely on professional psychologists, scholars, and lawyers. These educated women tended to be un- or underemployed and were more likely to have the ability to understand Western theory and practice. Without widespread grassroots feminism, activists had little local feminist activism to build on, but instead found a way to package the crisis center as a response to the widespread crisis that most Russians, living through dramatic inflation and infrastructural collapse, felt (Hemment 2007, 101). They addressed not just gender violence, but broader needs such as alcoholism, poverty, and depression. In an artistically skilled society, they used new approaches, such as art therapy, to address gender violence.

As anthropologist Julie Hemment (1999) argued, they "helped themselves to liberal feminist discourse" but translated the global repertoire for action into a Russian crisis center, a new social service at the collapse of state social services. While building upon neotraditional gender assumptions of women as caregivers, they also helped women take radical steps not legitimated by neotraditionalism, such as leaving abusive partners and prosecuting rape. They accomplished a successful transplantation, adjusting the crisis center to fit the context even as the model continues to challenge the social order (Merry 2006a).

Almost all of the activists I interviewed spoke very positively of these kinds of transnational feminist interventions, even when they included ideas of "international solidarity" and assumptions of universalism. For many Russian feminists, transnational feminist networking was the best hope in this neotraditional society, a new kind of leverage against a still undemocratic state (Keck and Sikkink 2000). Almost all embraced the global feminist language of "women's rights are human rights" and expressed enjoyment of transnational feminist meetings and exchanges. Other observers of the Russian women's movement found more criticism of the pervasive influence of Americans, but they also found that these comments came from those activists outside the crisis center movement and in response to witnessing the infusion of cash into the women's crisis center movement (Sperling, Ferree, and Risman 2001).

## FUNDING FEMINISM, 1998–2001

### Crisis Center Proliferation

In the late 1990s, most women's crisis centers expanded their activities. In 1998, Moscow-based ANNA was a thriving crisis center with twelve staff members and dozens of volunteers providing hotline and some group consultations, helping over two hundred women a month (Henderson 2001). By 2001, ANNA's leaders had become national advocates, having participated in a whirlwind of interactive conferences on domestic violence across Russia. These conferences, facilitated by the Moscow-based American Bar Association Central European and Eurasian Law Initiative (ABA-CEELI) gender program, brought together social service providers (psychologists, social workers, healthcare providers), law enforcement, and women activists. ANNA also ran two large national media and public education campaigns. The growth of other already existing crisis centers was less dramatic, but many took on new roles, such as social accompaniment programs, encouraged by Women, Law, and Development International and then ABA-CEELI, in which crisis center activists would accompany domestic violence or rape survivors.

Most dramatically, this period was marked by an escalation in the rate at which activists established new women's crisis centers. Reflecting this growth, the RACCW network expanded to forty members by the summer of 2002, but there were dozens of other centers that self-identified as crisis centers to international donors or to the Russian women's movement. In 2002, one RACCW leader estimated that there were 120 organizations across Russia involved in addressing gender violence.[15]

The proliferation of crisis centers can be illustrated by developments in Barnaul, a southwestern Siberian city of 780,000 residents a few hundred miles from Kazakhstan, China, and Mongolia, where not one but three centers emerged (Johnson 2006). Barnaul—and the region of Altai of which Barnaul is the capital—represents fairly typical post-Soviet Russian urban life since the collapse of Soviet rule: an economically depressed region that must rely on financial subsidies from the federal government.

The Women's Alliance in Barnaul (Zhenskii Al'ians), founded by Nataliia Sereda in 1998, was the result of the restructuring of a women's organization first founded in 1993.[16] Inspired by and modeled on the first-generation crisis centers, this second-generation crisis center's primary activity was a hotline, but Sereda and her staff continued other services, including on-site counseling and support groups, from the original women's organization. With support and training from ABA-CEELI, she added a program to escort victims to the police and court. Between 1998 and 2002, with only a handful of paid staff and no more than a dozen volunteers loosely affiliated with the center, the center had helped "6,500 victims—most of them female victims of violence."[17] The Women's Alliance is the best-case scenario of crisis centers that emerged in this period.[18]

The two other new centers were Response (Otklik), a project of the local public university's sociology department, and the Altai Crisis Center for Men, a state social service that was revamped to also address domestic violence (Johnson 2006). The latter—not a women's crisis center but headed by a man affiliated with the movement (Kostenko 2003)—was particularly remarkable for being the first crisis center for men and illustrated a new kind of responsibility for taking action against gender violence. That so many organizations chose to focus on domestic violence illustrates just how popular the issue had become. On the other hand, these organizations were hybrids—part state, part NGO—receiving public funding while simultaneously representing themselves to donors as NGOs.[19] By 2004, RACCW leaders acknowledged that one-third of organizations affiliated with the RACCW, which had once resisted state centers, were similar types of hybrids. By the end of 2001, the Russian Ministry of Labor and Social Development was supporting fifteen government crisis centers to address violence in the family (Zabelina et al. 2007, 103).

Although these hybrid organizations have been obstacles to grassroots feminist organizing in other similar contexts (Hrycak 2006), in Russian practice they extended mobilization against gender violence. In a resource-poor environment, activists found new ways to fund activism, illustrating the power of even relatively small grants in terms of increasing not just financial capital, but reputation and legitimacy.[20] In a contrast to the Western advice to privatize social support, these hybrid organizations represented new responsibilities for the Russian state and drew funds to do so from the very government (the United States) that was advocating the dismantling of the Russian welfare state. Further, hybrid organizing also brought in new blood, including more traditional women and men who worked with the state and who became politicized by contacts with the autonomous women's crisis centers. The risk, however, is that these kinds of entities contribute to the corruption and lack of transparency that plague Russian politics and that Russian citizens, taught to be clever discerners of government deception, will understand this maneuvering and be even more suspicious of the foreign-funded women's crisis center movement.

Even religiously affiliated organizations got into the game. In 1997, the Presbyterian Church, as part of its missionary outreach to Russia, created a training center, Opora (Support), in Moscow, which provides counseling training for Russian social service providers on treating alcohol and drug addiction, sometimes in collaboration with federal and local government social services.[21] Geared toward all types of Christians (but open to atheists), the extensive training includes a module on domestic violence. Similarly, Project Kesher, a network based on the post-Soviet Jewish communities, began to take the once-taboo issue of domestic violence more seriously in its women's groups across Russia.[22]

Another important trend was the explosion of new crisis centers in Northwest Russia, an area that was one of the most militarized during the Cold War. Whereas arctic Murmansk hosted a first-generation crisis center, by 2001, there were at least ten women's crisis centers in the Barents regions of Karelia, Murmansk, and Arkhangelsk (Liapounova and Drachova 2004). Six were autonomous NGOs, and four were municipal institutions. Three of the ten had short-term shelter space, for a total of nineteen individuals at one time.

In 2000, scholar-activists affiliated with these northwestern Russian developments conducted a detailed survey of these centers plus two others in St. Petersburg that provides a snapshot of the women's crisis center movement (Liapounova and Drachova 2004).[23] All had hotlines and provided psychological counseling; ten out of twelve (83%) also offered legal counseling and self-help groups, and included volunteers in addition to social, psychological, and legal professionals. Not the sister-to-sister groups advocated in global feminism, they construed their assistance as professional and were not particularly concerned about overriding the wishes of the client in some circumstances (Liapounova and Drachova 2004, 65; Saarinen, Liapounova, and Drachova 2003a). Although focused on domestic violence, almost all centers also addressed sexual abuse, incest, rape, and, less often, sexual harassment. While "advocating women's rights," Russian activists understood that the central problems facing women were financial problems, housing, and unemployment.

They also found notable differences between government and autonomous crisis centers in Russia (Liapounova and Drachova 2004). The autonomous crisis centers tended to be more activist oriented: slightly more likely to identify as feminist and much more likely to have links to women's movements abroad (46). They also tended to be more flexible and less hierarchical than government centers, but not without hierarchy (especially in terms of information distribution) and conflict (47). Their success was highly dependent on the management and fundraising abilities of the director(s). On the other hand, government centers benefited from more constant (albeit often very limited) funding, but were heavily regulated by higher authorities and were subject to the whims of the politicians who funded them (48). Liapounova and Drachova (2004) also argued that personnel at the government centers were less competent, having received no training on gender violence prior to the center's opening. In terms of funding, the government centers had received no grants, and only one autonomous crisis center had received (limited) municipal funding. One crisis center was completely dependent on unpaid work.

By 2001, relative to Russia's weak society, the crisis centers were success stories. There was committed leadership spread out in a dozen organizations that had been around for more than five years. Although not meeting the ideal form of social movement with a broad constituency observed in the 1970s in Western societies, the women's crisis centers were well networked through flexible as well as more enduring coalitions and had an effective mobilizing structure. These women were in the marginalized third sector, the housework of politics, but they were also organizing as women (instead of returning to the home), and most saw themselves as activists if not feminists. Further, they were supported by other organizations in the women's movement, government crisis centers, and religious interests in addressing gender violence.

### Transnational Feminist Networks + Democracy Assistance

As earlier, transnational feminist networking was necessary to this stage in the women's crisis center movement development, though the source of attention shifted toward Europe with the creation of the Vienna-based Women against Violence Europe (WAVE, www.wave-network.org). After receiving start-up funding in 1997, WAVE has linked activists, policymakers, and others with an interest in reducing violence against women in nearly all European countries (Brunell and Johnson 2007). It serves as a discursive space for information exchange among professionals and activists, a library and archive, and a database of addresses, as well as a resource for women who are victims of domestic violence to find help within specific countries. From the beginning Russian crisis centers, including Syostri and later ANNA as the Russian focal point, were involved, solidifying the Russian crisis center movement's participation in global feminism.

More crucial was democracy assistance, which expanded and reshaped the movement.[24] Funding began to pour in from a variety of charitable foundations and development agencies. One deep-pocketed donor was the New York-based Ford Foundation, which had been funding women's organizations in Russia since

1994, but turned to women's crisis centers in 1998 (see table 3.2). For instance, through Ford's human rights program, ANNA, the Moscow-based crisis center whose activities were greatly expanded during this stage, received more than half a million U.S. dollars from 1998 to 2001, a relationship that would continue. Another quarter of a million was dispersed to centers in Irkutsk and St. Petersburg. A second big donor was USAID.[25] In 1998, Hillary Clinton had traveled to Moscow for a Russia–United States conference on domestic violence and promised support for the women's crisis centers. The result was almost one million dollars in aid, from discretionary funds, distributed between 1999 and 2002 to thirty-five crisis centers across Russia, for start-up and expansion of advocacy.[26]

A third important initiative—an innovative mix of transnational feminist networking and democracy assistance—came from the Nordic countries, where in 1999 activists created the Network for Crisis Centres for Women in the Barents Region (NCRB) (Saarinen, Liapounova, and Drachova 2003b). Since some Nordic countries had been late to join the European Union and Norway and Iceland remain nonmembers, the Nordic countries, which are close to northwest Russia, had their own multilateral relations with Russia. Built upon an already existing transnational feminist network, Femina Borealis, NCRB came with approximately $300,000 from European Union and Nordic sources, some of which went directly to the women's crisis centers in northwest Russia.[27] This aid was sister-to-sister, part of a collaboration of organizations addressing domestic violence in Finland, Sweden, Norway, and northwest Russia through conferences and information technology.[28] The NCRB drove the expansion of the movement into the Russian Northwest.

As expected, some funding explicitly designed to foster mobilization did not produce the intended results. For instance, a 2001 EU Tacis grant of approximately $200,000 was given to the Italian Association for Women in Development (AIDOS) and their Russian partner, Focus, for the "[c]reation of a Russian network to fight gender based violence."[29] Though they partnered with several already existing women's crisis centers, translated a handful of American psychological texts on sexual and domestic violence, and held a 2003 conference, they did not create an effective new network or deepen existing networks. Focus's report on this primary goal even justifies their limited focus and impact on women's mobilization: "Russian women are very patient, and as long as they continue to tolerate violence, its scale will not decrease" regardless of changes in the state response.[30] In contrast to the NCRB, AIDOS appeared as global feminist opportunists. AIDOS was a gender and development NGO that had no previous experience working with domestic and sexual violence and no experience in Russia. They took advantage of the new global commitment to addressing gender violence but came from a parafeminist perspective in which gender violence could be cast as a psychological problem requiring only a state social service response.

For the most part, though, the infusion of funds greatly supported the crisis centers' "viability," "capacity," and "governance," categories that Sarah Henderson (2003, ch. 4) used to evaluate the effectiveness of foreign aid on Russia's civil

**TABLE 3.2.**
*Ford Foundation Grants to Gender Violence Activism in Russia, 1998–2006*

| RECIPIENTS | TOTAL | 1998[a] | 1999[a] | 2000[b] | 2001[b] | 2002[b] | 2003[b] | 2004[b] | 2005–6[b] |
|---|---|---|---|---|---|---|---|---|---|
| TOTAL | $1,695,100 | $122,600 | $350,000 | $284,500 | $93,000 | $295,000 | $150,000 | $150,000 | $250,000 |
| ANNA | $1,289,600 | $87,600 | $200,000 | $227,000 | $75,000 | $150,000 | $150,000 | $150,000 | $250,000 |
| Irkutsk crisis centers | $378,500 | $35,000 | $150,000 | $30,500 | $18,000 | $145,000 | | | |
| St. Petersburg Legal Aid* | $27,000 | | | $27,000 | | | | | |
| Council of Women at MSU^ | $95,000 | | | | | $95,000 | | | |

*Note:* Not adjusted for inflation.

* To establish 10 new crisis centers in Siberia and the Far East.

^ MSU=Moscow State University. The grant was to research the incidence of domestic violence in Russia.

*Source:*

[a] Henderson (2003, 128–29)

[b] Ford Foundation annual reports, available online through http://www.fordfound.org/. The most recent are searchable, online at http://www.fordfound.org/grants_db/view_grant_detail.cfm [accessed February 6, 2006].

society. Centers, which without this support would probably have shut down following Russia's 1998 economic crisis, paid more staff and expanded their activities. New centers were founded, sometimes with some government support. All centers, relative to other post-Soviet NGOs, interacted with the population. While also causing some problems found in the broader women's movement and civil society—such as fostering oligarchical leadership, "building unsocial capital" (distrust between organizations), and "mission drift"—funding to women's crisis centers was some of the most effective (Henderson 2003, ch. 5). While NGO-ized and somewhat fragmented, women's crisis centers were also political and networking. For the critics who studied civil society as a whole and who knew of the women's crisis centers movement, the women's crisis centers were different, perhaps even "a moderate success story" because so many provided necessary social services and advocated for social and political change (Richter 2002, 79; Sundstrom 2002; Henderson 2003). For Henderson (2003), "the support for the crisis centers was most effective in that centers established other sources of support, developed a cadre of dedicated volunteers, and were slowly implementing mechanisms for affecting public policy" (147).

Other places suffered without transnational feminist networking and funding. In Orel, another regional capital just five hours by train from Moscow, a rural Russian woman, based on her experiences with abuse and activism in her village, linked up with the gender expert at ABA-CEELI. Although the resulting conference in 1999 led to much attention from the media and the local administration, without local feminists, TFN involvement, or foreign assistance no women's crisis center was founded. In Kaluga, only a few hours by car or train from Moscow, a crisis center was thriving in 1999, so much so that they enticed one of the most powerful woman politicians in Russia to a conference on domestic violence. But though they received one small grant from IREX, they could not sustain their funders when USAID decided that they were not sufficiently professional, and by 2004 the center had vanished.

## DE-FUNDING FEMINISM, 2002–?

### Collapse of the Alliance

Just as the movement was set to take off, international donors began to shift gears. Following the September 11, 2001, attacks on the United States, many donors, who had already grown weary of funding postcommunist civil society, redirected funds toward new hotspots. In 2002, USAID, which had been such a boon to the crisis centers, suddenly stopped funding them.[31] Other donors, hoping to wean postcommunist recipients, began focusing on teaching fundraising and on the elusive goal of "sustainability." By 2003, across the world, donors became less interested in funding women's rights, although more funding was allocated to Central and Eastern Europe and the issue of gender violence than other issues in other places (Clark et al. 2006, 11–12). Without international support, in most Russian regions, the only domestic source of wealth is the state. Charitable donations from Russian business or the "new Russians" were highly improbable, especially following the 2003 imprisonment of oil baron turned philanthropist Mikhail Khodorkovsky.[32]

Of the previous commitments to supporting autonomous crisis center mobilization, only two main sources of funding remained. The first were EU-funded projects, such as AIDOS-Focus and the Nordic NCRB for northwestern Russian centers, which required European partners, who often received a large part of the grant, and most of the attention was turned to the East and Central European societies that would become EU members in 2004. The second was the Ford Foundation, but only for Moscow-based center ANNA. The disappearance of many funding sources left most crisis centers, at the height of the movement's mobilization, scrambling for other sources of and methods for securing the minimal funding for existence. The global alliance between transnational feminists and democracy assistance donors to fund domestic and gender violence was over.

## The Global Antitrafficking Campaign

As democracy assistance disappeared, possibilities appeared for antitrafficking grants. In the earlier stages of the Russian women's crisis center movement, with little funding available for antitrafficking efforts, very few crisis centers had taken on the issue of trafficking in women even though the high point of the problems appears to have been in the late 1990s (Khodyreva 2004). The new global attention to trafficking, especially the new U.S. legislation, changed the financial incentives. Embracing the new opportunities, centers in Moscow, Petrozavodsk, Ekaterinburg, and Krasnodar secured funding from USAID for "trafficking prevention and information dissemination" (2001–2004).[33] Crisis centers in Barnaul and Saratov won an additional grant from USAID for public awareness campaigns and the introduction of crisis intervention services.[34] A similar grant supported some thirteen women's organizations in the Russian Far East and Siberia "to address the trafficking problem through short-term training programs in job skills and small business development, awareness raising activities, targeted information dissemination, and individual services and consultations for women at risk."[35] A fourth, much smaller grant went to a Novgorod crisis center to compile a trainer's portfolio on trafficking, which was completed in 2004.[36] Other funds went to individuals as part of an "International Visitor Exchange Program on Trafficking of Women and Children" that brought Russian experts to Washington, D.C., for exposure to U.S.-based programs. In general, these interventions were modeled on earlier gender violence interventions in Russia and funded through traditional development channels.[37]

However, the new kind of funding available through the new U.S. State Department's Office to Monitor and Combat Trafficking in Persons (G/TIP) went to a new player in the anti-gender-violence campaign in Russia, the MiraMed Institute and its Angel Coalition. Founded in 1991 in Moscow by American doctor

Juliette Engel, MiraMed is registered as both an American nonprofit and a Russian nongovernmental organization. Originally focused on improving Russian birthing centers and orphanages, MiraMed turned to the issue of trafficking in women and young girls in the late 1990s, founding the Angel Coalition to link twenty member organizations combating trafficking in 1999.[38] By the beginning of 2004, the Angel Coalition claimed thirty-three members in Russia.[39] Seven of these organizations collaborated to provide hotlines, and five ran temporary "safe houses" for trafficked women who are deported back to Russia.[40] According to their April 2006 newsletter, their members have helped 3,700 victims of trafficking since January 2003, and their shelters have housed 87 victims since 2004.

Although most members of Angel Coalition were organizations unaffiliated with the women's crisis center movement, six organizations were also members of RACCW, and several more were members of the broader Russian women's movement.[41] For example, the Psychological Crisis Center in St. Petersburg, under the direction of Natalia Khodyreva, an early crisis center leader and the official president of the Angel Coalition, was coordinating one of the safe houses. In 2003, they had a hotline to counsel people considering working abroad and a nine-woman shelter offering psychological counseling, medical assistance, and education and job training.[42] In contrast, in Kazan, the capital of the Russian Republic of Tatarstan, Angel's affiliate was a micro-financing woman's organization previously unaffiliated with the crisis center movement. Their safe house was a rented apartment, which housed one woman who had been deported back to Russia in the summer of 2004. For some women's crisis centers, joining the Angel Coalition was simply a pragmatic decision, a quest for more resources. For others, joining meant a new status that they had been unable to obtain within the movement. Several women's organizations had no recollection of giving MiraMed/Angel the green light to add them to their list.

### Global-Local Controversy: The U.S. Antiprostitution Pledge

Especially in a country as large as Russia, some competition between organizations may be healthy for civil society, but the emergence of the Angel Coalition and, more significantly, the Bush administration response gave transnational, institutional, and ideological dimensions to the movement's personality conflicts and competition for scarce resources. In the fall of 2002, an ally of the Angel Coalition, American professor Donna Hughes, accused the U.S. government, because of its support through USAID of women's crisis centers such as Syostri, of a covert policy to secure the continued provision of prostitutes (Hughes 2002). Hughes expressed her claims in an online version of the neoconservative American magazine the *National Review,* describing a "pro-prostitution mafia: the U.S. State Department, U.S.- and Dutch-funded nongovernmental organizations (NGOs), and a Russian political party—the Union of Right Forces."[43] She argued that these pro-prostitution views and coalitions explained why the Angel Coalition, after securing funding in the first few years of their activities, had their applications rejected by USAID. The MiraMed director echoed these claims in one of the key online news sources for observers of Russia.[44] These accusations rallied supporters, many of them evangelical Christians, to send letters to U.S. Congress members, and the U.S. Embassy in Moscow was repeatedly called on to explain its actions.[45]

Things got so heated that then U.S. ambassador to Russia, Alexander Vershbow, tussled with Hughes in the *Washington Times,* accusing "Miss Hughes" of "slander," "libel," and "innuendo" and defending both the U.S. embassy and USAID.[46] But the G/TIP office had more influence with the Bush administration. In January 2003, the U.S. secretary of state sent out a memo to field missions of the USAID that said that no more antitrafficking funds would go to "organizations advocating prostitution as an employment choice or which advocate or support the legalization of prostitution."[47] The memo further announced that funding would be cut for all projects construed as supporting "trafficking of women and girls, legalization of drugs, injecting drug use, and abortion." Rearticulated as a requirement that all recipients of USAID vow their opposition to prostitution, this antiprostitution pledge was inscribed in U.S. law in 2003.[48] The Bush administration also came out in explicit support of the Angel Coalition, inviting them to a Washington, D.C., conference on trafficking[49] and singling them out for support in a speech by the secretary of state in June of 2004: "The State Department supports the Angel Coalition."[50]

The foundation of the allegations was that the women's crisis centers, especially Syostri, had advocated the legalization of prostitution in Russia, but there is no evidence that any of the women's crisis centers, USAID, or USAID-funded intermediaries actually did this.[51] They had been open to discussing this option, and they were more committed to a comprehensive feminism. In contrast, MiraMed, with its programs to assist young single mothers through a partnership with a local Russian Orthodox Church, has transmitted the view that motherhood and marriage should be women's preeminent goals, suggesting little challenge to the dominant sex-gender order.

This controversy left the women's crisis centers, especially Syostri, to defend themselves to both their American funders and Russian supporters. It created a painful rift, both institutional and ideological, between many women's crisis center leaders and the MiraMed/Angel Coalition. In the next round of U.S. antitrafficking funding (2004), the Angel Coalition scored a grant of almost half a million dollars (to develop more shelters), while only one women's crisis center—affiliated with RACCW, in Siberia—received anything: $6,060.[52] The American antitrafficking politics left the Russian president of the Angel Coalition, a longtime women's crisis center advocate, critical of these ways that transnational feminist antitrafficking organizations "subordinate the Eastern organizations . . . to their standards and frameworks," making funding dependent upon ideological agreement (Khodyreva 2004, 245). Because of the lines that were drawn, the conflict led to the closing off of most long-term, feminist women's crisis centers from U.S. funds.

By 2005, the national government was supporting some twenty-two women's crisis centers (Zabelina et al. 2007, 21, 103), but prospects were bleak for most autonomous women's crisis centers, especially those committed to comprehensive feminist goals (see Hemment 2007). By year's end, some eighteen had closed (Open Society Institute 2007, 32). One movement leader acknowledged that since "crisis centers survive only on the springs of foreign donors," this was a "new stage [in the women's crisis center movement] in which only the strongest organizations survive."[53] Other than antitrafficking funding, there were few, unpromising survival tactics, which I illustrate through brief case studies of three movement organizations in disparate regions.

### Moscow-based RACCW: Begging from Europe

Up through 2001, the crisis center network RACCW and the Moscow crisis center ANNA were intermingled, with overlapping leadership and shared resources, but after criticism from USAID about this organizational structure, the organizations were severed. This change meant that RACCW would have to support itself without the Ford Foundation and the very effective fundraising of leader Marina Pisklakova.[54] Although they had received some USAID funds for an antitrafficking hotline, the controversy had closed that door. Fortunately, because of previous transnational feminist networking, RACCW found a new feminist partner, Women's Aid, the British network of organizations working to end domestic violence, which came with British and EU funding.[55] In July 2003, they, in collaboration with a handful of other feminist crisis centers, started a large, multiyear project to target ethnic minorities and migrant communities.

However, from the onset, the project was an odd fit for Russia, where activism against gender violence had only just begun, the rule of law is sketchy, and racism (especially against those from the Caucuses) remained widely accepted even among the intelligentsia. Not understanding the Russian context, British partners were surprised that ethnic groups, especially unregistered immigrants, were particularly resistant to turning to either the NGOs or the state for help, or even to acknowledging that domestic violence existed within their community.[56] In Russia, such an admission would legitimate common Russian assertions that ethnic minorities are to blame for society's ills, especially for violence. Instead of introducing questions of intersectionality—how race and racism might impact gender violence—this approach threatened to foster racist arguments that domestic violence was a problem *only* for ethnic groups (or a problem related to the Chechen conflict). When the project came up for renewal, EU officials conducted what the Russian activists characterized (in exaggeration, one hopes) as a "nine-month audit worse than the KGB."[57] Claiming the RACCW had failed to meet its goals—goals that underestimated the obstacles in Russia to shelters and the involvement of policymakers—the Europeans terminated the grant.

The fully autonomous, feminist RACCW was left without support. In the fall of 2005, the center existed only on the volunteer labor and small donations of its two top leaders. All of the paid staff had been let go, and by 2006, they lost their Moscow office. Similarly, autonomous feminist crisis centers with whom RACCW had been collaborating—in Saratov, Kazan, Nizhny Tagil, Voronezh, and Barnaul—lost their primary external funding. Even ANNA, the best-funded example of this kind of organization, was increasingly being drawn away from service provision toward becoming professional feminists disconnected from the women they professed to serve. It was the end of the era of autonomous feminist mobilization against gender violence.

### Fatima in Kazan and the Women's Alliance in Barnaul: Turning to the State

In response to these dire conditions, some formerly autonomous feminist organizations turned to the state. One such organization was Fatima, located in Kazan, the capital of the Republic of Tatarstan, an ethnic homeland of approximately 48 percent mostly Muslim Tatars and 43 percent Russian ethnics deep in the heart of Russia. Although the movement had mostly been dominated by Russian ethnics, by 2004, women's crisis centers had expanded into communities where ethnic minorities have more sway, such as Tatarstan, Buriatiia, Udmurt Republic, and Republic of Komi. Founded as part of the second generation, much like the Women's Alliance in Barnaul, they had emerged as an active center, quickly joining the RACCW. As Kazan appears to be a hotspot for trafficking women (e.g., to or through Turkey, whose language is similar to Tatar), Fatima tried to secure antitrafficking funds, but got only small grants through RACCW.[58] Generous with their time, the Fatima activists were also working with the Angel Coalition affiliate in Kazan. In the summer of 2004, for the one deported trafficked woman staying at the safe house, they were providing psychological support, attempting to find her employment and housing, and trying to keep her from the mafia. Unlike most women's crisis center leaders, the directors, Venera Ibragimova and Guzel' Sharapova, were not ethnic Russians, but Tatars, making them good candidates to work with RACCW on the ethnic minority project.

By 2004, they had created a tenuous base of support. The small grants through RACCW gave the directors some compensation for their time, while a sympathetic director of a local social service agency granted them office space. In Kazan, one of the wealthiest Russian cities outside of Moscow and St. Petersburg, authorities could afford to be a little generous. But although Angel's affiliate received foreign assistance, Fatima's leaders were working for free. Once RACCW's EU grant was terminated, the state support proved insufficient, the founders left, and the organization turned to antitrafficking funds.

In the southwestern Siberian regional capital of Barnaul, where domestic violence activism had led to the emergence of three entities to address domestic violence, including state-NGO hybrids, by 2005 the autonomous and openly feminist Women's Alliance was also left virtually unfunded once the EU grant to the RACCW was terminated. In 2003, forced to move when they could not afford the increased rent, the center was struggling to find and maintain office space

(Sperling 2005, 173). Their financial problems existed despite their international recognition by American women's magazine *Marie Claire,* which in 2004 declared staff member Elena Shitova to be one of the top ten women in the world. As director Natalia Sereda scrambled for financial resources, the regional administration decided to support a government crisis center for women, and eventually invited Sereda to become the new government center's director.[59] Although funding is limited to salaries for a few specialists and the rent, Sereda thought that she could use these resources to continue supporting her advocacy. As a condition for accepting the job, Sereda insisted that she be able to continue her connection with the autonomous women's movement. However, soon growing frustrated with the state's focus on only social service provision, Sereda returned to the Women's Alliance.

Considering Putin's campaign to establish control over society, moving toward the state may be the only long-term tactic for Russian activists as the state becomes "the only game in town." But there are huge risks. Government leaders or whims may shift suddenly, as they did for a similar government center in Arkhangelsk. Even if funding continues longer term, in a state so resistant to feminism—and foreign influence—such movement toward the state runs the high risk of cooptation of the activists, bringing them "into the process but . . . not render[ing] policy the movement desires" (Stetson 2002, 12).

### Bridges of Mercy in Arkhangelsk: Retaining University Support

The most stable base for feminist women's crisis centers is probably affiliation with public universities. Such support had long been a part of the crisis centers' resources as many of the founders were academics.[60] Some crisis centers, such as Moscow-based Yaroslavna, had been built within universities, while others, such in Tver, seemed to be moving in that direction (Hemment 2007, 147). With some subsidy of space and faculty's time, crisis centers could exist on relatively little other financial support.

In the fall of 2005, one surviving crisis center built within a university was Bridges of Mercy in the far northern city of Arkhangelsk. Founded in 1999 using a borrowed phone line, the organization was formally registered when a senior professor at the local university used her influence to obtain an office at the university.[61] With this base of support, they were able to secure some funding from USAID and more through Nordic sources and the Nordic-Russian NCRB. Bridges of Mercy was also lucky to partner with an American shelter that ran a small fundraiser to fund the necessary renovations to their very cold room. This partnership had emerged serendipitously through the Russian American Rule of Law Consortium, which happened to bring to the region American legal officials who were also domestic violence activists.

In 2005, when Nordic funding was halted—the NCRB project ended in 2005 and Nordic officials decided that Arkhangelsk would no longer be included in future Barents Region projects—Bridges of Mercy had no financial resources. Led by the three founder-professors, they were surviving because the university was continuing to allow them use of the office and to pay for the phone line. They reciprocated by providing work experience for university social work and psychology students. Because of the involvement of the Russian American Rule of Law Consortium, they were also beginning to collaborate with the university's new free legal clinic (which itself had received external grants through long-term United States–Russia cooperation).

Although such university affiliation may be the best long-term tactic, the Arkhangelsk case illustrates that this option represents a scaled-down feminist mobilization. Without additional funding, the crisis center is limited to providing crisis counseling without much advocacy. The feminist leaders were exhausted, and most of the volunteers I met in the fall of 2005 saw their work as practical, a step toward acquiring necessary job experience.[62] They described their varying hotline strategies, most often trying to reveal or create more options for the woman living with violence. In some cases, the hotline counselors were able to arrange for temporary shelter at a local homeless shelter or help the victim trade apartments in order not to live with her abuser. But only one of the three felt that raising awareness was central to their work. Without this additional component, hotline counseling runs the risk of reinforcing the neotraditional gender roles, where women are responsible for peace in their families.

———

By the middle of the decade, the women's crisis center movement was embattled. There was some expansion in the number of organizations. In 2004, the RACCW had expanded to some 47 organizations as more NGOs and state hybrids found out about RACCW and filled out the necessary paperwork, but in the fall of 2005, it seemed the network and at least some members would soon cease to exist. By 2004, ANNA had created its own overlapping loose network of 121 organizations in Russia with whom they had trained or collaborated (Amnesty International 2005, 2). In 2004, at what may be the high point of the movement and including all antitrafficking organizations, the movement included 229 distinct organizations addressing violence against women and/or trafficking in women, covering sixty-one out of the eighty-nine regions.[63]

However, these increased numbers of organizations are undermined by the increased fragmentation in the movement and the tenuousness of the existence of most of the feminist crisis centers. Only thirty-eight of these organizations had proven longevity by lasting more than a couple of years. Even among the relatively well-founded northwestern crisis centers (through 2005), one center had ceased focusing on gender violence and there had been high staff turnovers because of low salaries: 50 percent of the centers paid their staff at or below the official minimal "living wage" (approximately $108/month in Arkhangelsk in 2005), and an additional 40 percent of the crisis centers in the region had no paid staff (Liapounova and Dracheva 2005). In 2007, activist leaders found only nineteen NGO women's crisis centers remaining (Open Society Institute 2007, 33). These included all the centers listed on the map as active centers (map 1), except Nizhny Tagil, which closed in 2005, as well as seven other centers, including ones in the

Siberian republic of Buriatiia and far eastern Vladivostok. The decrease was perceivable to the population beyond its direct impact. Russians in 2006 were much less likely to recognize that their city had a shelter, crisis center, or trust line than five years earlier (Zabelina et al. 2007, 86).

## ASSESSING THE IMPACT OF INTERVENTIONS ON FEMINIST MOBILIZATION

Of the three interventions, assistance through international development agencies and large charitable foundations was clearly the most effective at fostering feminist mobilization. Global feminism and transnational feminist networking helped the movement get off the ground, but it took feminist alliances with democracy assistance donors to create a women's crisis center movement, an unusually successful segment of Russia's weak civil society. Despite some problems, the most dire concerns raised by critics of democracy assistance—that NGOs would be used to legitimate neoliberal privatization policies by replacing state services—were not realized for women's crisis centers, many of which remained both service providers and advocates for change. The best testament to the success of these initiatives is that when these funds were most available, the Russian local and federal social services began to mimic the autonomous women's crisis centers with their own crisis centers. In a country where women's organizations are not even allowed to use the word "feminist" in their official names,[64] the creation of a broad network of women's crisis centers and some government counterparts is a remarkable change. Working with antitrafficking crusaders shaped by states more concerned with sovereignty, security, and border control, on the other hand, pushed the de-radicalization of the movement and embroiled it in geopolitics, funneling support to organizations least concerned with feminist mobilization.

What made the alliance with democracy assistance more successful than the states' (and the EU's) antitrafficking initiatives was the greater influence of global feminism and transnational feminists on the process. Although far from perfect, this kind of alliance, in which feminists were involved in the grant-distributing process and gendered implications of intervention were considered, led to the most feminist intervention. The Nordic NCRB project in northwestern Russia illustrates the potential of a real partnership, not just alliance, between transnational feminists and donors, creating the most responsive and most inclusive intervention. In a context of already existing feminism, the involvement of transnational feminists helped donors see a little past their "shareholders'" interests for short-term observable outcomes because they are committed to broader, longer-term goals. In contrast, there was less global feminist influence on antitrafficking initiatives in terms. The lack of consensus among transnational feminists meant no coherent ideology on how to address the problem, and an issue first raised by feminists was preempted by states for pragmatic and ideological reasons. This Russian case illustrates that the transnational women's movement, at its best, has become more reflective and responsive to the concerns of those beyond the Global North/West.

# CHAPTER FOUR

# Sexual Assault:
## The Limits of Blame and Shame

THE 1998 PUBLICATION OF Margaret Keck and Kathyrn Sikkink's *Activists beyond Borders* affirmed global activists' hopes that new global norms, such as those that frame gender violence as human rights violations, could have important long-term impact on state behavior. Aspirations more than reality, such norms represent a new transnational consensus about what it means to be civilized, and activists hope that their creation means new incentives for states concerned about their international reputation. Non-state actors—organizations or networks, global or local—can draw upon global norms to hold states accountable. Does the creation of global feminist norms against gender violence—and their monitoring by transnational feminists and human rights organizations— bolster domestic activism, boost public awareness, and promote state policy reforms that address violence against women? If not, why?

The study of the politics of sexual assault in the new Russia shows that the consensus on global norms, even with the support of transnational and local feminist activism as well as human rights monitoring, is not sufficient to significantly change popular or state response to violence against women. After a short burst of attention toward rape and sexual harassment by foreign and local activists in the early 1990s, these issues were virtually ignored by policymakers, and Russians, if anything, became more likely to blame women for their own sexual assault. The global feminist campaign against gender violence can legitimate local activism and some public discussion of sexual assault, but feminist entrepreneurs, both Russian and foreign, with only limited funds and without credible sanctions, could not induce meaningful compliance. Julie Mertus (2004) in *Bait and Switch: Human Rights and U.S. Foreign Policy,* shows that the U.S. policymakers "talk the talk" of human rights, but continue to see human rights through the lens of American values and national interests, applying human rights standards only to other states. Despite self-representation to the contrary, the European Union has had similar double standards, especially toward new member states since the breakdown of communism in Europe (Williams 2004). This Russian case study suggests that even states of moderate sovereignty—not the most or least powerful—can effectively ignore these new human rights norms. For those who are wary of any type of substantial foreign intervention and yet hope for feminist policy reform, this suggests that there is a tradeoff: global norms are not enough.

To clarify, I am using the term *sexual assault* as shorthand to refer to a variety of types of sexual violence committed by individuals, strangers or intimates, against adult women in intimate relationships or at work. I exclude trafficking in women, including trafficking for the provision of sexual services, reserving this issue for another chapter. I include what U.S. feminists have called rape, such as acquaintance rape, date rape, wife or spousal rape (which I summarize as *familiar rape*), and sexual harassment. Although there are important differences between these phenomena, sexual harassment, at least one form of it, is understood as much more like rape in Russia (where it has been proscribed in criminal law) than in the United States (where it is regulated through anti-discrimination civil law).

## GLOBALIZING NORMS

### Expanding Norms against Rape

For centuries, women's movements around the world have made sexual assault, especially rape, a central concern. In Russia, the mid-nineteenth-century women nihilists and the revolutionary feminist Alexandra Kollontai even advocated absolute equality in love and sex; they created alternative forms of relationships, from loveless, sexless fictitious marriages that allowed women unusual independence from their parents and social expectations to extramarital serial monogamy (Noonan and Nechemias 2001, 47). In the West, the issue of rape gained new prominence in the second wave of women's activism in the 1970s and 1980s. In the United States and the United Kingdom, along with the proliferation of rape crisis centers came Take Back the Night/Reclaim the Night marches that revealed atrocities and made new claims upon the state. But the resurgence of the issue was not reserved for the Global North. For example, rape also became a key issue for Indian women's movements, while in Brazil women's organizations linked sexual violence to state repression, getting the newly installed civilian government to create special police stations to assist women who had suffered from sexual violence (Basu 1995, 11–12). The consolidation of the concept of "violence against women" provided a way to connect these concerns, helping activists from the Global North to overcome claims that they were only a middle-class white movement and those from the Global South to undermine assertions of violence as cultural practice (Weldon 2006). When activists succeeded in getting violence against women included into U.N. documents in the 1980s and 1990s, rape was explicitly included (see appendix 1).

The central innovation in the global feminist consensus was the global recognition of the use of rape in war. Even at the Nuremberg and Tokyo war trials following World War II, the systematic deployment of rape during war had been ignored. In the aftermath of mass rapes of women by Iraqi soldiers in Kuwait in 1991 and by Serb forces in Bosnia in 1993, transnational feminists working with human rights activists created enough pressure that key perpetrators were brought to trial for their policy of raping Bosnian women and that such rapes were reclassified as crimes against humanity. This politicization of war rape also led to the creation of the second postsocialist women's crisis center in 1990, the Belgrade SOS hotline (Corrin 1996) (the first was founded in Zagreb in 1987). That the human rights community had to be persuaded to take seriously rape in war, the most public and visibly violent form of rape, revealed the hypocrisy in the widespread formal condemnation of rape. In practice, while officially criminalizing rape, most societies limit rape prosecutions to "honorable" victims and to only certain forms of forced sex.[1] These "real rapes" differ from the more widespread and often ignored "simple rapes" between those who know each other and where less explicit force (outside the rape itself) is employed (Estrich 1987). Most societies have been quite skeptical of women's actual assertions of rape.

In 2002, the Special Rapporteur on violence against women to the High Commission on Human Rights issued the boldest critique of rapes outside of war.[2] Whereas U.N. documents had condemned rape without specifying what constituted rape, this report condemned marital rape, honor killings of raped family members, gang rapes of lower-caste women by upper-caste men, forced marriages (including those through rape), the exoneration of rapists if they agree to marry the woman they rape, incest, and the punishment or abuse of women who transgress boundaries of what is accepted as appropriate sexual behavior. While the other condemnations of rape met with widespread and facile support, this report evoked far more outcry because it "moved into a new domain of behavior, that of sexuality and its regulation, and challenged cultural practices considered acceptable by at least some members of societies" (Merry 2006a, 62–65). Official representatives from many South Asian countries were disgruntled, some even hostile, as the report claimed that the international community had the right to challenge societies' regulation of women's sexuality and family life, issues that had not necessarily been raised by the more pedestrian statements on rape and sexual abuse. The critiques also provoked resistance because they "resonated with colonial critiques of family and gender practices, ranging from assaults on *sati* to child marriage" (65).

Activists also have a history of challenging sexual harassment in the workplace. In post-Revolution Russia, Bolshevik feminists were concerned about employers forcing women to have sex, leading early Soviet leaders to criminalize this behavior as part of other sexual violence (Juviler 1977). But it was not until U.S. activists took up the issue in the 1970s that sexual harassment came to represent the distinct phenomenon understood today, "[u]nwelcome sexual advances, requests for sexual favors, and other verbal or physical conduct of a sexual nature." Their activism led to the introduction into U.S. anti-discrimination law of two forms of sexual harassment, for which both the individual harasser and the employer can be held liable. The first is quid pro quo (or blackmail) harassment, which exists when there are explicit or implicit threats that submission or rejection of these sexual behaviors will affect employment decisions. The second, hostile work environment, covers the more subtle sexual intimidation—through sexually charged comments and images—that creates a hostile or offensive environment.

The American construction of sexual harassment as well as resistance to recognizing individual claims of sexual harassment was broadcast globally during the hearings for the nomination to the U.S. Supreme Court of Clarence Thomas, whose alleged sexual harassment did not derail his appointment. By the 1990s, women's groups across the world were pursuing reform, albeit with different understandings of the problem. For example, French feminists in the early 1990s included harassment based on sexual orientation and stressed women's rights to "dignity, their moral or physical integrity, their right to receive ordinary services to the public in full equality" (quoted in Saguy 2002, 253). In response to the various activists' pressure and conceptions, countries adopted very different reforms. France adopted labor and penal code articles against sexual blackmail in 1992. The European Union, framing the problem as a "violation against workers' dignity" and part of a conflict-ridden workplace where workers sometimes terrorize others, required that all members adopt legislation by 2005 (Zippel 2006). This was not just a North American and European phenomenon; the 1997 Vishaka decision in India, a result of the Indian Supreme Court's commitment to the Convention on the Elimination of All Forms of Discrimination Against Women (CEDAW), led to the drafting of sexual harassment legislation in 2004.

Even with these different viewpoints, sexual harassment was incorporated into the key U.N. documents on women's status (see appendix 1). The Nairobi Forward Looking Strategies for the Advancement of Women (1985) called for "appropriate measures to prevent sexual harassment on the job or sexual exploitation in specific jobs, such as domestic service" (para. 139). The Vienna Declaration and Programme for Action (1993) linked "gender-based violence" with "all forms of sexual harassment and exploitation" (part I, para. 38). Whereas these earlier documents decried sexual harassment, the 1993 U.N. Declaration on the Elimination of Violence against Women clearly attached sexual harassment to the concept of violence against women (art. 2).

By the 1990s, these global norms against sexual assault were read into international law, especially CEDAW, the international bill of rights for women, which did not initially refer to gender violence. In General Recommendation 12 in 1989, the CEDAW Committee requested that states include information about measures to assist and protect women from "sexual violence" and "sexual harassment at the workplace." General Recommendation 19 from 1992, which elaborates how violence against women violates the articles of CEDAW, explicitly includes both "sexual assault" and "sexual harassment." Most importantly, the recommendation asserts an international definition of sexual harassment that encompasses both forms as discriminatory.[3]

Yet, these international documents, even those that officially constitute international law, do not represent legally binding laws with the same power of state-based law, which, in functioning states with credible commitments to the rule of law, is backed up by state machinery to enforce compliance. This is true even in countries like Russia, where international law signed by Russia theoretically carries the force of law within Russia. International laws come from supranational institutions such as the United Nations, which is only a collection of states, has no coercive mechanisms, and, in some places, has little legitimacy. Even CEDAW, which requires periodic reports of states' compliance and their assessment by the CEDAW committee, has no teeth. Global feminist frustration with this limitation led to the passage of the 1999 Optional Protocol. This protocol allows individual women, under certain circumstances, to appeal to the CEDAW Committee and permits this committee to investigate particularly serious violations of women's rights, perhaps creating the potential for more direct influence over states. Signaling some commitment to these norms, Russia is a signatory to both CEDAW, without reservations, and the 1999 Optional Protocol. The United States ratified neither CEDAW nor the Optional Protocol.

Instead, the domestic impact of international documents is more indirect. In the language of international relations constructivists, these international documents constitute a *global norm*—"a standard of appropriate behavior for actors within a given territory"—that can influence beliefs, behavior, and sometimes even the identity of individuals, groups, and institutions (Katzenstein 1996, 5; Checkel 1998). Such a transnational normative consensus, complemented by international conventions, may constrain state behavior as states become socialized into the international arena (Klotz 1995). The process through which this happens is *norm diffusion,* and success is observed as a *norms cascade,* the growing acceptance of these norms among different actors and states. Fostering this norm diffusion are dynamic networks of social relationships at the local, national, and global levels that are often summarized as *transnational advocacy networks* (Keck and Sikkink 1998)—the generic form of what this book calls transnational feminist networks. These collaborations of social movements, interested professionals, and, sometimes, firms work together on a campaign to "'frame' issues to make them comprehensible to target audiences, to attract attention and encourage action, and to 'fit' with favorable institutional venues. . . . They also promote norm implementation, by pressuring target actors to adopt new policies, and by monitoring compliance with international standards" (Keck and Sinkink 1998, 2–3). For Keck and Sikkink, they tend to create a *boomerang pattern,* in which "domestic NGOs may directly seek international allies to try to bring pressure on their states from outside" to both raise the issue and formulate a policy response (12). Others have suggested a kind of *ping-pong* model in which norms bounce back in forth between the supranational institutions and nation-states (Zippel 2006, 120).

In the language of social movement theory, these international documents signal a global *collective action frame* of the problem, an "action-oriented" set "of beliefs and meanings that inspire[s] and legitimate[s] activities and campaigns" (Benford and Snow 2000, 614). The new frame is among the different types of international institutions that "offer resources, opportunities, and incentives" to domestic activists (Tarrow 2001, 1). The corresponding transnational advocacy networks can also foster the recognition of—or *certify*—identities and public activities as legitimate (15). They can *model* "forms of collective action or organization in one venue that have been demonstrated in another." For social movement theorists, campaigns succeed when such frames *resonate,* that is, when the target population sees the movement's arguments as credible, salient, and not in conflict with national myths or ideologies.

Whereas the first approach undertheorizes the domestic process as it is focused on international relations, this second approach focuses on domestic activism, undertheorizing the transnational. The second approach and sometimes the first neglect the ways that global norms can be powerful interventions. Norms are exercised not just by domestic organizations and their transnational network collaborators; their use can be imposed by transnational activists and other international organizations. Most importantly, most social movement theorists' emphasis on resonance misses the point that too much resonance means that the new norms lose their radical critique. For example, until they were qualified with radical claims about marital and date rape, the new global feminist claims about rape met with acceptance because, of course, most everyone agrees that (real) rape is unjust. I agree with Sally Merry (2006a, 10): the most effective translation processes are those that can balance the need to challenge the social order with adaptation to the given cultural context. If a norm has much resonance with local traditions and beliefs, it ceases to be a challenge in that particular setting; if it has no resonance, then the norm has no rhetorical power in that society. In practice, this often means "that the rights framework does not displace other frameworks but adds a new dimension to the way individuals think about problems" (180–81).

In the language of legal anthropology, international documents are *culturally constitutive* in that they produce "cultural meanings associating with modernity and the international" to which states have incentives to subscribe (Merry

**TABLE 4.1.** *Blame and Shame Model*

| PROCESSES | LEADING FOREIGN AGENTS | MECHANISMS |
|---|---|---|
| localizing activism/ vernacularization | feminist entrepreneurs and transnational feminist networks | global norms as modeling and certifying activism, activists appropriating and translating |
| raising awareness | | |
| reforming policy | human rights and rule-of-law advocates | monitoring |
| reforming practice | | |

2006a, 89). Their power comes from their consensual nature and their ability to elicit shame. Global norms come to matter when they are *made into the vernacular* (Anderson 1983). This process of *vernacularization* includes *appropriation* and *translation* (Merry 2006a, 219). National political elites, human rights or feminist activist leaders, service providers, legal professionals, or academics—as the key intermediaries between global and local—appropriate global norms. They then must translate these norms into the vernacular, "adjusting the rhetoric and structure of these programs or interventions to local circumstances" (135). These processes can also be *localized*, as they are when women's groups, especially poor urban and rural women, claim entitlement to these rights.

This book summarizes the process of the new global feminist norms coming to matter in Russia as *blame and shame* (see table 4.1). I assess how transnational feminist networks and global norms may model collective action strategies and can certify domestic activism in the process of localizing activism and vernacularization of global norms. I evaluate the agency and effectiveness of feminist entrepreneurs, transnational feminist networks, and the alliance between transnational feminists and human rights activists. I gauge whether these agents and processes have led to significant changes in public awareness, state policy, or practice.

## APPROPRIATING, BUT NOT TRANSLATING, GLOBAL NORMS

### Localizing Anti-rape Activism

The issue of sexual violence was raised in 1991 at the very beginning of the post-Soviet women's movement in Russia. It was one of the issues of violence against women that was unscheduled, but added to the agenda of the watershed event in the Russian women's movement, the First Independent Women's Forum in 1991 (Nechemias 2001). Already by the mid 1990s, several women's organizations—especially Moscow-based FALTA and Syostri as well as Saratov-based Interregional

Association of Women Lawyers (IAWL)—were working to bring more attention to the issue among the broader public. They were, respectively, running their own consciousness-raising groups and translating Western theory on related problems into Russian; holding workshops for young people, healthcare personnel, and law enforcement officers while creating public service announcements; and producing a regional television program as part of a local (1995) "16 Days without Violence" campaign with local law enforcement organs. As do other anti-rape campaigns around the world, all sought to create awareness of forms and aspects of sexual violence, such as date rape and incest, that were previously taboo.

For the leaders of these organizations, initial interest in addressing sexual violence arose locally. In some cases, they had experience with sexual violence, against either themselves or someone close to them, that led them to imagine creating an organization. One Syostri founder, who first began assisting women in 1989, was encouraged by over 1,500 letters she received from rape victims in response to articles she published. In the words of another leading activist at the center, "it was through her work and correspondence with survivors that she developed a vision of an independent crisis center staffed by professional psychologists and trained volunteers" (Zabelina 1995, 266).

Nonetheless, from the onset of anti-rape activism, their campaigns were linked with the transnational feminist movement. Even before the Soviet collapse, participants at the First Independent Women's Forum included feminists from the United States, Great Britain, Canada, and India who broached the issues of sexuality and violence. A 1993 seminar on "women, youth, violence" brought several Canadian lawyers to the Russian crisis centers to discuss Russian experience and the history of North American anti-rape movements, leading at least one Russian activist to analyze sexual violence using ideas modeled on North American feminism.[4] In those years, Westerners collaborated with Russians to translate Western feminist texts to Russian, producing scores of booklets, articles in the Russian women's movement's new journals, and books on sexual health and violence. Although these projects sometimes included discussion of the differing Russian situation, almost always the texts were translated and reproduced uncritically. The Russian anti-rape campaigns even modeled themselves on Western anti-rape campaigns. For example, Moscow-based crisis center Syostri—in pamphlets, workshops, articles, and interviews—confronted "myths" about sexual violence in Russian society with the "facts."[5] In one adaptation to the Russian society and culture, activists frequently linked the blaming of women to Russia's particular taboo about discussing sexuality.[6]

These kinds of transnational feminist interventions tended to be viewed positively by Russian leaders who viewed themselves as transnational feminists. As explained by one leader, she was "feminist by birth," but Western feminist theory and practice gave her new ways of understanding and responding to sexual violence.[7] Although critical of the impact of foreign assistance on feminist organizations, she spoke uncritically of Western feminist ideas and models and the global campaign against gender violence. She understood this stage of activism as one during which "Russia was integrated into the [global] war against violence against women."

By 1999, the global norm framing gender violence in terms of human rights had entered into the campaigns and rhetoric of organizations and activists. In collaboration with other crisis centers and the gender program at the Moscow affiliate of the American Bar Association Central and Eastern European Law Initiative (ABA-CEELI), Syostri produced a series of brochures called the "Rainbow of Rights."[8] These brochures linked sexual violence to Russia's international rights obligations under CEDAW and the European Convention on Human Rights. Syostri's website (http://www.owl.ru/syostri/) then added an extensive section on rights, including reproducing the U.N. Declaration on the Elimination of Violence against Women and parts of the Beijing Platform for Action.

Feminist entrepreneurs and venues for transnational conversations were essential to the process of localizing activism. In the early 1990s, the frequent trips by Western feminists to the region brought Western feminist ideas about sexual violence.[9] American entrepreneur Martina Vandenberg not only provided startup resources for Syostri, but also shaped their activism "based on her experience as a rape crisis counselor in California and England" (Zabelina 1995). American Dianne Post at ABA-CEELI was the driving force behind the "Rainbow of Rights" brochures. Other interactions occurred at transnational conferences, workshops, and trainings, and then congealed into collaborative publications and websites.[10] To a lesser degree, there were exchanges in which Russian leaders traveled to visit U.S.-based crisis centers.

### Localizing Anti–Sexual Harassment Activism

After receiving distress calls from women, by the mid 1990s Russian women's movement scholars and activists also grew concerned with the issue of sexual harassment (e.g., Khodyreva 1996; Pisklakova 1996). For example, at a 1993 seminar on women's unemployment at the Moscow Center for Gender Studies (MCGS), one attendee publicly requested consideration of the problem she and her friend had faced in a one-factory town where the manager would hire only women who would have sex with him (Khotkina 1996, 19–20). But these movement participants were not the only ones interested in collectively responding to the problem. In Moscow, a husband-and-wife team not connected to the women's movement founded the first organization, Diana, to address sexual harassment (Khotkina 1996, 16–17). Valerii Vikulov, working at a popular newspaper, had been confronted by the problem when women began to arrive in his office to complain that want ads he published had led them to jobs for which sexual, not professional, services had been required. In addition to helping some one hundred women find suitable jobs, Diana began lists of "moral" and "immoral" private firms.

This Russian problem encountered U.S. approaches at a 1995 MCGS seminar on sexual harassment, the first such event held in Russia; it was funded by American organizations, the ABA-CEELI and the NIS-US Women's Consortium

(Khotkina 1996). The American participants named the problem as sexual harassment, but as was true even in Western Europe (Zippel 2006), translating American/global norms into the Russian experience was difficult. The obstacle was more than just a linguistic problem (although that too was a problem).[11] On the one hand, because the closest piece of Russian law to sexual harassment is a criminal article on "sexual compulsion" (*seksual'noe ponuzhdenie*), it was easy for the Russians to imagine sexual harassment as a form of gender violence with perceivable bodily harm, the way that global norms framed the problem. Under the Soviet version in effect until 1997, this article "exclusively protected women in cases where they were compelled into sexual relations for fear of losing property or work related possessions [i.e., losing their job, not being hired]" (Suchland 2005, 151–52). On the other hand, most of the foreign attention to sexual harassment in Russia was coming from the United States, where sexual harassment is framed as discrimination, and the phenomena brought to the activists' attention more closely resembled a form of economic discrimination in which only women who were willing to provide sex were hired. As argued by Jennifer Suchland (2005), this kind of sexual harassment would be more effectively regulated through a legal mechanism that recognizes the economic consequences, such as through labor law. Trying to incorporate all approaches to sexual harassment, the conference volume editor begins with the definition established by American feminist legal theorist Catharine MacKinnon, links this kind of discrimination with the criminal article on sexual compulsion, and then blames the overall gender system (Khotkina 1996, 14, 20).

Following this conference, for Russian activists and scholars sexual harassment uncomfortably blends what Americans might call sexual violence with economic discrimination, leading to some frustrating results from the perspective of global feminists (Suchland 2005). For example, a sociologist with the Russian Academy of Sciences in St. Petersburg in what was the next major work on sexual harassment also begins with the MacKinnon definition of sexual harassment (8), but at the same time manages to blame women for often provoking the sexual harassment used against them (Kletsin 1998).[12] Similarly, the one crisis center (in Tula) that published a booklet on how to defend oneself from sexual harassment also simultaneously blames women for provoking harassment, such as by flicking their hair.[13] The failure to successfully translate the global norm against sexual harassment into the Russian vernacular helps explain why here was much less Russian activism against sexual harassment than rape despite the salience to many women's lives of widespread sexual harassment.

## Attention Wanes

By the beginning of the 2000s, women's crisis centers were much less focused on sexual assault. While others continued to address the issue as part of their other work, only one crisis center (Syostri) remained that was devoted to combating sexual assault. The issue also disappeared from women's crisis center campaigns.

Whereas a 1994 article by a Russian activist titled "Violence against Women" addressed only sexual violence, a 2002 well-received dictionary of gender terminology included no entry on rape or sexual violence.[14] By 2002, most women's crisis centers identified themselves as addressing violence against women but meant, in practice, primarily nonsexual domestic violence.

Part of the problem was the extensive resistance to discussing sex, which evolved into a moral panic under Putin.[15] But this retrenchment also reflected shifts in funding possibilities for such activism. Until 1999, donors were at least as willing to fund organizations addressing sexual violence as those funding domestic violence; however, the USAID funds that helped the movement grow were designated only for those organizations that address domestic violence. While a tremendous boon to the women's crisis center movement, this decision left organizations such as Syostri that focused on sexual violence with few resources.

Attention toward sexual harassment also waned somewhat. By the late 1990s, the center Diana, which had been providing information about "moral" businesses, had closed (Suchland 2005, 178). Similarly, the women's crisis center in Tula appears to have done nothing further on the issue. Yet, because harassment remains a common feature of post-Soviet women's lives, new interest emerged; another organization in Rostov-on-Don had a sexual harassment hotline, which in 2005 reported receiving one hundred calls a month (Duban 2006, 85). In Kazan in 2004, a one-woman dynamo was teaching groups of unemployed women who were involved in a fifty-four-hour job retraining program with the regional Ministry of Labor about the global women's movement and sexual harassment.[16]

## NOT RAISING AWARENESS

Did these new campaigns transform society's awareness of sexual assault? Were these new norms reflected in the media? Did they penetrate into people's opinions or change the dominant discourses about rape and sexual harassment? For the answers, I examine the impact of the anti–gender violence campaigns on public awareness by reviewing newspaper coverage of the issues from 1995 to 2004 (see appendix 2), summarizing the available public opinion surveys, and observing the dominant discourses about gender violence.

### Media Coverage of Sexual Assault

In the early years, women's crisis centers were remarkably successful at getting coverage in local, regional, and national newspapers. For example, in 1997, according to their files, the work of Syostri or Syostri's founders was reported in fifteen English-language articles, in United States and Russian news, and thirty-nine Russian-language articles, dating from a 1991 publication. That the articles were published in some of the most important and popular news sources—*Argumenty i Facty, Ogonek, Izvestiia,* and *Nezavisimaia Gazeta*—illustrated that the women's crisis centers had early been able to command attention toward sexual assault.

TABLE 4.2. *The Incidence of Various Terms for Rape in* Izvestiia, *1995–2005*

| SPECIFIC TERM | 1995 | 1996 | 1997 | 1998 | 1999 | 2000 | 2001 | 2002 | 2003 | 2004 | 2005 |
|---|---|---|---|---|---|---|---|---|---|---|---|
| rape (*iznasilovanie*) | 38 | 26 | 42 | 26 | 12 | 37 | 26 | 32 | 110 | 91 | 69 |
| date rape (*iznasilovanie na svidanie*) | 0 | 0 | 0 | 0 | 0 | 0 | 0 | 0 | 0 | 0 | 0 |
| rape in marriage (*iznasilovanie v brake*) | 0 | 0 | 0 | 0 | 0 | 0 | 0 | 0 | 0 | 0 | 0 |

Articles on rape appeared first, but in 1994 *Komsomol'skaia Pravda* published the first article in Russia that regarded sexual harassment with seriousness and as a social problem (Khotkina 1996). In the early to mid 1990s, the Russian mass media, newly freed from censorship, were enamored with writing about social problems that had previously been taboo and were even open to innovative ways of thinking about these problems.

Unfortunately, this kind and degree of interest did not last long. Of all the forms of gender violence discussed in this study, rape is the most commonly covered issue in national and regional newspapers and newswires, reflecting not a new awareness of the problem, but the long history of a (limited) understanding of rape. There has been no meaningful increase over the time that the crisis centers have been active. For example, coverage in the long-running national newspaper *Izvestiia* from 1995 to 2005 remained relatively consistent over time until 2003 (see table 4.2). The more recent increase in coverage, coming after activism had waned, reflected coverage of several high-profile cases, including a serial rapist "maniac" active around Moscow. As during the Soviet period, rapes such as these that are seen as particularly threatening to the social order receive a lot of attention, and most other articles refer to rape as a criminal problem or use the word as a metaphor for other problems. Very few articles cover rape as a form of violence against women or violation of women's rights, suggesting that the campaign against rape has very little impact on media coverage.

More telling, these news sources almost never used the new terms for familiar rape that activists wanted to introduce (Khodyreva 1996). Whereas there were over eight thousand articles from 1994 to 2004 that referenced rape in an entire database of national and regional newspapers (East View), only a handful used an activist term for "date rape" (*iznasilovanie na svidanie*), and none referenced "rape in marriage" (*iznasilovanie v brake*).[17] Neither of these terms appeared in *Izvestiia*. The Russian media do not recognize a broader construction of rape.

Similarly, activism against sexual harassment had no positive impact on media

TABLE 4.3.

*The Incidence of Various Terms for Sexual Harassment in* Izvestiia, *1995–2005*

| SPECIFIC TERM | 1995 | 1996 | 1997 | 1998 | 1999 | 2000 | 2001 | 2002 | 2003 | 2004 | 2005 | TOTAL |
|---|---|---|---|---|---|---|---|---|---|---|---|---|
| sexual overtures (*seksual'nye domogatel'stva*) | 4 | 6 | 6 | 24 | 5 | 21 | 6 | 15 | 30 | 23 | 15 | 155 |
| sexual harassment (*seksual'noe presledovanie*) | 1 | 0 | 0 | 0 | 0 | 0 | 1 | 0 | 1 | 1 | 2 | 6 |
| sexual harassment (in English) | 0 | 0 | 0 | 0 | 1 | 2 | 1 | 0 | 0 | 0 | 0 | 4 |
| sexual encroachment (*seksual'noe posiagatel'stvo*) | 0 | 0 | 0 | 2 | 0 | 0 | 0 | 0 | 0 | 0 | 0 | 2 |
| Total | 5 | 6 | 6 | 26 | 6 | 23 | 8 | 15 | 31 | 24 | 17 | 167 |

coverage of the problem. Albeit less than rape, sexual harassment was discussed quite often in print media. This would seem to be a significant accomplishment as sexual harassment, unlike rape, was a new concept, suggesting that any coverage might signal a change. The most common term for it was "sexual overtures" (*seksual'nye domogatel'stva*), the term chosen by scholar-activists at the 1995 seminar on sexual harassment.[18] However, the concept of sexual harassment appears to have been quickly picked up by the media, but almost never as a serious discussion of the problem as it relates to women (see also Zabelina 2002, ch. 5). For example, spikes in the references to sexual harassment in *Izvestiia* tend to reflect American events (see table 4.3). The increased attention to the issue in 1998 was a response to the scandal over then U.S. president Clinton's relationship with a White House intern. The upsweep in 2003 and 2004 reflected the attention to the 2003 allegations of sexual misconduct by Michael Jackson and the 2004 American sexual abuse of prisoners in Iraq. More broadly, many articles that mentioned sexual harassment did so as part of either ridiculing the concept or casting it as a foreign idea, such as by mocking Americans and their "ludicrous" regulation of sexuality in the workplace. For example, a 1994 study reported in the news suggested that Russian "[w]omen view their bodies as a way of furthering their careers—that's just the way that it is. . . . Sexual harassment is absolutely not a real problem in Russia. . . . I assure you there is no opposition on the part of [Russian] women to this."[19] As elsewhere (Saguy 2002), "sexual harassment" was a domestic construct created by nonfeminist nationalists.

More important for global feminists would be a shift in the ways the public understands sexual assault. Unfortunately, since sexual harassment was not seen as a problem by mainstream sociologists, there is limited survey data and no data that is comparable over time. The little available data suggests some growing concern for sexual harassment, especially among women. For instance, a 1999 study conducted by the Institute for Urban Economics found—through a combination of surveys, interviews, and focus groups in various Russian cities—that privatization of the economy had severely disadvantaged women in terms of hiring, firing, and sexual harassment (Liborakina 1999).[20] Focus groups with working and unemployed women revealed that these women were quite critical of the job ads explicitly or implicitly demanding sexual services (Liborakina 1999, 59–62). Similarly, a 2002 survey found that most Russians see the problem of quid pro quo sexual harassment as a serious impediment to women's advancement in education and the workplace (Zabelina 2002).[21] Seventy-two percent of the 1,528 respondents thought that a woman who resisted sexual advances from an employer or teacher would likely lose her position; 53 percent thought that this might destroy her career (56–57). Only 3.3 percent thought that there would be no negative consequences.

However, this growing concern reflected an apparent increase in the problem, not an increase in global feminist understanding. In the first study, none of the fifty focus group participants were familiar with the feminist concept of sexual harassment (Liborakina 1999, 59–62). Further, only one expressed outrage at having to appeal to management for assistance with a drunken boss's unwanted sexual attention, and she explained the support she received, to the extent that she did, as because of her "excellent reputation," drawing upon earlier morality-based critiques of such behavior. In the second study, although most respondents (83%) thought that demands for sexual services in order to be hired or accepted into institutions of higher education constituted a form of violence (56),[22] this construction of quid pro quo harassment as violence mostly derives from the Soviet legacy of criminalizing sexual compulsion at work and protectionism toward women, not women's empowerment as rights-holding individuals (Suchland 2005).

Illustrating the lack of recent attention to rape, there have been no significant studies that focus on popular understandings of rape in Russia. The one scientific study that touches upon the issue is a 2003 survey by researchers at Moscow State University that examines sexual violence within marriages as part of their examination of violence in the family (Gorshkova and Shurygina 2003). Their survey of 2,200 people in more than fifty locations across Russia found that most Russians remained very skeptical of the idea of marital rape, albeit possibly less so than in the late Soviet period. Approximately 60 percent of the men and 50 percent of the women held that rape within marriage was simply impossible in principle (53). Although respondents had fairly egalitarian views of their own sexual practices (most women and men felt that they had sex when both wanted it), many (43%)

**TABLE 4.4.** *Opinions on Spousal Sexual Relations, 2003*

| PERCENTAGE OF RESPONDENTS WHO AGREED WITH THE FOLLOWING STATEMENTS: | SEX | AGE | | | | | AVERAGE |
| --- | --- | --- | --- | --- | --- | --- | --- |
| | | 18–24 | 25–34 | 35–44 | 45–54 | 55–64 | |
| Think that it's better if a wife doesn't refuse her husband sex even if she doesn't want it at that moment | W | 31.6% | 32.5% | 39.2% | 42.8% | 47.5% | 39.2% |
| | M | 46.2% | 42.0% | 43.0% | 52.5% | 55.7% | 47.2% |
| Think that a woman should not restrict sex with her husband to times when she herself expects to receive satisfaction | W | 26.6% | 37.2% | 37.0% | 37.0% | 32.1% | 35.6% |
| | M | 46.9% | 43.6% | 40.7% | 31.3% | 35.0% | 38.4% |
| Think that sexual gratification in marriage is not as important for women as for men | W | 25.3% | 23.0% | 31.0% | 39.5% | 57.1% | 34.3% |
| | M | 26.2% | 23.9% | 25.4% | 33.1% | 49.6% | 30.4% |

*Source:* Gorshkova and Shurgina (2003, 53).

thought that wives did not have the right to refuse sex if she did not want it (52). Perhaps illustrating some change over time, the youngest cohort of women were more likely to think that they deserved sexual pleasure and had a right to refuse sex than middle-aged women. Young men, though, were even less likely to take into consideration women's pleasure than older men (see table 4.4). Together, these changes suggest a sexual revolution, but might mean more sexual violence, as women seek sexual pleasure and men disregard women's desires.

## Lingering Skepticism

The media coverage and public reaction to two high-profile events illustrate how Soviet-period skepticism toward sexual assault has lingered. The first is the story of Aleksandra Ivannikova, who, following a common practice, flagged down a car in Moscow in 2003 to ask for a ride home in exchange for a small fee. According to Ivannikova, the driver, Sergei Bagdasaryan, agreed, but then stopped the car in a secluded space, dropped his pants, and threatened rape. Ivannikova stabbed him in the thigh, hitting an artery, and then ran for help. By the time the police arrive, Bagdasaryan had died. In 2005 when Ivannikova's case was going to trial, the case exploded onto the Russian blogs, newspapers, and then television media, becoming a frequent topic of conversation among Moscovites. After a two-year investigation by the prosecutor, Ivannikova received a suspended sentence of a conviction for a form of involuntary manslaughter and was levied a fine to be paid to Bagdasaryan's parents.

Various groups rallied to her side. Some surrounded the court building with signs declaring, "Save the nursing mother." Human rights groups wanted to draw attention to the lack of exoneration for self-defense in Russia. Nationalist and ultranationalists came to her defense, both because Bagdasaryan was an ethnic Armenian from Azerbaijan and because they wanted to use her to justify the right to bear arms. One radical group, the Movement against Illegal Immigration, despite the fact that Bagdasaryan was a legal resident, even raised money to give to Ivannikova's husband to pay for court costs. For these groups, she was variously a deserving mother, a damsel in distress, and a nationalist hero. (For the few against her, she was, in the words of one brash Internet commentator, a "homicidal bitch from hell.") The confluence of pressure led the city court to take the unusual step of canceling the verdict and later, the prosecutor to drop the charges.

This high-profile case shows how some cases of rape, even an attempted rape, continue to capture the Russian public, and how, in certain circumstances, people rally behind the (almost raped) victim (Johnson 2004). Ivannikova, ethnically Russian, married and, by the time of the trial, mothering a baby, was seen by most as a proper Russian woman. Her account of resistance and her attempt to get help were backed up by police and ambulance workers. Carrying on early post-Soviet practice, certain types of rape are seen as real, as in this case, especially those of the racially dominant women by disadvantaged males (because non-consent can be inferred). However, the case also illustrates how very little of the reaction reflected a new recognition of women's rights. Such an understanding of rape would have meant serious consideration of the reason Ivannikova was carrying the kitchen knife, reportedly a rape when she was sixteen, and the state's previous failure to assist her. According to an opinion piece in the *Moscow News* (June 15, 2005), the police had refused to accept her complaint of this earlier incident. The absence of the feminist discourse was exacerbated by the exclusion of Russian activists from the discussion.[23]

The second event is a sexual harassment case in the relatively poor southwestern Siberian region of Altai that brought national attention to the issue. In 2000, the local women's crisis center, the Women's Alliance in Barnaul, supported a group of women claiming a form of quid pro quo sexual harassment against director of the hospital, the primary place of employment in a small rural town. Jurists working at the center helped the women try various avenues, including appeals to local government and the labor unions and legal claims of moral harm, violation of the labor code, and sexual violence under the criminal article of sexual compulsion (Art. 133). After meeting much resistance, partially because the director was well-connected, the women, with the support of the Women's Alliance, convinced the trade union to review the case and dismiss him from his directorship (but not from the hospital).

This was a remarkable success for the women and the women's crisis center, so remarkable that a popular TV news magazine, *Russkie gorki c Mikhailom Taratutoi* [Russian hills with Mikhail Taratuta], decided to do a segment on the case. The segment began with a shot of a roller coaster to illustrate the rise and falls in a person's fate, and the women—what Americans might see as babushkas—were represented lined up on a bench against a wall. The segment framed the story as a "struggle against their boss . . . for all his sins" and suggested that the women were part of the (American and Western European) feminist movement. The events were construed as a "sex scandal" that these women had won, and the closing thought was that perhaps these were "just free [or loose] women." Recalling this case, a 2004 article in the national newspaper *Vedomosti* summarized the response: "The public opinion was unanimous: the ladies paid too much attention to American feminists and used that pretext to exact revenge on the boss who was only trying to bring the hospital into order."

Like rape, sexual harassment stories can titillate, but as in Ivannikova story, the Altai sexual harassment coverage reveals no support for feminist understandings of sexual assault. Here, feminism was discussed explicitly, but also derisively, as if it had been ridiculous for the women to complain and for officials to take their side (to the extent that they did). Neither the women nor the women's crisis center was given a voice in the segment. The specific allegations (which were quite veiled even in the affidavits) were taboo. There was also no discussion of the power the hospital director wielded in this poor town where state institutions, such as the hospital, were practically the only place of employment.

All in all, despite international and local feminist attention, there appears to be little global feminist consciousness of sexual assault in Russia. Instead, the public discourse suggests that the attention provoked a backlash against global feminist ideas against sexual assault.

## NOT REFORMING POLICY

As the women's crisis center movement was not successful at localizing activism and as the public perception of sexual assault had shifted so little, public pressure from Russians themselves to reform policy would be unlikely, even if the Russian political system were not so closed. Nevertheless, foreign intervention, especially from those international organizations that advocate or monitor human rights and the rule of law, could circumvent the domestic policy process. To what degree have the global and local campaigns created the opportunity for meaningful state reform of laws on sexual assault?

Since rape and sexual harassment are regulated by criminal law in Russia, the post-Soviet revisions of the Russian criminal and the criminal procedure codes are the most likely location for reform.[24] Expressing global feminist concern, Russian activists leveled two critiques of the rape laws in both the Soviet-period and draft codes.[25] First, they argued that the law excluded what the activists identified as psychological coercion, such as threatening to discontinue economic support or threatening to hurt the victim's children.[26] Second, these activist leaders criticized the law's lack of specificity about body parts or the act of penetration.[27] Feminist activists were similarly critical of the law on sexual compulsion for its limited understanding of coercion, arguing that it did not cover the now commonplace situations in which women were promised better work conditions or salary if they complied with their boss's demands for sex.[28]

Speaking these concerns to power was the Russian feminists' goal of the 1995 conference on sexual harassment. The foreign funding and attention attracted some key policymakers and legal experts, but the resistance to their feminist understandings of gender violence was unmistakable. For example, in contrast to the activists' call for a broader construction of sexual harassment, Aleksei Ignatov, a professor of criminal law and member of the advisory council for drafting the new criminal code, lectured that the understanding of sexual harassment in the Russian body of law is much narrower, not covering verbal jokes or even touching (Ignatov 1996, 45). Confused by the activists' use of the term "sexual overtures"— which also refers to the criminal code article—he seemed baffled by any discussion of hostile-environment harassment. Ignatov also disagreed with the feminists on rape. In contrast to their aspiration to include psychological coercion, he authoritatively explained that, for rape, there must be "physical threats" (Ignatov 1996, 45). He said that rape is distinguishable from other forms of sexual violence because rape is "intercourse between the sexes, intended for reproduction, that can cause a woman to become pregnant. All of the rest are different ways to satisfy sexual needs, but they are not sexual intercourse . . . if it's not sexual intercourse, that means it's not rape" (Ignatov 1996). In other words, Ignatov took great pains to distinguish penile-vaginal rape from other forms of sexual violence because, for him, the possibility of getting pregnant was very significant, evoking historical concerns about paternity. Ignatov also understood rape as connected to a woman's "morality" rather than human rights or other forms of violence. Resistance came even from those most likely to be the crisis center movement's allies, for example, Liudmila Zavadskaia, a member of the Women of Russia faction and the chair of the parliamentary subcommittee on the rights of the individual within the committee charged with reforming the criminal-legal system. Even though she was an advocate for socioeconomic issues relating to women, at the conference she explained that she did not consider sexual harassment a women's issue.

With these failures to persuade, it was not surprising that the new Russian criminal code, passed in 1996, reflected none of the feminist hopes. Although broadening the Soviet law on sexual compulsion, the revision moved it further away from being about quid pro quo sexual harassment.[29] The new article (133), with no new language about power in the workplace, included other types of sexual assault and other types of coercion, and incorporated conditions other than workplace or material dependence.[30] It also appears to be limited to supervisor-employee harassment, not coworkers, and excludes the giving of benefits in exchange for sexual favors (Naumov 1997, Art. 133, comments 6–7). This suggests that while the demand for sex with a threat of negative employment action is a crime, the demand for sex with a promise of positive employment action is not. Disregarding feminist claims that sexual harassment is about power, this commentary clarifies that intent is required and that the motive of this crime is "the satisfaction of sexual passion." The revised article also decreased the punishment from imprisonment to fines. There were no meaningful changes to the rape law.[31]

The only unquestionably progressive reform of the sexual assault articles was the decriminalization of male homosexuality, a result of pressure from human rights and rule-of-law advocates who had focused their attention on this issue. Other changes reflected odd compromises between what lawmakers understood as progressive and unreformed attitudes about sex. For example, new laws criminalizing forced sodomy and "forced lesbianism" as well as reckless HIV transmission were left so ambiguous as to allow for the prosecution of individuals for homosexual acts (Essig 1999, 14).

### Worsening the Criminal Procedure Code, 2001

A few years later, when legislators got serious about revising the Criminal Procedure Code, crisis center Syostri again raised concerns with Russian policymakers and international observers about how reforms would impact rape victims.[32] The Soviet code, as an essential part of the totalitarian system, had what legal scholars call an accusatorial bias, in reality a presumption of guilt, leading to incredibly low rates of acquittal at trial, 0.4 percent even into the 1990s (Solomon 2005, 90). Although an obstacle to human rights in general, for victims of rape, the Syostri director argued, this bias had the benefit of facilitating prosecution. In such a system, the man on trial for rape—standing in a cage after a lengthy pretrial detention, deprived of any sort of real legal defense, and forced to listen to charges (often read out loud by the judge) crafted by a prosecutor with almost unlimited investigatory powers—had virtually no way of undermining the accuser's credibility, a common tactic in rape trials elsewhere. The bias against anybody caught up in the system, combined with strong incentives for indictments and convictions, overrode much skepticism toward rape victims that Soviet police and prosecutors surely had. This accusatorial bias was the central concern of international rule-of-law and human rights organizations, such as the ABA-CEELI and the Council of Europe, who by the late 1990s were actively pressuring for reform. Considering how democratic systems have allowed legal procedure to protect men's right to inflict bodily harm against some women (Estrich

1987; Pateman 1988; Elman 1996), gender violence activists' concern that fostering a presumption of innocence might create a similar bias against sexual assault victims in Russia was reasonable.

The sexual assault activists' concerns fell on deaf ears. U.S. organizations and officials raised no gender issues. The Duma commitment charged with reforming the code issued no response to Syostri's repeated pleas. Women's crisis center activists were not even allowed to attend parliamentary hearings. As a result, without acknowledging that women's rights were excluded, leading jurists portrayed the new code as a compromise "between concerns with human rights and the interests of the agencies that uncover crimes" (Solomon 2005, 77). To the degree that the accusatorial bias was lessened and there were no new provisions countering the institutionalized skepticism toward rape, the new code provides the police and medical examiners even more opportunities to avoid helping women. In contrast to the global feminist consensus, this reform illustrates that, in some important ways, many Russian and international human rights advocates have not fully incorporated women's rights into their conception of human rights.

There were no other changes to the procedures for rape or sexual harassment. For example, another problem was that the Soviet procedural code distinguished "simple rape" from other types of violent crimes by stipulating that this kind of rape case is initiated in no other circumstances than when a victim brings a complaint (1960 RSFSR Criminal Procedure Code, Art. 27). Much as for domestic violence victims in the United States, this difference meant that rape victims were particularly vulnerable to pressure from their rapists to withdraw their complaints. The new criminal procedural code also maintains the distinction between simple rape and all other forms of violent crime (Russian Federation Criminal Procedure Code, promulgated July 1, 2002, article 20.3).

## NOT REFORMING PRACTICE

Even without formal legal reform, the state response to gender violence can be transformed through pressure on the state to change its procedures or on the individual state agents immediately involved with responding to gender violence. In other places, pressure from women's organizations, what Merry calls the "social service approach," is supplemented by a "human rights advocacy approach led by lawyers and political elites" (2006a, 138). Such an approach often includes setting up human commissions on women's rights, transnational workshops or trainings to educate the judiciary about human rights standards and treaties, and demands for country reports such as CEDAW to make governments take stock (166). Have these kinds of pressure reformed Russia's practice?

### Monitoring Women's Rights

International human rights advocates quickly brought attention to the problem of sexual assault in Russia. The Women's Rights Project of U.S.-based Human

Rights Watch, a product of the alliance between transnational feminists and human rights organizations in the United States, released the first critique in 1995 as part of a larger study of employment discrimination. Appalled by government attitudes toward gender violence, researchers returned to Russia in 1996 to produce the more extensive report "Too Little, Too Late: State Response to Violence against Women" (1997). Using typical human rights monitoring strategies, this report laid out Russia's obligations to international law, examined Russia's laws pertaining to domestic and sexual violence, and, based on extensive interviews, summarized the criminal-legal system's negligence of violence against women.

These reports helped enlist the U.S. State Department and USAID in the human rights advocacy–friendly environment of the Clinton administration (which brought funding to the women's crisis centers), but they also inserted the United States into Russia's gender-violence politics. The American lens on sexual assault framed the problems as mostly criminal issues rather than results of the shrinking welfare state, sidelined sexual harassment (which in the United States is distinct from sexual violence), and dismissed Russians' assertions that translation was required to fit the Russian context. In the long run, paradoxically, this American involvement also helped shift the attention away from sexual assault toward other gender violence issues, such as domestic violence and then trafficking in women, which became more salient for the United States.

### Feminist Entrepreneurs and Bottom-Up Reform

Other attempts at reform came from feminist entrepreneurs, notably a take-no-prisoners feminist, Dianne Post, the gender expert at the ABA-CEELI, who hoped to skip the rigmarole of working with high-level officials in the still heavily bureaucratized Russia and focus directly on the line staff who respond to gender violence. From 1998 to 2000, Post zigzagged across Russia with crisis center leaders, upon the invitation of local women's organizations, to hold conferences and seminars with state employees, such as police officers, medical examiners, other doctors, social workers, psychologists, prosecutors, and judges, as well as lawyers and anyone else who might be interested.[33] Post, who had been a parole office, social worker, and domestic violence and then legal aid lawyer, astonished the more reserved women's crisis center leaders with her energy and broke taboos about sexuality by demonstrating and describing each item in an American rape kit for emergency personnel to collect evidence of rape, something that was not available to Russian doctors.

Even having access to the state personnel who are the frontline of attending to sexual assault is remarkable in a polity where social organizations are new and often excluded, but these interventions and trainings also resulted in some remarkable changes. In Orel, a once flourishing but now impoverished city with no independent women's crisis center, Post and the women's crisis center leaders were met with a very limited conception of rape (as only stranger rape) and blame for the women for provoking the rape. For example, a psychologist at a city center for youth explained, "I don't talk about guilt with my patients. . . . But if a woman is to walk in the forest with some men that she doesn't know and she begins to talk about sex, she is provoking a response." After a contentious debate with the women's crisis center leaders and the formal workshop, a representative from the same youth organization spoke of "destructive behavior" instead of "provocation" and ended with a plea for special crisis centers for women because "human rights include women's rights."

According to Post (2002), the transformation was even more marked in other places, especially where an independent women's crisis center already existed or was founded in response to the workshop.[34] Some of those that she met already had feminist understandings of gender violence, such as rejecting the idea of provocation, but had had no language or logic to articulate their arguments. Some had felt alone and used the events to legitimate their work. Others were empowered by Post's can-do attitude, a transformation explained to me in Barnaul three years after Post's conference there. Some policymakers were shamed, such as a public relations person for the local prosecutor's office in the Siberian city of Tomsk, who, after challenging questions, acknowledged that, although girls' immorality (drinking with boyfriends) might make them more likely to be raped, "it is not the girls' fault." Illustrating the greater potential for influence in far-flung regions, in the far northern city of Norilsk, Post was lauded for simply coming to the hinterland where few travel. Even the crisis center leaders, trained in a Soviet system in which people "read lectures" (*chitaiut lektsie*) to passive audiences and hold conferences to discuss already crafted resolutions, began to imitate Post's style when they participated, requiring audience participation and demanding plans of future action. In 1999, Moscow-based Syostri, for example, was conducting periodic trainings at a Moscow police academy; activist lawyers and psychologists were leading similar police trainings in St. Petersburg.

### Russian Resistance, More Monitoring

Although these feminist entrepreneurs and women's crisis centers worked tirelessly, there is only so much that a small number of individuals can do in such an immense country. Their inability to reach the high levels of government was evident in the 2002 exchange between the CEDAW committee and government officials over Russia's CEDAW report (Russian Federation 1999). Recognizing the global attention to violence against women, the official report talks the talk of addressing gender violence, expressing a desire to increase criminal responsiveness, to provide more social services, and to collaborate with women's NGOs, but there is little evidence of real reform. For example, the report (Art. 6) casts as progressive the revision of the Soviet article on sexual compulsion. It also boasts of establishing a "network of agencies providing social services for women and children," but closer evaluation of these social services, even from official reports, reveals that by the end of 2001, none focused on sexual assault.[35] In other cases, the government takes responsibility for the women's crisis centers' achievements.

In response to the report, the CEDAW committee focused on Russia's failure to enact any real reform, asking the important question of why there had been no specific legislation on any types of gender violence or no new procedures to hold police accountable.[36] The Russian representative from the Ministry of Labor and Social Development then admitted that too little had been done, but blamed "centuries old mentality" and inadequate government infrastructure, and then backtracked, saying the gender violence was a "burning issue" that the government was working to address.

Following this exchange, human rights monitoring of Russia's response to gender violence increased. For the first time, a Russian human rights advocate, the Moscow Helsinki group, took up the issue of gender violence (Lukshevskii 2003). The Geneva-based World Organisation against Torture, a transnational network of human rights organizations, released a study that included a section on violence against women in Russia (Benninger-Budel and O'Hanlon 2004). In 2003, Amnesty International began a transnational Stop Violence Against Women campaign, leading to a report on the problem in Russia (Amnesty International 2005). Additionally, ABA-CEELI, which had developed a CEDAW Assessment Tool to evaluate a country's compliance with CEDAW, applied it to Russia (Duban 2006). This last report was extensive and well documented. The new gender expert at the ABA-CEELI Moscow office conducted 180 interviews and seven focus groups in 32 municipalities (in all seven federal districts) in addition to surveying recent scholarly articles and these human rights reports. All of these reports, except Amnesty's, included substantive sections on sexual violence.

### Little Change in Law Enforcement Behavior

Together, these studies show that very little has changed since the first Human Rights Watch reports. Official rape rates are even lower because women had learned not to expect assistance from the authorities at all levels.[37] Although law enforcement remains plagued by widespread corruption, inclined toward abusive practice, and without legitimacy (Beck and Roberston 2005), their failure to help women who have been victims of sexual assault reflects continued skepticism toward women and sexual assault. For example, a recent informal poll of male prosecutors in Irkutsk revealed that 81 percent thought that women often change their minds after consenting to sex and then falsely accuse their partners of rape (Duban 2006, 105). Police and prosecutors continue to ask repeated, humiliating questions of women alleging rape that exhibit their belief that women are almost solely responsible for preventing their rape. Unsurprisingly, rape cases are not initiated if the victim is a prostitute because consent to all men is assumed.[38] As before, virtually no women pursue criminal or legal options when they experience sexual harassment (86).

Instead of effectively pressuring law enforcement to respond better, the independent and government crisis centers have unwittingly become excuses for the police to do nothing. According to the ABA-CEELI (Duban 2006), staff at government crisis centers recommend that women not report rape to police (arguing the process would be too traumatic) while providing minimal psychological or legal support, in essence leaving women to fend for themselves. Similarly, some local police were handing out Syostri's phone number, but only after telling women that there was nothing the police could do.[39] At the same time, the police were no longer allowing Syostri to conduct trainings at the police academy. More so than under the totalitarian state, sexual assault was privatized as women's individual misfortune.

## ASSESSING THE IMPACT OF GLOBAL NORMS

In sum, blame and shame is not enough. Scores of individuals and a hundred organizations, both foreign and domestic, have been involved in the campaign against sexual assault in Russia since the collapse of the Soviet Union in 1991. Feminist entrepreneurs and other activists have given heroic amounts of time and energy to learning more about sexual assault, trying to raise public awareness and shift public blame from women, and influencing state policy and practice. For more than a decade, international human rights advocates have been monitoring the Russian response to sexual assault, and now even Russian human rights advocates have taken on some concern for gender violence.

From the perspective of global feminists, the results have been frustratingly little, so much so that, in the mid 2000s, human rights monitors began a new round of blame and shame. The new talk about gender violence by government officials in the CEDAW process—what might appear as a success—is undermined by their inaction and their tendency, when they do focus on gender violence, to mean only domestic violence. Putin's 2006 off-the-cuff remarks seemingly congratulating the Israeli president—under investigation for harassing and assaulting several women—for his sexual prowess illuminate the powerful resistance to global feminist norms.[40] (According to one Russian report, Putin, who thought the microphone was turned off, said that the Israeli president "turned out to be quite a powerful man. He raped ten women. I never expected it from him. He surprised all of us. We all envy him.") Even if this was a joke, as Putin asserts, it was callous, and this kind of callousness about gender violence is widespread.

Foreign intervention was designed to support reform "from below" by stimulating local activism, but this kind of intervention could not sustain activism in Russia's inhospitable environment. Foreign intervention to encourage reform "from above"—such as monitoring policy and practice—led to no meaningful reform for sexual assault. Local women's crisis centers, although networked transnationally, were not strong enough to create successful collaborations with Russian human rights organizations. Even now, there is little sense among these Russian human rights advocates that women's rights or gender violence are an essential part of human rights. More significant, by 2006, women who had been sexually assaulted were worse off vis-à-vis the criminal justice system than when the Soviet Union fell apart.

# CHAPTER FIVE

# Domestic Violence: The Benefits of Assistance

I F GLOBAL NORMS AND foreign intervention to help monitor, blame, and shame a government for its failure to address gender violence are not sufficient, perhaps more intrusive interventions could promote increased awareness and reform of policy and practice. Development agencies and large charitable foundations may join human rights advocates and transnational feminist networks, providing financial support to domestic violence activism and supporting public awareness campaigns. States and non-state actors can offer to train police, prosecutors, judges, social workers, and healthcare personnel. Do these foreign investments in local gender violence politics—in this case, domestic violence politics—boost the process of blame and shame to promote more effective domestic activism, increased public awareness, and significant state reform? If so, why and how?

The examination of the politics of domestic violence in post-Soviet Russia shows such assistance is much more effective than the process of blaming and shaming by itself. When donors intervened to promote a greater awareness of domestic violence in Russia, there were notable shifts in the public knowledge and understanding of the problem. In localities where donors invested in changing state behavior, law enforcement, judges, and prosecutors altered their practice. When there was sustained and funded pressure for domestic violence reform, Russian authorities created state crisis centers, passed regional legislation, and created local and national working groups on the problem. Although there was no new national domestic violence law, activists were able to translate the global norm into Russian vernacular, suggesting the possibility for more meaningful reform in the future. While some (Western) feminist observers have been particularly concerned about the impact of this kind of targeted funded intervention (e.g., Ghodsee 2004; Hemment 2004a; Kay 2004; Rivkin-Fish 2004), at least when local interest already exists and activists are able to translate the global norms, assistance can promote feminist social change without too much of a backlash. In Russia, funding supplemented transnational feminist networks and human rights advocacy. Reform also was fostered by the Soviet legacy of state parafeminism.

In this analysis, I use the term "domestic violence" with some trepidation. As Ann Jones has argued, "'[d]omestic violence' is one of those gray phrases, beloved of bureaucracy . . . a euphemistic abstraction that keeps us at a dispassionate distance, far removed from the repugnant spectacle of human beings in pain" (Jones 2000, 80). Not as evocative as "wife beating" or "wife torture," the term "domestic violence" also conceals the gendered power—the power of the men who intimidate, batter, and rape the women they profess to love and of the states that condone such abuse—that activists denounce. But "domestic violence" is the term transnational feminists, human rights advocates, and local activists most often use these days, giving it the most currency.

## GLOBALIZING NORMS, ENLISTING DONORS

### Creating Norms

As with sexual assault, a critique of domestic violence has become a global feminist norm, the cornerstone of the broader concept of gender violence crafted by global feminists. For more than two centuries, women in the West and in Russia had fought for more rights within marriage, including the right to divorce to escape violence and control. Beginning in the 1960s in the West, battered women's movements (also called shelter or refuge movements) re-articulated this struggle in terms of domestic violence. By the 1980s, such movements existed in thirty-five out thirty-six stable democracies, including a strong, autonomous movement in India (Weldon 2002, 77). As a result, domestic violence (or "family violence" or "abuses in the family") was incorporated into the U.N. documents that condemn violence against women, such as the General Recommendations 12 and 19 from the Committee for the Convention on the Elimination of All Forms of Discrimination against Women (see appendix 1). Recently, domestic violence has been attached to European human rights norms, for example, by the Council of Europe.[1]

Consequently, as with sexual assault, these global and regional politics meant the availability of global norms from which *feminist entrepreneurs* and *transnational feminist networks* (TFNs) could draw to influence national governments.

Global intervention can be seen in how activists *localize activism* and remake the norms *into the vernacular* using models of raising awareness in other contexts. The norms may help *certify* domestic activism. Alliances between transnational feminists and human rights monitors may lead to the process of *blaming and shaming* that I analyzed in chapter 4. These political strategies may give meaning and muscle to international documents and international law.

More so than for rape, global feminist norms helped define domestic violence, a problem most societies had not historically criminalized. While their conception still varies, TFNs and human rights advocates concerned about domestic violence tend to share a focus on violence against women within the family or other interpersonal relationships. The forms or acts of domestic violence can be physical, psychological, or sexual:

> from simple assaults to aggravated physical battery, kidnapping, threats, intimation, coercion, stalking, humiliating verbal abuse, forcible or unlawful entry, arson, destruction of property, sexual violence, marital rape, dowry or bride-price related violence, female genital mutilation, [and] violence related to exploitation through prostitution. (Coomaraswamy 1996, II.C.11)

Many activists make a distinction between domestic violence (by current or former boyfriends, husbands, or partners of adult women), which they see as a mechanism of gendered power, and other forms of violence within a family, such as child abuse, incest, or elder abuse.[2] Some others, such as UNIFEM's East and Southeast Asian regional office, make no such distinction but include *economic violence,* such as economic blackmail or control over the money a woman earns.

The global norms also elaborated a consensus on what needed to be done to combat domestic violence. First, the new global norm suggested that activists should work, for example, through the yearly 16 Days of Activism against Gender Violence Campaign, to raise awareness of the problem understood to be obfuscated by culture and tradition (Merry 2006a, ch. 1).[3] Second, as spelled out in the 1993 Declaration on the Elimination of Violence against Women, states are called to provide social assistance, such as shelters and hotlines, to women subjected to violence. Third, as articulated in "A framework for model legislation on domestic violence" by the U.N.'s special rapporteur on violence against women, countries should adopt comprehensive legislation that allows for "flexible and speedy remedies (including remedies under special domestic violence legislation, penal and civil remedies)" (Coomaraswamy 1996, para. 2e). Specifically, the rapporteur called for criminalization of domestic violence, the establishment of ex parte restraining and protection orders, systematic law enforcement record keeping, training of police and judges, the recognition of victim's testimony as sufficient evidence, and the provision of medical care and crisis intervention services to ensure health and safety of women facing domestic violence. This support was echoed by the next special rapporteur, who identified as crucial "specific legislation on domestic violence, providing for full protection of victims, unhindered access to medical, social and legal services, and for perpetrators to be held accountable" (Erturk 2006, 23).

Even as some skepticism emerged among North American activists (e.g., Matthews 1994; Coker 2004), prominent TFNs advocated a particular model to respond comprehensively to domestic violence, a *coordinated community response.* This structured collaboration, requiring state criminal justice and human service agencies to work with the women's shelter movement, was developed by the Domestic Abuse Intervention Project in Duluth, Minnesota. While nodding to the need for adaptation, TFNs, such as the Minnesota Advocates for Human Rights, suggest some constants: the need to first develop a common understanding of domestic violence and the centrality of core intervention principles such as holding the offender, not the victim, legally accountable.[4] This well-elaborated, U.S.-initiated model was particularly attractive to U.S.-based donors.

### Adding Assistance

By the mid to late 1990s, domestic violence became the gender violence issue that donors most wanted to fund. International development agencies' willingness reflected a new sense among many industrialized long-term democracies about the need for national legislation on domestic violence.[5] In the United States, the biggest donor to Russia,[6] attention from USAID to domestic violence activism emerged simultaneously with the passage of the first national legislation on domestic violence. While U.S. president Bill Clinton advocated the 1994 Violence Against Women Act, his wife, Hillary Clinton, heading the U.S. delegation to the U.N. Conference on Women in Beijing, "created a flurry of activity within USAID [leading to] the creation of the Gender Plan of Action (GPA) in 1996," a plan to integrate gender concerns, including domestic violence, into all USAID activities.[7] As a result, USAID and the U.S. State Department began to invest in a variety of programs to raise awareness about domestic violence and to shift policy and practice as part of their women in development, democracy assistance, and rule-of-law programs.

Other donors who fund feminist initiatives—such as UNIFEM, the Ford Foundation, and Open Society International—similarly turned to the issue of domestic violence.[8] Even the U.S.-based cigarette manufacturer Philip Morris (Altria), a more conservative donor with no prior commitments to women's issues, in the late 1990s decided to target its charitable donations to domestic violence service and public awareness programs, both domestically and abroad, as a ploy for publicity.[9] U.S. conservatives could criticize domestic violence as part of their rhetoric about promoting families.

Adding this substantial assistance to the blame and shame model from chapter 4 suggests the following intervention model:

**TABLE 5.1.** *Investing in Blame and Shame*

| PROCESSES | LEADING FOREIGN AGENTS | GLOBAL NORMS | ASSISTANCE |
|---|---|---|---|
| localizing activism/ vernaculization | feminist entrepreneurs and transnational feminist networks | global norms as modeling and certifying activism, activists appropriating and translating | financial support for activism and awareness campaigns |
| raising awareness | | | |
| reforming policy | human rights and rule-of-law advocates | monitoring | supporting interdisciplinary collaborations, training of state personnel |
| reforming practice | | | |

The assessment of the effectiveness of assistance speaks to a second concern expressed by observers of democracy assistance and postcommunist civil society. The concern was not just that such funding was taming what should be a dynamic civic sector, but that the most vibrant movements within postcommunist civil society turned out to be the ones the West least wanted: religious and nationalist movements (Kaldor 2003, 79). Targeting women's activism was one way to shape civil society to support constitutional liberalism, an essential part of democracy imagined by the Western promoters of democracy assistance.

## APPROPRIATING, TRANSLATING, AND DIFFUSING NORMS

### Localizing Activism

As with sexual assault, the issue of domestic violence was raised at the watershed event of the women's movement in Russia, the First Independent Women's Forum in 1991, and activism began in earnest following the Second Women's Forum in 1992 (Racioppi and See 1997; Sperling 1999). From the onset, activists understood a central first task to be the naming of the problem in Russian.[10] In the language of social movement theory, this meant generating a frame to be used in movement discourse that rediagnoses the problem, identifying the individuals and processes responsible for the problem in a new way (Benford and Snow 2000). Instead of creating something from scratch, Russian activists turned to global norms against domestic violence. One movement founder from Moscow-based ANNA, who was not fully fluent (yet) in English, claims to have simply and literally translated the English term "domestic violence" (*domashnee nasilie*) even though the term sounded as awkward in Russian as it does in English.[11] As in most domestic violence activism around the world, she, believing that many women in Russia felt responsible for family harmony, wanted to invoke a new understanding that shifted the blame away from women to the perpetrators and to larger structures of society.[12]

Therefore, as with sexual assault, although some of the Russian interest was based on personal experience, domestic violence activism in Russia, from the beginning, was transnational, drawing upon global feminist norms and linked to transnational feminist activism. This was explicit for ANNA, founded by the Moscow Center for Gender Studies (MCGS), an organization that defines itself as part of global feminism.[13] Many of the same transnational (especially North American) feminist entrepreneurs involved in supporting the founding of crisis centers and advocating against sexual assault were also essential to domestic violence activism in Russia. As the Cold War had focused on U.S.-Russian differences, the collapse of the USSR had fostered U.S.-Russian dialogue and fascination, leading to, especially in the beginning, a particular American flavor in Russian activism. In particular, early Russian activism drew upon Catharine MacKinnon's theories of violence against women.[14]

To distribute the norm among the broader women's movement, the activists turned to the movement's new magazines. A 1993 article presented domestic violence and "violence in the family" (*nasilie v sem'e*) as forms of violence against women (*nasilie nad zhenshchinoi*), as "yet another weapon against women."[15] Taking a strong stand, the article contends that other family members are complicit in hiding the violence, because they do not want to start a family quarrel or because they are "afraid to spoil the reputation and career of the family terrorist." In contrast to the early movements in Great Britain and the United States, Russian activists immediately connected femicide—the murder of women by their current or former domestic partners—with domestic violence.

### Funding Awareness Campaigns

Whereas Russian sexual assault activists struggled to raise awareness with little funding, three donors stepped in to support three sizable domestic violence campaigns that would not have been possible without their support. In 1997, with a grant from the Ford Foundation, crisis centers in Moscow and St. Petersburg coordinated the first attempt to raise consciousness of the problem of domestic violence, utilizing the new terminology, among wide sectors of the population.[16] Modeled on a San Francisco–based Family Violence Prevention Fund's (FVPF) campaign, the Russian campaign included the distribution of posters, stickers, brochures, safety cards, radio spots, and television public-service announcements, employing the "There's No Excuse for Domestic Violence" slogan on black and blue background.[17] Using gender-specific language and images, the campaign linked domestic violence to women's human rights. And as evidenced by a higher number of calls to the crisis centers following the radio and TV announcements, the campaign brought attention to the issue of domestic violence and the work of the crisis centers.

A second national campaign was conducted from 1999 to 2001 by transnational information access-promoter Internews, in consultation with the women's crisis centers.[18] With a quarter million dollars from USAID, the campaign included the broadcast of radio jingles in seventy cities and eight reports on already existing popular radio programs, inclusion on ten national and fourteen regional television programs, and the production and distribution of two documentary films and five public service announcements. In response to the growing attention, some of the most popular TV programs even requested information from Internews about domestic violence.[19] As with the first campaign, the purpose of the campaign was to inform the population of the existence of domestic violence and to combat what the activists saw as the Russian myths: that domestic violence is a private problem, that women are solely responsible for family tranquility, and that women provoke domestic violence. Illustrating the expansion of activism, the regional crisis centers were the ones negotiating with the local TV and radio stations. For example, the Barnaul Women's Alliance produced a TV series that offered new, more peaceful models for family relations and a two-part tribunal on domestic violence to hold the local administration accountable for addressing domestic violence.

A third, regional campaign was coordinated at the turn of the millennium by the Nordic Network for Crisis Centres for Women in the Barents Region (NCRB), also "to increase awareness of violence against women" (Saarinen, Liapounova, and Drachova 2003b, 7). During the 16 Days of Activism in 2000, twelve northwest Russian crisis centers distributed information on violence against women and the crisis center activities through bulletins, articles, and interviews in the local media, presented their research, organized roundtables with local and regional authorities, gave public lectures at various educational institutions, and exhibited literature, art, posters, photos, and video materials (35). Being in the Network gave the Russian crisis centers increased funding for these campaigns as well as access to new ideas employed by the Nordic crisis centers. In contrast to the earlier campaigns, these campaigns were broader in scope, explicitly including violence against children.

These three public awareness campaigns were then reinforced by other foreign-funded programs. Late 1990s initiatives from the U.S. State Department, for example, included Sister Cities International, of which several city-partnerships focused on domestic violence.[20] They also included training for healthcare providers treating and counseling women victims of domestic violence through the American International Health Alliance.

### Translating Domestic Violence

All along, some crisis centers had been invoking ideas more consonant with dominant ways of thinking about women in Russia. Regional crisis centers, even those that identified as feminist and drew upon human rights rhetoric, were more likely than those in St. Petersburg or Moscow to employ neotraditional, especially maternalist, gender ideologies, often signified in their use of the Russian term "violence in the family" rather than "domestic violence." For example, in the Volga city of Saratov, the crisis center campaigned using slogans on posters such as "Defend my mother" (Johnson 2001). Better than other issues raised by global feminists, this framing of domestic violence could also resonate with the maternalist women's groups that had first emerged under Gorbachev (Hrycak 2002).[21] But because this framing was so resonant with Russian ideas about "protecting of women and children" that did not hold abusers accountable, the more radical movement leaders were skeptical of such organizations and this way of talking about domestic violence.[22]

By 2001, encouraged by shifts in leadership, expansion of the movement to the regions, and the realization of the costs of appropriating global norms virtually unchanged,[23] the movement as a whole began to tactically employ these kinds of maternalist ways of framing domestic violence, more often using the translation of "violence in the family." Although some of the new crisis centers stimulated by the infusion of democracy assistance were simply maternalist, the new leadership balanced maternalism and global feminism (Johnson 2007a). As explained by the Saratov crisis center director who became a national leader, using maternalism was the best way to bring attention to domestic violence because "women [as a category of rights-bearing citizens] are not heard in Russia."[24] Reflecting the activist leaders' Soviet heritage, translation of the global norm also included the incorporation of economic violence—"the refusal to allow the woman to go to work or pressure to stop working; complete control over the woman's income."[25]

In other words, with global feminist support, the movement's leaders translated global ideas about domestic violence into the Russian vernacular. In the language of social movement theory, they had *amplified* their frame of domestic violence by drawing upon already existing values in Russian society.[26] But, at the same time, as elsewhere in the global movement against gender violence, they had developed a *double consciousness*, articulating their claims in different ways in different domestic and global contexts (Merry 2006a, 3): using maternalism and "violence in the family" in Russia, and what American activist Elizabeth Schneider (2002) called the radical feminist frame and the more globally recognized term "domestic violence" to global feminists, donors, and human rights advocates (Johnson 2007a). The women's crisis centers, while seeking a transformation of gender ideology by holding (men) batterers more accountable than (women) victims, simultaneously tapped into existing gender ideology, especially the neotraditionalism that extols women's contributions as mothers. Much as with the activists' transplantation of the crisis center model, the movement adjusted the global concept of domestic violence to fit the Russian context even while continuing to challenge the gender order. While earlier interventions might have curtailed opportunities for such translation, global feminist calls for recognizing autonomous self-organization (Weldon 2006) meant that such localization was at least tolerated, if not promoted.[27]

This negotiation between neotraditionalism and feminism may be activists' best hope for protesting domestic violence and gender after communism, especially in societies that remain less than democratic (Johnson and Robinson 2007). As Chela Sandoval (2000) found for U.S. women of color and third-world women, "shifting" between different ideologies and frames may be the most effective challenge to the dominant, often binary, ways of thinking. In Sandoval's words, "[t]he idea here, [is] that the citizen-subject can learn to identify, develop, and control the means of ideology, that is marshal the knowledge necessary to 'break with ideology' while at the same time *also* speaking in, and from within, ideology."

In 2002, as donors began to withdraw their support, the importance of this international funding for feminist activism became more apparent.[28] The new funding environment supported only small feminist actions, such as a booth at family day by the Russian Association of Crisis Centers for Women (RACCW) in 2004, or larger actions by those less radical, such as the Altai Crisis Center for Men's 2005 white ribbon campaign, in which they distributed informational materials about nonviolence within families. The only major public awareness campaign was part of the unsuccessful RACCW–Women's Aid project on domestic violence among ethnic minorities.[29] One hopeful sign is that, after years of pressure from gender violence activists, the Council of Europe initiated a two-year campaign against gender violence across its member states, including Russia, 2006–2008.

## RAISING SOME AWARENESS

Perhaps unsurprisingly, intervention helped provide the inputs for public awareness campaigns: the slogans and images for pamphlets, fliers, posters, and TV or radio spots on domestic violence. The tougher question is whether these campaigns, as influenced as they were by foreign ideas and moneys, nudged society toward change in its perception of domestic violence.

### Media Coverage

From the early years of domestic violence activism, Russian activists were remarkably successful at getting coverage in newspapers relative to their organizational strength. In the mid 1990s, crisis centers secured sympathetic coverage in English-language Moscow- and St. Petersburg–based newspapers, as well as in a variety of popular Russian newspapers.[30] Coverage then seems to have increased over time (Lukshevskii 2003). Between 1995 and 2005, there were at least 1,600 articles referencing these various terms for domestic violence in national and regional newspapers and newswires (see appendix 2 for method). Somewhat reflecting the movement's terminology, the literal translation of "domestic vio-

**TABLE 5.2.**

*The Incidence of Various Terms for Domestic Violence in* Izvestiia, *1995–2005*

| SPECIFIC TERM | 1995 | 1996 | 1997 | 1998 | 1999 | 2000 | 2001 | 2002 | 2003 | 2004 | 2005 | TOTAL |
|---|---|---|---|---|---|---|---|---|---|---|---|---|
| violence in the family (*nasilie v sem'e*) | 1 | 2 | 0 | 3 | 1 | 5 | 4 | 3 | 10 | 14 | 4 | 47 |
| everyday violence (*bytovoe nasilie*) | 0 | 0 | 0 | 0 | 0 | 1 | 0 | 9 | 2 | 1 | 0 | 13 |
| domestic violence (*domashnee nasilie*) | 0 | 0 | 0 | 0 | 0 | 0 | 0 | 0 | 0 | 5 | 1 | 6 |
| family violence (*semeinoe nasilie*) | 1 | 0 | 0 | 0 | 0 | 0 | 0 | 0 | 0 | 0 | 3 | 4 |
| spousal violence (*supruzheskoe nasilie*) | 0 | 0 | 0 | 0 | 0 | 0 | 0 | 0 | 2 | 0 | 0 | 2 |
| Total | 2 | 2 | 0 | 3 | 1 | 6 | 4 | 12 | 14 | 20 | 8 | 72 |

lence" was the second most popular way of referring to domestic violence, following "violence in the family," the term the movement began to use more recently. Whereas in 1995 there were only two references to domestic violence using terms acceptable to the women's crisis center movement (rather than euphemisms, such as "family scandals") in the high-circulation national newspaper *Izvestiia,* there were twenty in 2004 (see table 5.2). In the aftermath of the foreign-funded campaigns, as argued by two leading Moscow-based journalists, journalists are now much more educated about domestic violence, and mass media as a whole are now actively engaged in discussing the problem as well as helping to prevent it (N. I. Azhgikhina and S. R. Svistunova in Rimasheevskaia 2005).

One follow-up survey documents this increase in domestic violence coverage in newspapers as well as in other media (Zabelina et al. 2007). Respondents in 2006 were more much likely to assess that newspapers, radio, and television "often" report on "domestic violence by men against women" than five years earlier (83–34). Some 23 percent of men and 49 percent of women in 2006, for example, thought this was the case on the radio and on television respectively, compared to 5 percent and 24 percent in 2001. Regarding the most powerful medium in Russia, only 5 percent of respondents in 2006 thought that television programs never referred to domestic violence. These survey results, although indirect in their measure of media coverage, are more meaningful because they suggest that people are becoming more conscious about media reporting of domestic violence.

It is not just that there are stories on domestic violence, but that people recognize and recall these stories.

These shifts in public awareness did not come easily and have not been complete. Again and again, reporters would call the crisis centers to cover the issues of domestic violence and the activists would spend hours talking to them to try to disabuse the reporters of their assumptions about domestic violence. Even into the new century, news coverage would often repeat the myths, especially the idea that women need to be held accountable for domestic violence because they "provoke" it in men. Even as many articles covered domestic violence, most "certified" rather than "analyzed" the problem, reporting the incidence but not explaining it as a violation of women's rights (Zabelina 2002, 69).[31] However, increasing references to the problem and the use of new terminology—which Russian researchers attributed to the existence of strong women's organizations (Lukshevskii 2003)—contrasts with the previous taboo against even raising the issue in public.

## Surveying Public Awareness

More importantly, the available survey data suggest a shift in public consciousness of domestic violence. A 2001–2002 survey, funded by UNIFEM and conducted by a scholar-activist at the Moscow Humanities University, found widespread awareness that domestic violence was a national problem (Zabelina 2002). In contrast to earlier skepticism and confusion over the new terminology, 92 percent of the 1,528 respondents (both male and female) agreed that "violence in the family" existed in Russia (40). Awareness was not just in the capital city, but also in the central Russian cities of Tula and Dubna and the Republic of Komi. The survey also indicates more than a superficial understanding of domestic violence. Regarding the activists' claim that domestic violence included economic violence—the deprivation of funds necessary for basic needs—approximately 40 percent agreed. City residents especially were likely to include as violence what activists call "verbal violence" (*verbal'noe nasilie*) (40). Most respondents also saw real consequences of violence for the women's health (65% of the men, 80% of the women) and psychological trauma or stress (78% men, 92% women) (46).[32]

A second, slightly larger survey conducted a year later by researchers from the Moscow State University Women's Committee (with funding from the Ford Foundation), similarly found that almost all married Russians (more than 90%) thought that physical violence was either a crime or a social evil (*sotsial'noe zloi*) that the state has a responsibility to respond to or to protect abused wives from (Gorshkova and Shurygina 2003, 36).[33] Providing more evidence of the impact of foreign-funded domestic violence activism, people in the regions in the study where such activities have been the strongest, Moscow and the Republic of Karelia near Finland, are the least likely to justify domestic violence. Almost half of the respondents also hold the belief that a husband's assault of his wife is a private matter, perhaps a reflection of continued skepticism regarding the criminal-legal system or of the correct understanding that the criminal procedure continues to classify most domestic violence cases as requiring private prosecution (*chastnoe obvinenie*), where the victim must bring charges herself.[34] More troubling is that approximately one-third to one-half of the married respondents thought that wife battery could be justified: that wives might be responsible because they started the argument (47%), that sometimes wives need to be punished for bad behavior such as adultery or substance abuse (32%), or that some wives simply deserve to be beaten (38%) (36). But women, who are perhaps more likely to have taken in the awareness campaigns, were nearly half as likely as men to hold such views.[35]

Even these second findings allow for the possibility of change over time. In contrast to the one-third to one-half of Gorshkova and Shurygina's (2003) respondents, a small-scale 1995 survey found that more than half of the respondents thought women were at least partially responsible for the domestic violence they suffered (Attwood 1997).[36] There are also some remarkable differences in opinions among age groups. Younger husbands (34% and 25% of those between 18 and 24) are much less likely than older husbands (48% and 43% of those between 55 and 64) to think that there are some women who deserve to be beaten or that a battered woman should reflect on her culpability in her own battery (Gorshkova and Shurygina 2003, 38). Similarly, younger wives are less likely than older ones to excuse a husband who batters.[37] At a 2002 discussion of domestic violence in St. Petersburg, Russian activists-scholars agreed that young women are less tolerant than older women.

In 2006, researchers involved in the first survey conducted a follow-up study, this time interviewing 450 people (half women, half men, all between 25 and 45) on the streets of Moscow, Samara, Dubna, and Tula (Zabelina et al. 2007). Although they used a different method (interviews versus questionnaires) with a somewhat different target population, the results provide some additional evidence of increasing awareness over time.[38] In this third survey, twice as many men considered profanity and cursing to constitute violence in 2006 than five years earlier (65% as compared to 30%) (78). Smaller but significant increases were found for women and men on all questions about whether the various behaviors constituted violence, including the following: compelling a person to take drugs or alcohol, threats and intimidation, prohibitions about meeting family members and friends, refusal to give money for the purchase of daily necessities, and prohibition on getting a job (79–80). As these later respondents were answering face-to-face, the increases may be overstated as presumably people would be more likely to be politically correct in person than on an anonymous questionnaire. Yet, even this modification in talk (if not thought) reflects a notable increase in awareness in a country where jokes have often been made about beating wives constituting love.

## New and Lingering Discourses

Media treatment of the second survey (Gorshkova and Shurygina 2003) illustrates the increased attention mixed with lingering nonfeminist views about domestic violence.[39] Upon release, the survey received serious attention and genuine curiosity about the problem of domestic violence from two progressive newspapers and only one story that reported on the survey as validating the Russian myth that women are more likely to beat men. In the next year, four more articles included serious and balanced discussion of the survey results and of domestic violence, including one article from a more traditional newspaper that discussed the survey as part of a larger discussion about changes in the institution of the Russian family. Coverage even included a discussion of the problem and consequences of economic violence among the rich and the poor alike, that the family in Russia was like a war zone and that domestic violence was the leading cause of death for disabled young and middle-aged women.

Significant national attention, however, came to the survey only in 2006, when a popular women's column in *Komosmol'skaia Pravda* presented some of the survey's findings on the seriousness of domestic violence and included phone numbers for both autonomous and governmental crisis centers, but also played up the women-beat-men angle. The response was huge, with readers wanting to hear more about why women beat men. The article received so much feedback, from letters and on the internet, that the columnist followed up with a second story, this time allowing one of the survey's researchers to put this women's aggression in the context of men's more serious and more common aggression against their wives. Fully transforming people's understanding of violence and gender takes a long time.

## REFORMING SOME POLICY

Considering the strength of local activism and this notable (if not complete) shift in public awareness, policy reform could come from domestic forces as well as directly from intervention. More so than for sexual assault, foreign human rights and rule-of-law advocates drew attention to Russia's inadequate laws. Have foreign-funded activism and this kind of foreign attention led to meaningful legal reform?

### Stalled Autonomous Legislation on Violence
### in the Family, 1994–1997, 1999

For Russian and international activists alike, the most important legal reform would be comprehensive legislation on domestic violence.[40] The pressure began one year before the 1995 U.N. conference in Beijing and was surprisingly successful. In 1994, the Women of Russia faction introduced draft domestic violence legislation into the Duma's Committee on Women, Family, and Youth, making domestic violence the first gender-related issue raised in the new parliament.[41] Partially, the opportunity was a fluke in that the Russian president's 1993 bombing of the recalcitrant Soviet-era parliament and hasty constitutional referendum had created a political vacuum. But, as brought by local activists, the global feminist attention to domestic violence also resonated with those formerly Communist Party women who mostly constituted the faction and with their allies concerned with protecting women and children in the social ministries.

Unfortunately, this proposal was premature, coming before activists had sufficient support and before they had been able to campaign for a new awareness of domestic violence. Even their allies had not accepted the transformative global feminist call for gender violence to be seen as a violation of women's rights. Over the next few years, when the bill was drafted and redrafted some forty-eight times, the working group moved the bill further and further away from the activists' interpretation of domestic violence as about gendered power and control.[42] The final version of the bill construed family violence as a psychological (and medical) problem requiring medical and psychological treatment for the victims and the perpetrator (Art. 11). It proposed a primary reliance on the welfare state, specifically the placing of victims of violence and minors in temporary shelters (Art. 10) or in permanent specialized institutions (Art. 13).[43] The primary role of the criminal justice system was to force into shelters victim-mothers who were unwilling to leave their homes. As if that were not enough to alienate the feminist women's crisis center leaders, the bill also called the NGO crisis centers brothels (Human Rights Watch 1997, 18–19).

Even the bill's less-than-feminist approach to domestic violence was too much for the Duma and the powerful state institutions of the General Prosecutor's Office, the Supreme Court, and the Ministry of Internal Affairs.[44] The speaker of the Duma declared, "We shouldn't meddle in family matters. The family always sorts itself out." Other Duma deputies made jokes about the bill or complained about the bill's cost. In 1997, the bill was effectively tabled. In 1999, the new chair of the Committee on Women, Family, and Youth, tried to build upon Beijing and reopen debate by holding a committee hearing and introducing a packet of bills ostensibly designed to address violence in the family, but really focused on child abuse. This 1999 attempt too went nowhere.

The failure to pass comprehensive legislation against domestic violence in Russia is a huge setback for global feminists. There is no doubt that passing such a bill, even with some nonfeminist provisions, would be a remarkable step in reforming domestic violence, especially if it included substantial budget outlays. Russia's failure to do so illustrates the consequences of moving to legal reform before there has been much success at transforming public awareness. Nonetheless, passing a law is not always necessary to enact changes in state behavior, and real reform requires more than a law, especially in a country such as Russia where laws can effectively be ignored by authorities.

### Neglecting the Criminal Law and Procedure

There was less attention focused on reforming the criminal laws regarding domestic violence when the parliament was revising the Soviet-era criminal code in the mid-1990s. Neither the embryonic women's crisis center movement, the Women of Russia faction, nor international human rights advocates were directing criticism toward the criminal assault articles for including no specific reference to domestic violence. Even more importantly, rule-of-law advocates, such as the Law Enforcement Section of the U.S. Embassy and ABA-CEELI, who were lobbying for changes in the code, did not bring up domestic violence. Gender issues were not their concern. Unsurprisingly then, the 1996 criminal code reform brought no global feminist reform. All of the articles in the Soviet code that applied to domestic violence remained in the post-Soviet code basically unchanged.[45]

In 2001, when the parliament turned to revising the criminal procedure code, the women's crisis center movement was at its height and, with the help of Human Rights Watch (1997), had leveled a critique of the code's relegation of domestic violence to the criminal articles not requiring public prosecution. However, as in the case of the criminal code reform, there was no support from the mainstream international organizations directly involved in the reform of the criminal procedure code and no impact on the final reform. The new criminal procedure code retains this private-prosecution provision and the provision for cases to be dropped if the abuser and abused reconcile.[46] Much as with sexual assault, the absence of gender violence insight into the process led to unintended negative consequences. In this case, an important part of the procedural reform was the institutionalization of the new justices of the peace, who were assigned the criminal articles most often used for domestic violence. As these courts are only for less serious crimes and are required to attempt reconciliation and mediation (Solomon 2005, 86), domestic violence is likely to be further minimized by the criminal justice system and women are likely to face increasing pressure to reconcile with their abusers.

More recently, the international community has ramped up its critique of domestic violence criminal laws. Amnesty International (2005) issued a strong critique of Russian criminal law's failure to address the specifics of domestic violence (e.g., the relations between the perpetrator and victim, the cumulative impact of repeated assaults) and the procedural hurdles (such as private prosecution, the allowance of character references for the accused). The Moscow Helsinki Group advocated the elimination of private prosecution (Lukshevskii 2003). While the proposals for domestic violence came too soon, this pressure came too late, after the big reforms of the codes had already taken place.

## State Parafeminism and State Services

Interventions, backed up with foreign funding, have had a greater impact on the so-called soft ministries. The first sign was the 1998 U.S.-Russian conference on domestic violence (in Russian, "violence in the family") held in coordination with the Russian Ministry of Labor and Social Development. Built upon U.S.-Russian connections made during the 1995 U.N. conference on women in Beijing, the conference was scheduled during then U.S. first lady Hillary Clinton's visit to Russia, and brought together government official from all branches and thirty-two regions of Russia, leaders from the women's crisis center, and American feminist entrepreneurs. Although the ministry had not previously expressed much concern about domestic violence,[47] the conference resolution declares that the government of the Russian Federation "recognizes the problem of violence against women, including domestic violence, as one of top priority, which is of special concern in Russia."[48] It called for new independent legislation on domestic violence, partnership with NGOs, and a government campaign to raise awareness of domestic violence.

By the new millennium, activists had also found allies in the little parafeminism that remained from Soviet times. The most important was the Commission for Women, Family, and Demography, created in 1993 in advance of Beijing and chaired by Ekaterina Lakhova, a feminist who also had connections to the women's crisis center movement and who was head of the Women of Russia faction that had initially proposed the domestic violence legislation.[49] Another ally was the Department on Women, Family, and Children, which held several annual conferences, in collaboration with RACCW, to foster the exchange of local and foreign experiences with addressing family violence.[50]

These new allies, in the face of global feminist pressure, added domestic violence to official plans to improve women's lives. The "National Action Plan on Improving the Status of Women in the Russian Federation and Promoting their Role in Society" was called for in the Beijing process, first drafted in 1996, and revised in 2001 by the Ministry of Labor and Social Development for 2001 and 2005. The second plan called for a variety of responses to violence in the family, including coordination between this ministry and the Ministry of Internal Affairs and the General Prosecutors' Office. The plan also called for the widespread establishment of state-supported crisis centers and shelters. Although underfunded and still rare—23 out of 3,371 crisis centers in 2005 were exclusively for women (Duban 2006, 102; Zabelina et al. 2007, 21, 103)—these state-supported centers represented a new commitment to assisting women living in violent relationships during a period of widespread welfare state retrenchment.[51] In 2006, twelve of these provided temporary shelter for women (and their children) suffering from domestic violence (Zabelina et al. 2007, 21).

## Regional Legislation

In addition to this national initiative, there have also been some regional reforms, mostly a result of international pressure.[52] In contrast to the national level, where there have been no criminal law reforms, at least two of the eighty-nine regions, the Republics of Chuvashiia in 2003 and Mordoviia in 2004, had modified their administrative codes to respond to some of the weakness of Russian criminal law (Duban 2006, 90). Both introduced articles on "domestic rowdyism" (*bytovoe deboshirstvo*), intended to allow for a fine to penalize unruly behavior, including loud noises, swearing, and "humiliation of a person's dignity" in a residence.[53]

In Mordoviia, where there is one women's crisis center, the change was adopted based on the realization that the police did not see "minor hooliganism" as including family violence.

Other regions have adopted social legislation on domestic violence. For example, the far northern region of Arkhangelsk adopted legislation in 2003 to expand the social services offered to those suffering from violence in the family.[54] Similar to the stalled national legislation and the national plan, the Arkhangelsk law called for the establishment of crisis centers for women and for men, a social help center for family, and a temporary shelter, some of which had been implemented by 2005. Not a response to local activism,[55] the law seems to have been a response to all the United States and Nordic attention to domestic violence in Arkhangelsk. Regional authorities, especially in poor regions, were more susceptible to the positive incentives offered by foreign interveners than the national government, but as with the national response, the policy seems more a promise than reality.

In other regions, developments resulted from a combination of local activism and international attention. In St. Petersburg, where local activism around the issue had led to the founding of a city shelter in 1995,[56] a law was passed in 2000 calling for coordination of the RACCW with the Committee on the Family, Childhood, and Youth in the city administration on the social defense of the family and childhood (Balibalova, Glushchenko, and Tikhomirova 2001).[57] Their project was both more effective and radical, including projects for institutionalizing a culture of rights among government officials.

In Khimki, a small suburb outside Moscow, a shelter was opened as a result of the foreign-funded Internews public awareness campaign. During one of the talk shows sponsored by this campaign, a city official had denied that domestic violence was a real problem.[58] When a woman called in to the show, with her husband pounding on her door and then breaking through the door to beat her up, the official recanted. As the mayor of the region, a survivor of the war in Afghanistan, was sympathetic, a shelter was established in 2000 under the city committee of social protection. Yet, even though foreign assistance helped lead to the shelter's founding, the director is resistant to foreign intervention, even global models, telling me in 2004, "Our experiences are totally different. It is not possible to adapt your experiences to our reality or our experiences to your reality."[59]

## SOME REFORMS OF PRACTICE

More so than on reforming Russia's laws, domestic activists and foreign interveners were focused on reforming the practice of state actors. They hoped to reform both the practice of law enforcement and the legal system and of social services. More so than in the case of sexual assault, these advocates had resources to back up their strategy of blaming and shaming the Russian government for its failure to adequately address domestic violence.

## Monitoring Women's Rights, Feminist Entrepreneurs, and New Cooperation

From the mid 1990s, those human rights advocates concerned with violence against women have spotlighted the behavior of Russian law enforcement personnel. Human Rights Watch reports in 1995 and 1997, the first such reports, covered the law enforcement failures regarding domestic violence almost as much as they condemned law enforcement response to sexual violence. Police behavior is a central issue for the several high-profile human rights campaigns that have followed. The Moscow Helsinki group, with support from the United Kingdom, found domestic violence to be a "very serious problem" to which police refuse to respond (Lukshevskii 2003). The World Organization against Torture condemned the Russian police claim that domestic violence is decreasing—a claim based on their receiving fewer complaints (Benninger-Budel and O'Hanlon 2004, 308). Of these new human rights campaigns, the most weighty—from the organization with the most international pull—was the Amnesty International campaign initiated in 2003, which resulted in an extensive and well-documented report, published in both Russian and English (Amnesty International 2005).

Also, as for sexual assault, this monitoring by human rights advocates from above was matched by feminist entrepreneurs, such as Dianne Post from the ABA-CEELI gender program, working from below. Post was focused even more on domestic violence than on sexual assault as she crisscrossed Russia holding seminars, conferences, and trainings from 1998 to 2000.[60] Building upon global feminist claims about women's human rights, her most common programs were what she called "Domestic Violence 101," a multidisciplinary conference for social workers, psychologists, educators, and local crisis centers, or training sessions for non-lawyers to be advocates for domestic violence victims.[61] In other cases, she trained judges and lawyers, teaching them how to advise others or initiate suits (Post 2001). She also wanted to support local women's crisis centers, by including them in the events.

Both these interventions certified a new kind of public space in which activists could meet with state workers from both social services and law enforcement in order to do more of their own training. Bolstered by some foreign funding and the crisis center movement's new willingness to talk the language of "violence in the family," this new space led ANNA to work with the Ministry of Labor and Social Development, conducting joint research, training social workers together, and developing a government crisis center in southern Moscow.[62] By 2004, the successor ministry—the Ministry of Health and Social Development—was coordinating with the RACCW, for example, holding a 2004 conference on the role of crisis centers in working with social services to prevent violence in the family.[63] ANNA, through the Ministry of Internal Affairs, has also conducted trainings for the police training programs (T. V. Veligurova in Rimasheevskaia 2005).

Foreign intervention also came from programs explicitly designed to foster state-society collaboration along the model of coordinated community approach. One such program was through Vermont-based Project Harmony, which aims to promote community partnerships and provides hands-on training for law enforcement officials. With funding from the U.S. State Department's Bureau for International Narcotics and Law Enforcement, in 1998, they launched Domestic Violence Community Partnerships in Irkutsk, Petrozavodsk, and Volgograd.[64] The program first brought a group of lawyers, police, psychologists, medical professionals, and victim advocates to conduct two-week seminars for the Russian counterparts. Following the seminar, they help to set up a local coalition of state institutions and NGOs to address domestic violence. To follow up, in approximately a year, Russian officials and activists were then brought to the United States to meet and learn from their American counterparts. Through programs like these, police in more than a dozen localities around Russia have participated in various training programs on how to handle domestic violence.

Another type of intervention came from the Russian American Rule of Law Consortium (RAROLC), an American nonprofit that grew from a Vermont judge's interest in Russia to a seven-state partnership.[65] Since 1993, American judges, law professors, prosecutors, criminal defense lawyers, and legislators—volunteers—have traveled to Russia, and vice versa, with the goal of improving the capacity of Russian legal institutions. Four of the partnerships took a particular interest in domestic violence, leading RAROLC as a whole to focus on the issue in 2005. For example, the Maine-Arkhangelsk partnership, which began in 1997, has been addressing domestic violence for five years. In 2001, Maine professors, judges, prosecutors, and lawyers, with their Russian counterparts, conducted comparative mock trials, including a family law dispute concerning custody, residence, alimony, and child support.[66] Revealing the systemic problems facing women hoping to flee violent relationships, the Russian mock court, granting divorce, refused to make any child custody or support decisions and simply left the divorced couple in their shared apartment.[67] In 2003, Maine judges and domestic violence attorney-activists conducted a three-day training session for Russian district court judges on legal issues in dealing with domestic violence cases. Because of the great interest among justices of the peace, the Maine representatives returned the next year to discuss the issue more broadly, including coordinated community responses.[68] In 2005, Russian judges and law school officials traveled to Maine to shadow U.S. counterparts and to visit a domestic violence shelter.

These exchanges, especially the events in Arkhangelsk, enlisted much media attention. They also seem to have had real results. In 2005, staff at the three legal clinics in Arkanagelsk, established with technical support from ABA-CEELI and RAROLC and financial support from USAID, were familiar with the problem of domestic violence and were helping citizens with issues of divorce, custody, and private-prosecution cases, and a leading law school administrator was hoping to open a special domestic violence legal clinic, modeled on a Maine clinic, in the next year.[69] The new judicial awareness of domestic violence has meant that the local independent women's crisis center has been able to persuade judges to authorize women divorced from their batterers to trade their joint apartments for smaller, separate apartments even without their former spouse's agreement.[70]

Interventions have fostered other types of coordinated community approaches in other cities. In Saratov, a "system of interaction among various bodies working to prevent family problems including domestic violence" was developed (Lukshevskii 2003). In Ekaterinburg, the local crisis center was working closely with law enforcement, together inspecting abusers' homes (Pashina 2004). In Barnaul, a working group, including officials from the Ministry of Internal Affairs, was developed, which led to information sharing and collaborations between the local women's crisis centers and the police (Johnson 2006). In Tomsk, a coalition of Russian psychologists, physicians, journalists, law faculty, state social services, and gender experts with Amnesty International and Project Harmony developed a program where the local legal clinic, state youth center, and gender center provide comprehensive services for battered women and are attempting to enlist the justices of the peace.[71] Although the Russian criminal justice system remains skeptical of domestic violence, the women's crisis centers and these interventions have initiated what Keck and Sikkink (1998) call "accountability politics." A 2004 discussion at the Ministry of Health and Social Development, with RACCW, re-raised the possibility of formal, national collaboration between state social protection and law enforcement institutions and independent women's crisis centers.[72]

## Some Steps Forward

To outsiders, it may look like nothing has changed. Amnesty's (2005) critiques of state practice, based on data collected in late 2004 and early 2005, were similar to the early Human Rights Watch reports. They found police inaction (such as the failure to enter an apartment when the abuser refused entry or refusal to accept a domestic violence complaint) and unauthorized use of force against the batterer (such as bludgeoning him) (30–35). They criticized lack of mechanisms, such as protection orders, for immediate defense of the victim (35–36); the rarity of state prosecution and conviction, which officials justify by means of bureaucratic rules (36–41); and the inadequate number of state shelters (41–44). The ABA-CEELI gender report also criticizes the emphasis of justices of the peace on reconciliation and the continuing housing problems and residency permit requirements (Duban 2006). Even though all citizens have a constitutional right to free and accessible healthcare, state medical personnel are often unwilling to treat injuries they know are a result of domestic violence (102). The network of state centers dedicated to social services to families and children have little knowledge of domestic violence, often treating the problem only through psychological treatment for the woman victim, whom they see as to blame (102–103). Although most authorities now will admit that domestic violence is a problem, few have been willing to take the responsibility to respond themselves.

Looking deeper, it is possible to see some steps forward. After years of global feminist pressure, there have been some procedural changes within the Ministry of Internal Affairs, the ministry charged with policing. Apparently (although not yet with results), the ministry began collecting and analyzing data about the relationship between the perpetrator and the victim of a crime, a step that would allow for the documentation of registered domestic violence cases (Russian Federation 2004, 18).[73] Further, as of 2001, a working group within the ministry has been meeting on violence against women, including domestic violence, "to assure the cooperation between federal executive bodies and social organizations engaged in these questions" (16). In 2006, the ministry launched a widespread campaign with the message, "Violence in the family? 'Beat cop' is from the word 'compassion.' . . . He will not remain apathetic to your problems" (see figure 5.1). Although perhaps more a promise than a reality, this is a far cry from the official denial of police responsibility dominant in the early years after the Soviet collapse. The parliamentary Committee on Women, Family, and Children has also recently been conducting roundtables with the relevant ministries and with the key Moscow crisis centers to discuss the problem of domestic violence (Open Society Institute 2007, 32).

Pockets of notable reform also include the following.

### St. Petersburg

Crisis center activists in St. Petersburg turned very quickly to the state and got fast results. In 1995, after activists lobbied the progressive mayor, the city opened a city shelter to provide "social assistance to women in danger."[74] The first director, a feminist academic, had been inspired to establish the shelter, because she "had been to America and knew that a shelter needed to be founded." Anticipating the decline in U.S. funding, she sought state support. She also believed that "it was important to hold the government accountable because they created the situation for domestic violence." The shelter holds up to thirty people, who have been officially allowed to stay up to two months (Amnesty International 2005, 43). In addition to physical shelter, as with the independent women's crisis centers, they also provide psychological and legal assistance via a hotline and in person.

Although the shelter was founded by those who self-identified as feminist, working with the city administration required compromises. For example, the city kept trying to use the shelter space for homeless immigrant women and children, and although the director wanted to help women only once they had made the decision to help themselves, the city social services started sending women to the shelter (and abrogating their own responsibilities). A central bone of contention was that many of the women who came to the center were older, and the government was "only interested in women of child-bearing age," leading to age limits and eventually a requirement that sheltered women have children.

**FIGURE 5.1.** Ministry of Internal Affairs campaign about violence in the family, 2006. Moscow, Russia. Photography courtesy of Elisabeth Duban.

But the center has lasted for more than a decade on the government budget, and the city's commitment to the shelter was reaffirmed in the 2000 law. Police in St. Petersburg, some of whom assisted Amnesty with their report, also appear to have a new understanding of domestic violence. These changes, primarily a result of the long-standing commitment of activists, were also fostered by norms and models from the West. In a city that sees itself as the gateway to Europe, the international prestige awarded to these local activists also certified their concerns.

*Karelia*
The Republic of Karelia, on the border of Finland, is another place in which there has been meaningful reform of state practice. Only three years after the St. Petersburg shelter was founded, Karelia established its own shelter for women with children who have suffered from domestic violence (Liapounova and Drachova 2004). The contribution of the local independent women's crisis center was recognized when its director was also given a post within the Ministry of Social Welfare (Merzova 2004).

Beginning in 1999, when the director of the Karelian Centre for Gender Studies organized a multidisciplinary seminar on domestic violence, more formalized state-society coordination on domestic violence has developed (Amnesty International 2005). Attended by local and regional administrators and social services, this first seminar brought official attention to the issue. A 2000 seminar conducted by the independent women's crisis center led to the establishment of a protocol about cooperation between NGOs, the Ministry of Internal Affairs, the Center of Family Planning, and the juridical clinic of the Petrozavdosk state university (Merzova 2004, 132). As a result, a woman police officer comes to the shelter when a woman first arrives, to help her understand her legal options and, with shelter staff, to support her decisions (Amnesty International 2005, 43). The police also "actively try to inform the population about violence in the family . . . and about the legal rights of victims of violence." The Karelian Ministry of Internal Affairs also introduced training on violence against women in the family for public safety officers and encourages officers to "work more proactively with female victims of violence in the family" (44).

According to the director of the gender center, these changes have led violence in family to be considered as "contradicting public acknowledged norms of morality, as violating human rights, not as a private but as a social matter" (Boichenko 2004, 17). With support from a republic commission on women and yearly fora on women, she argues that there is now widespread attention from all ministries, agencies, public organizations, schools, and libraries and what she considers the formation of a new social policy that is anti-violence, anti-discriminatory, and gender-equal.

The push for these changes came not just from dynamic activists but from international attention. RAROLC came out of links between Vermont and Karelia that date back to 1991 and that continue to thrive. The protocol emerged with support from Project Harmony's Domestic Violence Community Partnership Program. Facilitated by ethnic and linguistic ties and geographic proximity, support also came from the Nordic Network for Crisis Centres for Women in the Barents region, which brought Nordic activists and public administrators to talk about coordination just months before Americans came for the Project Harmony–sponsored conference. The Nordic Council and bilateral agreements with the neighboring Nordic countries have enabled the police to visit and cooperate with their Nordic counterparts (Amnesty International 2005). One police officer told Amnesty that such international experience "had shown him and his colleagues that with a different approach to violence and more preventative work, more serious crimes could be averted" (44).

### Barnaul and the Altai Region

Across Russia, in southwestern Siberia, the flurry of NGO activity in Barnaul that had produced new state social services targeted to both women and men in violent relationships has been accompanied by a new coordinated community-like initiative. In 2001, the director of the Altai regional department of the medical-social and family-demographic problems championed a working group on domestic violence.[75] The group brought together the crisis centers, social workers, administrative officials, health officials, educators, the head doctor of a private hospital, the head of the youth commission, and the deputy director of the krai administration of internal affairs. Along with multidisciplinary conferences held by the Women's Alliance, this working group created a new pattern of collaboration between state and societal social services and the police, who had, by 2002, begun to see the benefits of such a collaboration. By May of 2004, this group had led ten roundtables on "Safety in the Family: Time for Action," attracting a wide variety of both civic leaders and state officials from social services, education, and law enforcement. According to a journalist at the leading Altai newspaper, "The participants in the conversation [at the tenth roundtable] were unanimous that departmental segregation strongly hindered the war against domestic violence."[76] As a result, police in at least one precinct had been convinced to collect statistics on domestic violence. According to the journalist, this collaboration had raised the issue of domestic violence from a private problem to a problem worthy of state response.

Mutual cooperation was also fostered by the police officials learning about neighboring Kazakhstan, where special police forces dedicated to combating gender violence have been established (Amnesty International 2005, 46). Women's Alliance has trained police at the regional training center and Barnaul and nearby communities' public safety officers. Their goal is to broaden police officers' understanding of the causes and effects of domestic violence and highlight the obstacles women have faced when turning to the police. They simultaneously want to build up women's confidence that the police will assist them against violence in the family, helping them file complaints and appeal against court decisions.

The remarkable responsiveness in Altai has some domestic causes: the dynamism of local activists, the prevalence of patronage networks that fostered alliances, and the continuing popularity of social policy in the region. But what clinched the deal was the international attention and funding. The local activists gained their stature when they began to be invited abroad by transnational feminist networks and human rights advocates and received substantial foreign funding, especially from the United States, which pushed the multidisciplinary model. Further, their key ally in the administration had been radicalized by her participation in a national commission on women, a result of the Beijing conference. International modeling even came from Kazakhstan, reforms themselves resulting from U.S. involvement in training police in the region (Snajdr 2005).

---

These reforms stand in stark contrast to the policy areas where there has been little foreign attention and no reform: housing law, family law, healthcare, and forensic-medical experts. Although human rights advocates, from Human Rights Watch (1997) to the special rapporteur's 2006 report on violence against women in Russia (Erturk 2006), have pointed out problems in these areas, there has been much less monitoring, blaming, and shaming, and almost no funding to support reforms. Although the system was changed by federal law in 1993 and overturned several times by the new constitutional court, the official residence permits (*propiski*) system still exists, leaving many divorced women stuck in apartments shared by their abusive ex-husbands (Duban 2006). Family law still has no specific provisions to respect an abused women's rights in divorce (91). Healthcare providers deny any responsibility in addressing the cause of the domestic violence injuries they often see. Forensic medical experts deny that they have any responsibility whatsoever in combating domestic violence because there is no specific domestic violence law (L. V. Romanova in Rimasheevskaia 2005). In Russia, as in most places, there is a long way to go before women can live free from domestic violence.

## ASSESSING THE IMPACT OF
## GLOBAL NORMS + ASSISTANCE

In sum, despite these limitations, adding substantial assistance to the blame and shame of human rights advocates working with transnational feminists was much more effective than the blame and shame process alone. Foreigners gave local activists considerable financial support for their activism, for their campaigns to raise public awareness of domestic violence, and for their initiatives to transform law enforcement practice. Foreign entrepreneurs brought even more resources. Funding also went to state institutions and state personnel through conferences, law enforcement training, and programs to advocate coordinated community responses. Although much remains to be done, domestic activists were able to translate the global norm of domestic violence as a violation of women's human rights into Russian vernacular, resulting in notable shifts in media coverage and public awareness. Although there is no new domestic violence law—nor any substantial national reforms of criminal law—domestic violence is on the agenda of the Ministry of Internal Affairs and the Ministry of Health and Social Protection, and several regional governments have passed regional laws or implemented new procedures to respond to domestic violence. Even though less than global feminists might hope, these changes have the potential for transforming the sex/gender hierarchy. Global experience suggests that gender revolutions move at a glacial pace and not in a linear fashion.

Driven by intervention, this funded blame and shame process provided local actors with the necessary start-up resources. These included the ideational resources, such as the models for awareness campaigns and the certification of local activists' concerns, as well as the basic financial resources it takes to run any organization and advocacy campaign. Once established, some local organizations—similar to Keck and Sikkink's (1998) boomerang—pressured external organizations to put pressure on the Russian government. But this too was fostered by outsiders, as global feminist organizations had enough influence on donors to persuade them to be more inclusive of local activists as well as to fund awareness campaigns and to support programs designed to move Russia toward what global feminists understood as best practices. In 2005, the drop in references to domestic violence in Russian newspapers, the disbanding of several official institutions designed to help women, and the financial and legal difficulties of women's crisis centers demonstrated the consequences of donors pulling out of Russia's gender violence politics.

# CHAPTER SIX

# Trafficking in Women:
# The Costs of State Pressure

F FOREIGN ASSISTANCE COMBINED with local and transnational feminist activism made the process of blaming and shaming more effective, perhaps more powerful intervention could be even more helpful in promoting global feminist change. In addition to the positive incentives of grants from large charitable foundations and international development agencies, strong states can employ more traditional diplomacy, directly pressing other states to change their policies and practices. Instead of simply training law enforcement and other state personnel, strong states can lobby parliaments and threaten economic sanctions or even military intervention, using the justification of global norms. Do these higher stakes interventions into local gender politics enhance the chances of domestic activism, increased public awareness, and meaningful reform? If so, why and how? Does reform reflect the hopes of global feminists?

The analysis of the politics of intervention into the issue of trafficking in women suggests that these negative incentives can be quite potent, fostering some reform. After years of diplomatic pressure from Western states and the passage of a U.N. protocol on trafficking, U.S. threats of economic sanctions finally induced Russia to adopt legislation criminalizing trafficking. This new legislation led to a limited number of high-profile prosecutions, but regrettably not any national initiatives to protect victims or prevent future trafficking. Activism and intervention fostered increased awareness of the problem among Russians, but mostly as a nationalist reaction to foreign intervention. Perhaps helping a few women whose traffickers might be prosecuted, the intervention drew upon and reinforced sex/gender hierarchies, leaving the larger problem of gender injustice untouched. These heavy-handed interventions were never imagined by global feminists and were made without substantial global feminist involvement.

As with the terminology for domestic violence, there is no unproblematic way to discuss trafficking in women. In this case, such terms as "trafficking in persons," "sex trafficking," "sex slavery," and the like are laden with ideology. As I elaborate below, even the choice of terms to refer to those most likely to be trafficked, "prostitutes" or "sex workers," is contested. To be as neutral as possible, but to highlight the gender-specificity of the inquiry, I alternate terms and refer to the issue as "trafficking in/of women" or simply "trafficking." When discussing different groups' or institutional perspectives, I use their terminology.

## GLOBAL CONTROVERSIES AND STATE PREEMPTION

### Antiprostitution versus Sex Work Feminism

Western, especially American, feminists have a long history of being concerned about the issue of trafficking in white women (and children), particularly trafficking leading to sexual exploitation. The first wave of activism against "white slavery"—trafficking of women across borders for the purpose of prostitution—began around the turn of the twentieth century and resulted in several international agreements, including the International Agreement of 1904 for the Suppression of White Slave Traffic and the 1949 U.N. Convention for the Suppression of the Traffic in Persons and of the Exploitation of the Prostitution of Others. Although the latter was ratified by the USSR in 1953, convention supporters had trouble enlisting European countries to ratify the U.N. Convention (Ucarer 1999). As a result, this early activism succeeded in raising global attention to the issue but not in changing policy or practice.

The second wave of feminist activism in the 1970s and 1980s renewed feminist attention to the issue, but by the 1990s, when the Soviet collapse allowed dialogue between Russian and foreign feminists, the global feminist debate had become polarized. In practice, there are a variety of approaches to regulating, prohibiting, legalizing, abolishing, or criminalizing prostitution (see Outshoorn 2004, 8), but two views are constitutive both globally and especially in Russia. In one camp were transnational feminist networks (TFNs) such as the Coalition against Trafficking in Women, founded in 1993 and based in the U.S., which reject all prostitution as sex trafficking. Writing and speaking of "prostitution," "sex trafficking," and "sex slavery," their "antiprostitution feminism" subsumes the problem of trafficking (and mail-order brides) under prostitution, criticizing both as "sexual exploitation" (Chapkis 2005). They believe that "[p]rostitution victimizes all women, justifies the sale of any woman, and reduces all women to sex."[1] To address the problem, they propose raising women's status, "depenalizing the prostitutes, [and] penalizing the customer and anyone who promotes sexual exploitation, particularly pimps and procurers." They advocate "rehabilitation" for the former prostitutes.

On the other side were TFNs such as the Global Alliance against Trafficking in Women (GAATW), founded in 1994 and based in Thailand, who critique coerced prostitution while accepting what they see as voluntary sex work by adults. Speaking of "forced (reproductive or sexual) labor," "human trafficking," "trafficking in persons," GAATW broadens the understanding of trafficking to including trafficking for other forced labor.[2] Employing the term "sex work" instead of "prostitution," this "sex work feminism" articulates that "prostitution should be regarded as *work*" and that "new domestic and international law was needed to both advance the labour (and other) rights of sex workers and to protect victims of forced labour (for example in the trafficking for the purposes of prostitution)" (Sullivan 2003). The focus here is not the behavior (prostitution), but the coercion, "human rights" rather than sexual exploitation. Sex-work feminists fear that criminalization may drive prostitution further underground, making it more dangerous for women, and that "rehabilitation" of individual sex workers may deprive women of the most lucrative job opportunities, driving them to employment in perhaps just as exploitative labor conditions with lower wages.

The different approaches represent long-standing and complex disagreements about women's sex and sexuality and the best way to promote women's agency. As they believe that sexual violence (and by extension prostitution and trafficking) is the central tool through which women are dominated, antiprostitution feminists maintain that women's empowerment will come about only when all forms of sexual violence are eradicated. Sex-work feminists begin with some women's assertion that sexuality (and sex work) is empowering and wish to extend that empowerment to other women by creating new, supportive social, political, and cultural conditions. The first approach gives voice to the exploited women by clarifying the incorrect assumption of consent in many contexts such as prostitution; the second reinforces women's status as equal rights-bearing citizens by recognizing that women may give consent to sex or sex work. The former favors gendering the debate, focusing the discussion of trafficking on women (and children); the latter seeks to de-gender the debate so that women are not seen as particularly (or essentially) vulnerable.

Although there is no consensus on how to solve the problem, trafficking in women has long been part of the global feminist consensus on violence against women as a violation of women's human rights. It was the only form of gender violence explicitly condemned in the 1979 Convention on the Elimination of All Forms of Discrimination against Women (CEDAW) (see appendix 1). The U.N. Declaration on the Elimination of Violence against Women (1994) defined "trafficking in women as forced prostitution," one element of violence against women. The 1995 Beijing Platform established "effective suppression of trafficking in women and girls for the sex trade" as a "matter of pressing international concern" (para. 122). As part of the new alliance between global feminists and human rights advocates, the latter—including such giants as the Minnesota Advocates for Human Rights, Amnesty International, and Human Rights Watch—adopted the issue.

### The Global Compromise: The U.N. Trafficking Protocol (2000)

As global feminists rekindled the U.N.'s attention to trafficking through the yearly Commission on the Status of Women (Ucarer 1999), the conflict between antiprostitution and sex-work feminists shaped the debate. In 2000, after more than a year of contentious discussion, the U.N. passed a protocol on "Trafficking in Persons, Especially Women and Children." The conceptualization of trafficking in the final version represented an uneasy compromise. Throughout, while formally addressing "trafficking in [gender-neutral] persons" (more in line with sex-work feminism), the protocol frequently invokes the particular situation of "women and children" (more in line with antiprostitution feminism). More closely reflecting the stance of sex-work feminism, the Trafficking Protocol differentiated "prostitution" from "trafficking in persons," defining the latter as

> the recruitment, transportation, transfer, harbouring or receipt of persons, by means of the threat or use of force or other forms of coercion, of abduction, of fraud, of deception, of the abuse of power or of a position of vulnerability or of the giving or receiving of payments or benefits to achieve the consent of a person having control over another person, for the purpose of exploitation. Exploitation shall include, at a minimum, the exploitation of the prostitution of others or other forms of sexual exploitation, forced labour or services, slavery or practices similar to slavery, servitude or the removal of organs. (United Nations 2000)

But the protocol also appears to reflect the antiprostitution stance on consent and on criminalizing at least the use of prostituted persons.[3]

The protocol also reveals the greater influence of other interests and viewpoints on trafficking, especially those from the U.S. and Western European governments, who were most concerned about illegal migration and organized crime. The protocol, a part of the Transnational Convention against Organized Crime, is not a human rights agreement. First and with the most conviction, the protocol calls for criminalization of trafficking and prosecution of traffickers (Art. 5.1). Second, with less stringent requirements, the protocol calls for the provision of social services to those who have been trafficking (e.g., Art. 6.3). Third, similarly less stringently, the protocol calls for states to "endeavour to undertake" preventive action "such as research, information and mass media campaigns and social and economic initiatives to prevent and combat trafficking in persons" (Art. 9.2). The U.N.'s approach is not unique. Even the more social policy–friendly EU, especially its European Commission, has prioritized prosecution over assistance (Goodey 2004, 30).

Most global feminists sought these criminal justice and social policy reforms, what are commonly called the "3 Ps"—*prevention* of victimization, *prosecution* of offenders, and *protection* of and assistance to victims—but not with the same prioritization. By focusing on criminalization, states are given increased coercive powers (which are often implemented by men with guns) while women are cast as only victims, like children, who require protection (see Enloe 1993). The Trafficking Protocol includes frequent references to "protection," the need to protect victims of trafficking, especially women and children, a language not used to refer to adult men. The U.N. Trafficking Protocol empowered strong states' foreign ministers (nonfeminist and mostly male) to become entrepreneurs while disempowering TFNs, who were given no formal role. Unlike the international documents that constitute the global norms for sexual assault and domestic violence, the U.N.'s protocol denied global feminists descriptive representation even though they had broached the issue.

Nevertheless, the U.N.'s adoption of new antitrafficking legislation did inject some concern about human rights into an international debate once shaped by the view of trafficking as a migration problem. For instance, the intergovernmental International Organization for Migration (IOM), which had begun antitrafficking initiatives in 1994, had defined trafficking as fraudulent border crossing, prolonged stay often illegal, facilitated by a third party (Ucarer 1999, 232).[4] Focusing on the demand-pull factors that attract migrants to particular countries and the supply-push factors, such as poverty or instability, that encourage emigration, its migration approach led countries to beef up border control and to cast trafficked women as illegal migrants. Global feminist pressure to mainstream gender and the U.N. protocol led the IOM to adopt the protocol's definitions and to begin to collect and distribute information, in some ways similar to human rights monitoring. In 2002, the intergovernmental Council of Europe, of which Russia has been a member since 1996, also called on countries to examine their legislation and adopt the 3 Ps and emphasize victims' human rights.[5] In 2005, the council passed its own antitrafficking convention, leading to a new multinational campaign. Similarly, the Organization for Security and Cooperation in Europe (OSCE) has added trafficking as one of their main issue areas, including it as a human rights violation. Moving beyond the 3 Ps, the OSCE advocates a National Referral Mechanism, which formalizes cooperative partnership between state actors and civil society, including developing a system for referring trafficked persons to the variety of state and non-state services as a way to ensure their human rights.

While the human rights focus also classifies women as victims, it does so with a concern for the empowerment of the victim. As Jo Goodey (2004) notes, the re-classification of trafficked women, who had heretofore been seen only as illegal immigrants and shameful prostitutes, can be seen as a positive development despite some feminists concerns with this classification. For women trafficked abroad, being cast as a victim can given them important rights and privileges that they would not normally have in their destination or source country (34). Perhaps more problematically, for most states and intergovernmental agencies, social benefits of protection are dependent on the trafficking victim's cooperation with prosecution (31). A human rights approach can bring to light that this require-ment is both dangerous and unfair, with low prosecution rates for trafficking and the limited evidence that most trafficking victims have on the masterminds of their trafficking (37).

*U.S. Preemption, Adding Threats:*
*U.S. Trafficking Victims Protection Act (2000)*

While many Western governments had concerned themselves with the issue of trafficking, including initiatives in Eastern Europe and Eurasia by the European Union and Nordic Council of Ministers, the United States took the boldest stand with the 2000 Trafficking Victims Protection Act and its reauthorizations in 2003 and 2005. As with the U.N. protocol, the legislation reflects a compromise between the two global feminist approaches to trafficking as well as nonfeminist concerns. The particular U.S. flavor was interest from evangelical Christians, for whom "[t]he archetypal case—a young girl, tricked into leaving her impover-ished homeland by the promise of a respectable job, then brutally held captive, raped, and forced into prostitution—strikes deep moral chords."[6] Following the election of George Bush in 2000, these antiprostitution interests were promoted while other feminist voices were banned by the 2003 State Department memo—the antiprostitution pledge discussed in chapter 3—prohibiting working with or-ganizations promoting the legalization of prostitution.[7]

Following the terrorist attacks on September 11, 2001, antitrafficking efforts also became part of the "war on terrorism"; for the neoconservatives in the Bush administration, combating terrorism required combating international crime, under which trafficking in persons was subsumed. The "evangelical-feminist alli-ance" that created the law was usurped by the new U.S. administration's concern with insecurity. Without any feminists included in constructing the intervention, the U.S. evangelical viewpoint added, more explicitly than the intergovernmental approaches, the requirement that the trafficked women be a good victim, "inno-cent" and "deserving," that is, fitting into the mold of acceptable female behav-ior and acceptable female sexuality. There is no one to demand that the United States consider a more "woman-centered" approach, perhaps modeled on success-ful feminist anti–woman battery and anti-rape initiatives (see Goodey 2004, 42). This has led to an intervention that is, at best, a pseudofeminist policy, that is, a concerted response to problems women tend to face couched in language that appears feminist, but with no opposition to the sex/gender hierarchy. "[I]nter-national attention [even] on sex trafficking has . . . become distanced from the underlying global problem of violence against women" (35).

The most distinct element of the U.S. legislation was that it came with en-forcement mechanisms against other countries. A special task force, what be-came the State Department Office to Monitor and Combat Trafficking in Per-sons (G/TIP), was established to produce annual reports on trafficking. These Trafficking in Persons (TIP) reports were then used to place various countries in tiers based on their responsiveness to trafficking. Those countries not meeting minimum standards, nor making any significant efforts, would then be subject to the termination of non-humanitarian and non-trade-related foreign assistance, not just from the United States, but from the International Monetary Fund and the World Bank, the leading international lending institutions, upon which the United States has great impact. The president could even freeze assets located in the United States under the International Economic Powers Act (Mertus 2004, 174). For the first time on behalf of women, the United States explicitly legislated itself as the global policeman, threatening economic sanctions for noncompliance with U.S. legislation. This new kind of state power was combined with positive incentives, more than $300 million for antitrafficking efforts, including funding for NGOs, training for journalists, and U.S. embassy–led efforts to reform other countries' legislation.[8]

The first set of annual rankings began the process with some considerable methodological flaws, such as concentrating almost solely on sex trafficking, including no statistical data, and taking a country's promises of victims' services and legislation as good without considering their content, implementation, or effectiveness (Mertus 2004, 174). Not surprisingly, the United States also appeared to bias its assessments to reflect national interests, such as promoting to a higher tier those countries that became allies in the war on terror (e.g., Pakistan in 2002). In response to these problems, U.S. human rights organizations, especially the Women's Rights Project of Human Rights Watch, took the State Department to task in 2002, and in the 2004 report many of these methodological problems had been improved. A new tier was created (the Tier 2 Watch List) that put some of these allies on notice for their lack of antitrafficking practices. For Julie Mertus (2004), critical of many of the U.S. human rights standards used abroad, the U.S. TIP reports proved a place where human rights advocates had been remarkably successful. On the 2007 report, countries such as Iran, North Korea, Cuba, Venezuela, and Syria, which the Bush administration classifies as enemies, were placed in the lowest tier. However, Saudi Arabia, Malaysia, Kuwait, Oman, and Qatar were also on that list.

Overall, intervention on the issue of trafficking combined the assistance plus blame and shame politics elaborated in chapter 5 with the more coercive interventionist politics of state threats of economic sanctions. There are global norms available for feminist and nonfeminist entrepreneurs, transnational feminist networks, and local activists, who may use them to localize activism and to blame and shame governments. Donors, including states directly (not just through their development agencies), may bring assistance that can foster increased public awareness through funding of public awareness campaigns and reform of policy and practice through training. Finally, because there are so many other interests and approaches to the issue of trafficking, the United States can choose to exercise its new sanctioning option against other countries, or activists may try to recruit the U.S. into their own struggles. Together, this suggests the following intervention model:

**TABLE 6.1.** *State Pressure (in Addition to Global Norms and Assistance)*

| PROCESSES | LEADING FOREIGN AGENTS | GLOBAL NORMS | ASSISTANCE | THREATS |
|---|---|---|---|---|
| localizing activism/ vernacularization | feminist and nonfeminist (NGO and state) entrepreneurs, transnational feminist networks | global norms as modeling and certifying activism, activists appropriating and translating | financial support for activism and awareness campaigns | only anti-prostitution initiatives get U.S. funding |
| raising awareness | | | | |
| reforming policy | foreign ministers, especially U.S. embassy staff, law enforcement | monitoring, diplomacy | law enforcement training, lobbying parliamentarians | U.S. threats of economic sanctions |
| reforming practice | | | | |

As with the other interventions, threats of economic sanctions are not a guaranteed slam dunk. The use of sanctions—which can vary from boycotting events such as the Olympics to withholding diplomatic recognition or limiting diplomatic visits to imposing bans on trade or aid—to compel another state is a relatively recent, but increasingly common, strategy. Often justified as a more humane approach than military intervention, since Soviet collapse they also have become seen as a strategy to corral human rights violators and more often are used unilaterally by the United States (Colonomos 2004). Yet, analyses of the effectiveness of sanctions or the threats of sanctions suggest that they fail more often than they succeed, most likely by a large margin (e.g., Pape 1997). They can have the effect of rallying people in the target country against the coercer, a nationalist backlash that leaves people and their government willing to endure considerable pressure (107). In other cases, such as the 1990s sanctions against Iraq, elites can also protect themselves from the consequences of the sanctions, shifting the burden onto the less politically powerful and/or more economically disadvantaged. This reality, in turn, raises humanitarian concerns about sanctions as the population can be seen as indirectly suffering as a result of sanctions (Colonomos 2004). More so than with the other interventions, sanctions can be seen as unfair (or imperialistic) because they are imposed by more powerful countries against the weaker (Davis and Engerman 2003). These critiques have led to "smart sanctions," attempts to constrain the costs to the population, such as the U.S. threats to end only non-humanitarian assistance for countries not adopting the minimum antitrafficking initiatives. This chapter assesses whether smart sanctions—or even just the threat of sanctions—can achieve global feminist goals on this issue of not particularly high importance to Russia.

## Global Interventions

More so than for other issues, outsiders, not Russian activists, broached the problem of trafficking in women in Russia. Although as early as 1993 at least one crisis center began collecting information from their callers about their experience with trafficking (Khodyreva 1996), most did not include trafficking as one of their target issues. This was because the consequences of trafficking were most evident abroad, the embryonic movement had its arms full with sexual and domestic violence, and trafficking brought an additional element of danger, the involvement of Russian organized crime. According to the Russian Association of Crisis Centers for Women, the issue was first raised by global feminists at a 1996 United Kingdom conference, a follow-up meeting to the 1995 U.N. conference on women in Beijing.[9]

In 1997, a United States–based human rights nonprofit, the Global Survival Network, brought global attention to Russia in a conference planned to coincide with the release of their documentary film, *Bought & Sold,* a result of a two-year undercover investigation of the traffic in women from Russia for forced prostitution.[10] With invited participants from the Russian women's movement and officials from women's policy agencies, the program dramatically revealed the problem of trafficking in women to the disbelieving Russians.[11] The conference also spelled out what the Global Survival Network saw as "good practices," the multidimensional response later supported by the intergovernmental organizations (Caldwell, Galster, and Steinzor 1997).

Over the next few years, the leading Russian women's crisis centers became more engaged in the issue of trafficking in women. They extended their hotline counseling services to women seeking employment abroad. Movement leaders published the first journal issue dedicated to the problem, explaining the inclusion of antitrafficking activism in terms of their evolution, over the years, in their focus from sexual violence, to sexual harassment, and to domestic violence (Abubikirova et al. 1999).

## Localizing the Global Feminist Conflict

This special journal issue illustrates the movement's quest to both appropriate and translate the global feminist understandings of trafficking (Abubikirova et al. 1999). The editors employed GAATW's (sex-work feminist) definition, but, highlighting their understanding of trafficking as linked to new (1993) freedoms for Russians to travel abroad for work, the preface to the journal names the problem as the "illegal emigration of women" (*nezakonnyi vyvoz zhenshchin za granitsu*). While recognizing the incentives created by the "collapse of the [Soviet] social system," they place blame for women's ending up in the illegal sector of the economy on the countries of destination (in contrast to developed countries, which tend to blame countries like Russia). They see the problem as exacerbated by European countries' desire to restrict immigration, leaving women wishing to immigrate even more dependent on shady businesses who bribe European government officials. "This is how a woman, striving for independence and material wellbeing, finds herself, on the contrary, in servitude and dire straits, suffering both from violence and fear for her own life and the lives of those close to her" (3).

Over the next few years, the St. Petersburg Crisis Center for Women also began to take part in various international meetings on trafficking—in the Baltics, with the OSCE, and in front of the U.S. Senate—as they developed an antitrafficking project, including psychological, legal, and financial support to deported women (Khodyreva 2004). This center too did not fit easily in one global feminist camp or another. Its director, Natalia Khodyreva, has advocated the establishment of bilateral agreements to create temporary worker programs for Russian women abroad so that the women, who mostly want to earn money for their families, can have a better chance of not being manipulated by organized crime (241). She also highlights a particular Russian concern, the trafficking in women or women's body parts for reproduction. At the same time, she rejects the neoliberal discourse of choice, something she sees as alien to Russia and as essential to sex-work feminism. Acknowledging that sex-worker rights may work for citizen sex workers, she points out that legalizing prostitution would leave Russian sex workers outside of the regular labor market as most are likely not legal residents. For Khodyreva (2005, 245), the two feminist camps "do not contradict each other": antiprostitution feminists focus on long-term issues, while sex-work feminists focus on "palliative tactical measures to improve the quality of life for those women already engaged in prostitution."

But women's crisis centers in Russia could not long escape the global feminist divides. Not only did assistance increase suspicion and fragmentation, but funders took sides. Khodyreva elaborates: "[T]here are . . . structures that make the financing [of Russian antitrafficking initiatives] directly dependent on the ideological position . . . with respect to prostitution" (Khodyreva 2004, 243). It was this ideological (and funding) divide that solidified the conflict between many women's crisis center leaders and the Angel Coalition, the new coalition of antitrafficking organizations that emerged in the late 1990s from the U.S.-Russian NGO MiraMed and was officially headed by Khodyreva. MiraMed's director took a strong antiprostitution stance, and some funders, such as U.S. Agency for International Development (USAID) and the Ford Foundation, apparently at first refused to fund them. In contrast, the other women's crisis center leaders participated in international events organized by sex-work feminists.[12] Even though both the women's crisis centers and the Angel Coalition/MiraMed had been inspired by the 1997 conference and documentary, by the new millennium they were bitterly divided.

The divide between these two sets of organizations led to separate public aware-ness campaigns made possible by significant foreign funding. The crisis centers unaffiliated with the Angel Coalition increased their focus on spreading discus-sion of the problem through the Russian women's movement. In 2002, drawing legitimacy from the U.N. Trafficking Protocol, leading Moscow activists pub-lished a second special issue dedicated to trafficking in *We/My*, a long-standing East-West feminist journal on women.[13] They also turned to mainstream media, running a campaign with the Independent Radio Foundation and the news asso-ciation Internews, similar to the one they had done for domestic violence. In the words of a movement leader:

> It has long been understood that the mass media play a key role both in transmitting information, and also in the formation of images. Therefore, we see cooperation between the mass media and the Association as one of the key factors in our activity towards preventing violence against women in general, and in stopping human trafficking in particular. Our coopera-tion takes place on various levels: bringing in experts from the Association to educate journalists on these issues (through trainings and seminars) or to speak on radio and television programs at the national and local levels, and participating in talk shows. (Abubikirova 2002)

Launched in 2001 with funding from the U.S. State Department, the Internews campaign's public service announcement "Disappearance" won a grand prize at a Russian public service announcement festival.

In the Far East, projects—all with U.S. funding—have included broad-based media campaigns to raise awareness as well as "training for the trainers" programs for groups considered at risk. In Siberian Altai, for example, the Women's Alli-ance crisis center ran a series of educational seminars, dissemination of booklets, posters, stickers, and flyers, and public actions at local universities (2001–2002).[14] Another project focused on training NGOs to work with teachers, schools, and parents to prevent trafficking.[15] These leaders then worked with teachers and youth, coordinating street events and working in summer camps. More recently, programs have provided economic training programs to improve job search skills and self-esteem, seeking to empower at-risk women economically in order to pre-vent trafficking. The crisis center in Irkutsk conducted educational workshops and media campaigns, collected details about firms and marriage agencies that advertise jobs abroad, and disseminated practical info about how to protect one-self (Stoecker 2005, 23).

Meanwhile, the Angel Coalition/MiraMed was also working to raise awareness of the problem, among women's organizations, public officials, and the broader public. In the late 1990s, with a grant from UNIFEM, the MiraMed director co-ordinated one hundred showings of *Bought & Sold* and co-produced an episode of a popular television program with Vladimir Pozner.[16] In 2001, they initiated a multimedia public education antitrafficking campaign in six regional cities and began education programs in schools, colleges, and orphanages. Their message was "Don't get fooled by false promises—Get the facts!" an effort to help young women go abroad more safely. In 2002, northwestern Russian organizations cooperated with Nordic counterparts in a multinational campaign against buying sex from young women and children (Boichenko 2004). Since 2005, Angel Coalition, with the antiprostitution Coalition against Trafficking in Women and Project Kesher, has targeted the Upper Volga region for a gender violence campaign. In contrast to other crisis centers, Angel Coalition also focused on ending the demand for sex trafficking.

By 2004, some one hundred organizations across Russia were involved in some type of prevention or awareness-raising activity.[17] Particularly active were women's crisis centers and Angel affiliates in Moscow, St. Petersburg, Perm, Kazan, Barnaul, Irkutsk, Nizhny Tagil, Tula, and Karelia, which had conducted some two dozen projects between 1999 and 2005 (Tiuriukanova 2006, appendix). According to the leading Russian expert on trafficking, "[t]o date, NGOs have played the leading role in implementing practical initiatives to combat human trafficking and to provide support to victims" (65). In addition to the women's crisis centers' projects, the European Union supported radio announcements, the ILO supported economic empowerment for at-risk groups, and the IOM established some protection programs for already trafficked women. The Transnational Crime and Corruption Center (TraCCC) at American University in Washington, D.C., through its Russian affiliates in Vladivostok, Irkutsk, Saratov, and Moscow, solicited Russian experts to produce the first serious academic study of the problem (Tiuriukanova and Erokhina 2002).[18] These international organizations "play a crucial role . . . in Russia. They deliver up-to-date international experience and methodologies, in applying holistic, human rights-based approaches" (Tiuriukanova 2006, 66, 68).

## REFORMING POLICY

Simultaneous with the emergence of this activism, foreign actors were also putting pressure directly on administrators and policymakers to reform policy. Perhaps, together, domestic activism and foreign intervention could prove powerful impetus for policy reform. Or would the foreign intervention backfire, provoking national resistance and undermining the women's crisis centers?

### Parliamentary Roundtable on Trafficking, 1997

In 1997, one month before the Global Survival Network conference brought global feminist approaches to trafficking to Russian activists, the Russian Duma held its first roundtable on the subject. Co-sponsored by American University's TraCCC (Highlights from the Duma Roundtable on Trafficking 1999), the roundtable followed an April seminar on organized crime and the exploitation of women and children sponsored by the U.S. State Department's Bureau of International Narcotics and Law Enforcement Matters (INL), which provides technical support to Russian law enforcement (Human Rights Watch 1997, 49). These U.S. actors, including the TraCCC director, whose visible role in the roundtable was a first for an American, brought an understanding of trafficking in persons as predominantly about sex trafficking linked to organized crime.

The roundtable and the response to it illustrated the reluctance of most Russian officials to recognize the problem of trafficking in women in any way similar to the global feminist approaches. The first clue was the sponsorship by the Security Committee, rather than the Duma's Committee on Women, Family, and Youth, which brought mostly men affiliated with law and order, such as the military as well as security, intelligence, and law enforcement agencies, to participate (Shelley and Orttung 2005). The few Russian participants who acknowledged that individuals were being trafficked from Russia for prostitution dismissed Russia's responsibility or proposed solutions that would violate women's human rights. For example, speakers advocated increased border enforcement or condescending protection for "the most undefended category of our Russian citizens—women and children" (Highlights from the Duma Roundtable on Trafficking 1999). Russian authorities expressed nationalism, arguing that trafficking was the exploitation of the Russian national body such as through illegal transnational adoptions, missing Russian children, and the "national disgrace of trafficking of Russian women into prostitution" (Shelley 2005).

In the roundtable's aftermath, except a limited reform to address the trafficking of minors, Russian policymakers decided to ignore the problem.[19] When there was serious discussion of what the Russian politicians considered "trafficking in persons" in the Duma, the discussion referred to the problem of kidnapping in the Caucuses.[20] Yet, the roundtable established an unusual precedent for the involvement of foreign actors and local women's organizations in the policymaking process (Shelley 2005, 295).

### Threatening Sanctions, Adding Legislative Assistance

As the NGOs were deepening their focus on trafficking, the Russian Ministry of Foreign Affairs was quietly participating in various high-level diplomatic meetings on trafficking, such as through the OSCE. This international attention led this ministry to be "the first government structure to know about this problem" and Russia to sign the U.N. Trafficking Protocol in the first round of signatures in December 2000.[21] Nevertheless, the Russian administration did not acknowledge the roles of Russian law, practice, or citizens in the problem. Conceding that thousands of Russian-speaking women had appeared as prostitutes across Europe and the United States, officials repeatedly asserted that these women were from other post-Soviet states, not Russia.

Simultaneously, U.S. pressure for a more substantive response was increasing. In 1999, a State Department analyst wrote an influential report on trafficking into the United States, linking the problem to slavery and to Russian organized crime (Richard 1999). By 2000, the State Department's annual Country Reports on Human Rights were indicting Russia for its failure to address the problem of trafficking in persons. In 2001, the United States released the first Trafficking in Persons report, which placed Russia in Tier 3, the worst tier, indicating that the U.S. evaluated Russia as not meeting the minimum standards—nor was it moving in that direction.[22] In 2002, Russia remained in Tier 3, and an advisor to the U.S. secretary of state said that sanctions were probable.[23] These accusations and threats raised the ire of some Russian leaders. Following the 2002 Trafficking in Persons report, Russian labor minister Alexander Pochinok summarized the Russian viewpoint:

> To put it crudely, I would say this is libel. But more politely, these statements are based on unverified information. One can say to the authors of this report: Put the facts on the table. In Russia, unlike in those countries where people are kidnapped and sold in the hundreds of thousands, there have been only isolated instances and all receive the appropriate response of state organs and the media.[24]

Yet, the U.S. pressure had positive consequences: the Russian government formally requested legislative assistance from the United States to help draft a new law against human trafficking.

The resulting legislative working group introduced legislation on trafficking into the Duma in February of 2003, calling for the criminalization of trafficking, services for victims, public awareness campaigns, and prevention programs to alleviate the problems that encourage people to make decisions that facilitate their being trafficked.[25] The bill also required a broad range of ministries to get involved and, controversially, provided for the establishment of a federal commission to coordinate their work. It even called for governmental cooperation with NGOs.[26] Meeting the global feminist and human rights–based calls for the 3 Ps and a national referral mechanism, the proposed legislation was so good that leading intergovernmental organizations considered it a model for reform around the world (Shelley 2005).

Unsurprisingly, in Russia, where there has never been such comprehensive and socially inclusive legislation, legislators and Putin's administration were not persuaded. Seeking at least some reform, the working group changed tactics, choosing to piggyback the trafficking amendments on the president's proposals to amend the criminal code to reduce prison overcrowding. They reworked the legislation, calling for the criminalization of prostitution, of the dissemination of information about trafficking victims (their identity and location), and of trafficking and slave labor. And they waited. During the spring of 2003, the presidential administration did and said nothing. The United States, which had just promoted Russia to Tier 2 in 2003 with great fanfare in recognition of the formation of the working group, was hamstrung.[27]

In October of 2003, out of the blue, President Putin changed his mind. In an important policy speech, he announced a new commitment to the issue of human trafficking and then introduced his version of the trafficking legislation into the Duma. After some last-minute wrangling, the legislation was revised and resubmitted to the Duma and passed 353–0 in December.[28] The final legislation recognized, for the first time in Russian history, that trafficking in persons, including trafficking in women, and the use of slave labor was a crime, and it established punishments of up to ten years' imprisonment. Retaining the broadness of the Russian concept of trafficking, the new law includes the exploitation of men as laborers and kidnapping and forced labor in the Chechen military conflict (Shelley 2005, 301). By the summer of the next year, Russia had also ratified the U.N. protocol and passed victim/witness protection legislation, another first for Russia, that could provide some legal protection for trafficked women who bear witness against their traffickers.[29] This about-face on trafficking in persons was remarkable in light of most Russians' tendency to blame prostitutes and women seeking work abroad for their own exploitation. It was especially remarkable given that some Russian policymakers had been advocating the legalization of prostitution (Duban 2006, 47), including the key Duma deputy involved in the final wrangling over the bill, an owner of Moscow bars allegedly staffed with prostitutes.[30]

The U.N. Trafficking Protocol—and the global norm it represented—was part of the explanation. As Russian is one of the official languages of the United Nations, the passage of the Trafficking Protocol had created new opportunities for Russian awareness of the problem, especially among the human rights community and the Russian government.[31] The international consensus on the need for antitrafficking reform also legitimated the U.S. involvement, giving Putin a way to talk about the passage of legislation that did not subordinate Russia's sovereignty to the United States. For Putin, at this period, it was important for Russia to appear civilized.[32] Although they waited until almost the last minute to discuss antitrafficking legislation, the Russian parliament did pass legislation a few weeks before the U.N. protocol went into effect on December 25, 2003. "Without this outside pressure and the desire of Russia to conform to international standards, the trafficking legislation would have been developed much more slowly" (Shelley 2005, 299).

Also important were local activists. By 2002, their tireless work, with leverage from the global norms against trafficking, led Russia's special representative for human rights to characterize trafficking in women as a violation of human rights (Azhgikhina 2002). Their activism earned them spots in the working group, yet another first for Russian policymaking. Their alliances with transnational feminists led them to push for the multifaceted approach that was a part of the first draft of legislation. The Angel Coalition, too, claims impact, having mobilized U.S. evangelicals to rally the U.S. government and drafted and sent a "personal letter to Putin, signed by more than 200 international NGO's and human rights activists."[33]

Two policy entrepreneurs were more directly responsible. The first was Elena Mizulina, a Duma deputy, whom the United States approached to spearhead the drafting of legislation. Mizulina—a member of the West-leaning Union of Right Forces party and chair of the Central Federal District's Committee on the Affairs of Women, Families, Maternity, and Childhood—had led an earlier successful working group allowing input from the United States (Shelley and Orttung 2005). Although she knew little about the issue of trafficking,[34] Mizulina proved to be a savvy political player in an environment increasingly resistant to power outside of the president and his allies, repackaging the bill and inviting the Swedish director of the film *Lilja-4-ever*, which fictionalized a Russian trafficking tragedy, to screen and discuss his film in the Duma.

The second entrepreneur was an American, Tom Firestone, a Russian-speaking prosecutor for the Department of Justice in New York with experience prosecuting Russian organized crime, who had just arrived to be the resident legal adviser at the U.S. embassy in Moscow. After Putin proposed a much weaker version of the legislation,[35] Firestone called Mikhail Paleev, Putin's legal advisor, and, in essence, threatened Russia's demotion to Tier 3. After a three-hour marathon meeting, the Russian officials agreed to several changes that gave the legislation more teeth.[36] Both entrepreneurs tactically cast trafficking as linked to organized crime and the financing of international terrorism to enlist Putin's support.[37]

Following the passage of the criminal code amendments, the U.S. government kept up the pressure. In January of 2004, the American Bar Association Central and Eastern European Law Initiative (ABA-CEELI), with the sponsorship of President Putin's administration, arranged the First All-Russian Assembly of Non-Governmental Organizations on counteracting trafficking in persons. At the last minute, U.S. secretary of state Colin Powell was able to attend. In March, a group of Russian lawmakers was brought to the United States. The delegation came skeptical, but a New Jersey prosecutor's tape of traffickers as well as a speech from the former trafficker made the problem more real. The lawmakers returned home to pass the witness protection legislation. In January of 2005, additional criminal code amendments were signed into law that criminalize the organization of illegal entry and transit of aliens into and through Russia. Other recent amendments allow the confiscation of property in trafficking cases.[38]

## The Limits of Reform

The success of passing antitrafficking legislation, the only major national legislative reform on gender violence since Soviet collapse, was marred by the fact that so much of what global feminists regarded as good practices was not included in the final legislation. There were no national commitments to prevention or social services for deported victims, not even a mandate for federally funded safe houses. Even the victim/witness protection law, which includes some services, such as relocation, housing, and employment assistance, includes no specialized services for trafficking victims who may require additional support (Duban 2006, 47). There was no national plan of action. The question of consent, as laid out in the U.N. protocol, was also not sufficiently addressed, allowing the victim's consent to any part of the process of recruitment, border crossing, or work to become grounds for refusal to initiate a case (Tiuriukanova 2006, 19). The antiprostitution feminist wish for those who frequent prostitutes to be criminalized was also not included. Finally, there are also procedural problems, such as inappropriate use of civil law terminology, the requirement of specific intent, and the vagueness in the concept of exploitation (Tiuriukanova 2006). The director of the Moscow crisis center Syostri warned that the situation was actually worse than before because of the punitive nature of the law, leaving trafficked women even more likely to be arrested and prosecuted.[39]

The blame for these limitations must rest mostly on the shoulders of Putin and his supporters who refused the model legislation proposed by the working group, but the type of U.S. intervention may have exacerbated the problem, perhaps unintentionally pushing the legislation toward prosecution over prevention of trafficking and protection of deported women. Although those involved with the U.S. intervention advocated the inclusion in the Russian legislation of social services for deported victims of trafficking, it was their framing of trafficking as part of organized crime and international terrorism that resonated with the Russian administration. The U.S. pseudofeminist preemption of the issue, rather than including feminists in the intervention, meant that the key entrepreneurs were not feminists.[40] Clearly concerned about the impact of trafficking on women, they did not have transformative global feminist goals, nor did they think in terms of creating structures to respect women's agency. With the U.S. preempting the issue, even if human rights advocates had decided to monitor, blame, and shame, their normative power would have been dwarfed by the United States' efforts.

## RAISING SOME AWARENESS, BUT OF WHAT?

Did all this attention from foreign actors, Russian civil society, and Russian policymakers change the public awareness of trafficking in women? More so than for sexual assault and domestic violence, there is a second-level question: did foreign intervention contribute to feminist awareness, or did the multiple, foreign-influenced viewpoints on trafficking in women lead to shifts, but not necessarily in ways intended by (either of) the global feminist camps? Did the heavy foreign involvement promote nationalistic backlash?

### Media Coverage

Analysis of coverage of trafficking over time in the national newspaper *Izvestiia* suggests that attention to the issue mounted as a result of the parliamentary attention to the issue (table 6.2; see appendix 2 for method).[41] There was a small

**TABLE 6.2.**

*The Incidence of Various Terms to Refer to Trafficking in* Izvestiia, *1995–2005*

| SPECIFIC TERM | 1995 | 1996 | 1997 | 1998 | 1999 | 2000 | 2001 | 2002 | 2003 | 2004 | 2005 | TOTAL |
|---|---|---|---|---|---|---|---|---|---|---|---|---|
| trade in persons (*torgovlia liud'mi*) | 2 | 4 | 9 | 9 | 6 | 6 | 5 | 10 | 27 | 14 | 14 | 106 |
| sexual slavery (*seksual'noe rabstvo*) | 0 | 0 | 0 | 0 | 0 | 0 | 0 | 0 | 11 | 1 | 1 | 13 |
| traffic or trafficking (*traffik*) | 0 | 0 | 0 | 0 | 0 | 1 | 0 | 0 | 0 | 0 | 4 | 5 |
| illegal export of women (*nezakonnyi vyvoz zhenshchin*) | 0 | 0 | 0 | 0 | 0 | 0 | 1 | 0 | 2 | 0 | 0 | 3 |
| compulsion to prostitution (*prinuzhdenie k prostitutsii*) | 0 | 0 | 0 | 0 | 0 | 0 | 0 | 0 | 2 | 0 | 0 | 2 |
| Total | 2 | 4 | 9 | 9 | 6 | 7 | 6 | 10 | 42 | 15 | 19 | 129 |

increase in references to trafficking around the 1997 parliamentary hearing and a much larger increase during the Duma's consideration of a bill on trafficking in persons. There is a similar pattern across Russia: whereas in 1995 there were only three articles on trafficking in persons (*torgovlia liud'mi*) in national newspapers, by 2003 there were several hundred articles in both national and regional newspapers. This later interest reflects the conscious efforts of the Duma's working group, which held more than fifty press events in 2003 organized by a press liaison. With some 1,700 articles having used this term between 1995 and 2005, "trafficking in persons"—the official translation of the U.N. protocol—had become the agreed-upon way of talking about the issue. By 2004, trafficking had become the issue that the Russian press was more likely to report on, save rape.

However, a more detailed read of newspaper coverage illustrates that coverage did not equal outrage at the human rights violations involved in trafficking in women. Most articles are sensationalist, highlighting aspects of sex and scandal (Tiuriukanova 2006, 70). Focusing on sex trafficking rather than other types of labor trafficking, articles tend to blame the women for either being prostitutes (and thus bringing on the problem themselves) or being a part of a particularly downtrodden segment of society. Very few discuss human rights violations or the role of Russian nationals in the process. Many other articles mention trafficking but, especially before 2000, refer to the kidnapping of individuals for ransom and labor slavery in Chechnya or Afghanistan or refer to the large number of adoptions by foreigners as trafficking in children (see also Kleimenov and Shamkov 2005).

## Surveying Public Awareness

Unlike the case for the other forms of violence against women, there are absolutely no systematic public opinion surveys of the public's awareness of trafficking in women. Even with surveys repeated over time, it would be tough to sort out whether awareness was due to increased attention or to the increase in the actual problem of trafficking, which has also happened over the period since the end of the USSR.

Instead, survey data reveal much more about how some segments of the population are coming to understand trafficking. One 2000 study among workers in Moscow suggests that there was a great awareness of potential dangers of working abroad (Tiuriukanova 2005a, 105–106): one in four women workers believed that all jobs abroad were high-risk, and 40 percent believed that many immigrant Russian women found themselves in slavery-like conditions. But among those women actually seeking work abroad, there was much naiveté about their own prospects and the probability of facing coercion to work in the sex industry (Tiuriukanova 2005a, 100–102). Few of the women, especially those over twenty-five, wanted jobs that would require them to use sexuality (such as a stripper or bar waitress intended to flirt with customers to sell drinks), and almost none to sell sex. Nonetheless, most respondents were seeking jobs in service industries, such as in restaurants or hotels, or in domestic services (such as caregivers or maids), which have proven to be high-risk, and almost all thought it would be possible—or even easy—to find acceptable jobs. By 2000, sensationalized stories had evoked fear among Russians, but not a clear sense of how trafficking typically occurs or to whom. Some experts in Russia's regions also worry that information campaigns can have the perverse consequence of arousing more interest in traveling abroad (Tiuriukanova 2006, 73).

In Siberia and the Far East, almost all opinion leaders were quite aware of the problem. A 2000 survey in a number of cities in Siberia and the Far East found that only 7 percent of citizens had never heard of Russian citizens being transported abroad to be criminally exploited (Kleimenov and Shamkov 2005, 34–37). Almost one-half knew of similar cases, while more than one-third thought it was a widespread phenomenon. Respondents were most aware of the criminal transport of persons for exploitation in the sex industry, followed closely by labor exploitation, organ donations, and being kidnapped for ransom.

The evidence suggests that awareness comes from the media, personal experience, or crisis center activism. For example, a 1999 Angel Coalition survey, among those who had signaled interest in learning about trafficking by attending an Angel event, found that one-third of those who were aware of the problem gained this awareness because they had a close friend or family member who had been a victim of sex trafficking.[42] A few years later, an official from the Saratov Ministry of Health and Social Development, who spoke in detail about the complexities of the problem of trafficking at a 2004 women's crisis center conference, argued that the cooperation between her ministry and the Saratov women's crisis center (funded by USAID) had had a huge impact on the shaping of public opinion on the issue of illegal transportation of women abroad for sexual exploitation.[43]

## Marginalization of Feminist Discourses

That Russians tend to think more broadly about trafficking than Americans illustrates that Russians have appropriated and translated the concept of trafficking in persons into the Russian vernacular, but in contrast to domestic violence, the translated concept is so resonant to various national concerns that the transformative feminism is missing. Partially, their conceptualization reflects a legacy of Soviet concerns about economic exploitation that leads them to be more concerned with surrogacy and adoption in ways unimaginable to American feminists.[44] More significantly, the Russian notion stems from demographic concerns about the decreasing population in Russia, especially among ethnic Russians. Trafficking in persons is cast as the economic exploitation of the Russian national body, the stealing of Russian women, Russian children, and Russian body matter. Trafficking in women can easily be blamed on foreign demand and foreign exploiters (even if Russian nationals must recruit and transport women and Russian officials must be bribed). In light of these understandings, Russian women trafficked abroad become another purloined natural resource. These claims about national exploitation could then be linked to justifications for Putin's war on Chechnya. Feminists and feminism have no role.

A 2004 article from the Moscow weekly *Literaturnaia Gazeta* [Literary newspaper] illustrates this antifeminist dominant discourse about sex trafficking—both similar to and different from the U.S. conceptualization.[45] Subtitled "Fate Didn't Protect Them, but 'Angel' Heals," the article dramatizes the story of Tatiana, who was "lured from Russia" with the promise of a career as a dancer in a bar in Israel. She was coerced into sex slavery after her traffickers set fire to her parent's home back in Russia. Escaping through the desert to Egypt with a Bedouin guide, she has been placed in a psychiatric hospital, where she "periodically cries out in pain the names of foreign men" and suffers from "not only psychological problems but problems with her reproductive health." Based on information from the Angel Coalition, the article places this story within the context of some forty thousand persons who have fallen into "sex slavery" from Russia, lured by job ads for work as nannies, dancers, or models and the promise of learning a foreign language.

Not unlike the U.S. archetype and then mixed with Russian nationalism, the article highlights the naiveté of Russian young women and their love of Russia. "Our girls," the article asserts, "naively believe in the kindness of the 'uncles' and 'aunts'" who recruit them. Once they realize their situation, they of course "search for any way to return to their homeland. . . . Even the desert is no obstacle to them." Detailing some of the Angel Coalition's activities, the article also plays on the word "angel," casting the police raids and forceful deportation of women as "one of a few ways to be extracted from sex slavery in a civilized manner. . . . All [recently deported women] cried out of happiness when they found themselves in Russia."[46] In contrast to the Angel Coalition's reasonable suggestions about how to travel abroad more safely, the article ends with a call to "close the travel agencies . . . which can formalize foreign passports and legal visas in two days. . . . In truth, they work as part of the sex slave-holding mafia."

In contrast to the sympathy for Russian women trafficked abroad, the author reserves no concern for those women who work in a range of sex services, such as massage parlors and prostitution, in Moscow. He argues that these women are mostly "provincial," part of an unruly mass who have stormed into Moscow. Some of these "enraged young girls," ignoring the police patrols, who were only "trying to get in touch with them, . . . pounced on the police with their fists, once even overturning a police car." For these native prostitutes, some of whom may have also been trafficked, there is no exploration of the question of coercion or consent. As with sexual assault, prostitution and sex trafficking stories can titillate, but Russians tend to see the violence as real only when there is a clear foreign enemy.

## CRIMINALIZING PRACTICE

In a country with established rule of law, the new antitrafficking law would likely lead to some meaningful changes in behavior of state actors. In countries such as Russia where legislation can be completely ignored by state agents (while touted in international venues), foreign pressure may be necessary to persuade states to put their policies into practice.

### Intergovernmental and U.S. Monitoring

There has been almost no monitoring of Russian state practice from human rights organizations. There have been no significant reports or campaigns from the big human rights organizations such as Human Rights Watch or Amnesty International. The Minnesota Advocates for Human Rights have included trafficking in women as part of their campaign since 2003, but they have written no reports on trafficking in or from Russia. None of the major Russian human rights advocates has researched or campaigned against trafficking, including those organizations, such as the Moscow Helsinki Group, that had criticized the Russian response to domestic violence. In general, despite earlier interest in sexual assault in Russia, these organizations were now willing to leave trafficking monitoring to others. One small exception is the late 2007 Violence Against Women Monitoring Program of the Open Society Institute, which includes an assessment of Russia's antitrafficking efforts, albeit mostly based on others' empirical research.

More attention to the trafficking in adult women has come from intergovernmental organizations. In collaboration with the IOM and the OSCE, women's crisis centers in Moscow and Kazan have produced informational booklets on trafficking, contrasting Russian practice with international documents and practice in other countries in the region.[47] The ILO released a 2004 report on *Coercive Labor in Contemporary Russia: Unregulated Migration and Trafficking in Persons* (Tiuriukanova 2004). While not focusing just on trafficking in women, the report illustrates the links made by the ILO between sex trafficking and other coercive labor, including the trafficking of men to and within Russia as construction workers. Other monitoring has come through the CEDAW process. Only in 2006 did any of the international organizations release something akin to a human rights monitor, when a working group under the aegis of the United Nations and the IOM published *Human Trafficking in the Russian Federation: Inventory and Analysis of the Current Situation and Responses* (Tiuriukanova 2006).[48] Although assessing Russia's response based on a human rights and victim-centered approach, the report is only a review of the limited existing literature and includes no victim testimonies. As of 2008, the Council of Europe will monitor implementation of the Council of Europe Convention on Action against Trafficking in Human Beings, but as of June 2008, Russia had not even signed the convention.

The only sustained monitoring of Russia's problem has come from the United States' TIP reports released yearly starting in 2001. Although the first couple of reports were remarkably vague on details about country responses and focused almost solely on sex trafficking, by 2003, the reports were specific about the Russian government's failure to comply with what the United States established as minimum standards for addressing trafficking in persons, including trafficking beyond sex trafficking, based on the 3 Ps. However, unlike human rights reports, these do not focus on the human rights violations themselves or victim testimony but on government inaction. With no voice, the trafficked women and girls are cast as poor passive victims inherently vulnerable to trafficking.

## Trainings and Multidisciplinary Meetings

There have been several foreign interventions to foster increased responsiveness of state actors to the problem. The most active were from the United States. American University's TraCCC created training materials for a multidisciplinary audience, used at a 2001 seminar in Budapest attended by some investigators and prosecutors from Russia (Stoecker and Shelley 2005). The Saratov affiliate, with the local law school, compiled a training manual of existing criminal law cases. Other interventions came from organizations actively involved in other gender violence issues in Russia, such as the Consortium of Women's Nongovernmental Organizations, which was conducting law enforcement trainings, and the Russian American Rule of Law Consortium, which was working with judges and attorneys in the Russian Far East (Stoecker 2005, 24). With U.S. funding, the ABA-CEELI has coordinated meetings, including two national assemblies on trafficking, and created a directory of organizations addressing trafficking in order to foster partnerships between law enforcement and civil society, as recommended by the OSCE.

The U.S. Department of Justice was also actively involved. With hundreds of thousands of dollars per year from the State Department, they supported the U.S.-Russian antitrafficking task force that had pushed for legislation as well as training and coordination of law enforcement. Following the law's passage, the interagency task force, under the auspices of the Russian Duma committee on law and procedure, traveled around Russia to promote the law's implementation. Including representatives of various ministries, international organizations, and local experts, the group meets regularly to gather information and to discuss the implementation of antitrafficking legislation (Duban 2006, 50). In 2004–2005, the U.S. Embassy law enforcement project collaborated with the Russian Ministry of Internal Affairs (MIA) to provide training for Russian law enforcement in several Russian regions (Tiuriukanova 2006, 77).

Also involved were the Nordic countries, for which trafficking in Russian women has become a practical problem. The Nordic Council, the intergovernmental coalition of the five Nordic countries that has collaborated with northwest Russia since the Soviet disintegration, began a series of projects in the 2000s, including trainings and exchange programs with Russian law enforcement. In 2004, the council began to develop a Nordic-Baltic-Russian women's police network to better respond to trafficking in women. Other interventions have been more ad hoc, from individual Nordic countries or organizations. For example, several Swedish and Norwegian officials and activists took part in a 2005 antitrafficking multidisciplinary conference in Murmansk. Despite a call within the council to synchronize the response to the problem, the Nordic countries continue to have different approaches to trafficking and prostitution, from Sweden's antiprostitution stance to other less regulated societies such as Denmark. What unites them is not their interest in promoting women's rights, but concern over the influx of undocumented Russian women across their borders.

Some procedural reforms have resulted. It has become common to hold multidisciplinary meetings across Russia that include Russian women's NGOs, local and national officials, and regional and national law enforcement. Additionally, by 2002, a special unit within the MIA was formed to address violence against women and human trafficking, and according to the Russian government, it coordinates with nongovernmental organizations (Russian Federation 2004). In 2003, the Ministry of Labor, with Moscow crisis center Syostri, conducted a series of trainings of executive officials in seventeen regions across Russia. In early 2007, the MIA apparently created a federal antitrafficking unit (U.S Department of State 2007). At the same time, some of these initiatives, especially the U.S.-funded interagency task force, have created nationalist resistance.[49]

## Little Change

Despite the antitrafficking legislation and the Russian government's increased attention to the problem, there has been relatively little accomplished in practice (e.g. Duban 2006; Tiuriukanova 2006; U.S Department of State 2007). From the 2004 to 2007 TIP reports, for example, Russia remained on the Tier 2 watch list, meaning that, according to the U.S., the government has not fully complied with minimum standards, but is seen as making efforts toward meeting those standards.

### Prosecution

Russia's prosecution record is poor, even in comparison to its neighbors Ukraine and especially beleaguered Moldova. In 2004, trafficking cases initiated were limited to only sixteen of the eighty-nine regions in Russia and mostly to internal (Russian ethnic) cases of sexual exploitation trafficking, and the sentences were quite light (Tiuriukanova 2006, 78, 80). At the end of 2005, the Russian government declared that 80 human trafficking cases had been opened: 20 concerning forced labor and 60 sex trafficking.[50] In 2006, police conducted 125 trafficking investigations, mostly sexual exploitation cases, with approximately 53 prosecutions and 13 convictions (U.S Department of State 2007). In 2007, Russia seems to be taking government involvement in trafficking slightly more seriously. In March, the Federal Security Services reported that they had broken a large trafficking ring—run by a Russian official—which was trafficking people from Southeast Asia and former Soviet states through Russia to Western Europe.[51]

A typical successful prosecution is the following:

> Igor Khvan, an Uzbekistan citizen who resides in Primorye, was arrested in December 2004 for trafficking women from Uzbekistan. His two female assistants recruited young women in Tashkent, Uzbekistan, for hostess positions in Ussuriysk, Primorskiy Krai. Upon their arrival, Khvan took away the women's passports and forced them to work in prostitution. Khvan took all revenue from their activities, leaving the women an allowance of only $1.80 to $3.60 (47.7 to 95.4 rubles) a day for food. On January 25, the Ussuriysk Court sentenced Khvan to seven years in prison. His two associates were sentenced to the same term in Uzbekistan.[52]

Although there is no national analysis of the prosecuted cases, the evidence suggests that most prosecuted cases are for these kinds of small operations, and many are against non-Russians.

Part of the problem is inadequate training in how to investigate and prosecute such crimes, insufficient funding, and insufficient coordination of law enforcement and prosecutors' offices (Duban 2006). There is also low priority placed on investigations in a context of limited staff and resources (Tiuriukanova 2006). Although the 2005 TIP report (U.S Department of State 2005) recounts the development of an antitrafficking training manual and a draft field manual, by all accounts local officers tend to still deny that trafficking is a problem in their juris-dictions. They argue, dismissively, that the women knew what they were getting themselves into, and misidentify victims' refusal to cooperate as an indication of their criminal complicity. Despite anticorruption efforts, corruption is rampant; thus national reforms require little local change, and people's trust in law enforce-ment remains low (Shelley and Orttung 2005, 172).

Resistance to implementing change is deeply embedded in law enforcement's beliefs and practices. Since the Soviet collapse, prostitution and recruitment of women for traffickers appears to have been lucrative for a wide variety of govern-ment officials, from border guards to law enforcement officers and higher offi-cials. For example, after a long U.S.-Russian meeting with the MIA on the prob-lem of trafficking, several MIA administrators invited the American Firestone to relax with them, and offered him a prostitute.[53] There was not even a pause to consider whether these prostitutes were there voluntarily, even more remarkable considering the U.S. antiprostitution stance at these events. (When Firestone re-fused, the Russian said, "I never know what to expect from you Americans.") At the same time, at least in the Russian Far East, most law enforcement officials blame the women themselves, for example, suggesting that regulation should be targeted not against the recruiters or the men-clients, but against the trafficked women.

Even those whom the government totes out as experts on trafficking often ex-press only limited concern for the women's lives impacted by trafficking. Some when invited to contribute to materials compiled by the women's crisis center go off on tangents, discussing such things as the demographic problem and the threat to Russia's territorial integrity brought about by immigration of Eurasians into Russia. A key MIA official involved in many of these projects describes trafficking as a threat to the "national genetic fund" (Boris Gravrilov, e.g., in Rimasheevskaia 2005, 81). Repeating the victimized woman trope, another sympathetic MIA of-ficial sees trafficking as as a problem only for women who have lost their jobs and suffered from domestic violence.[54]

### Protection
Even more problematic is the lack of protection or assistance for women who have been trafficked.[55] Despite the new victim/witness protection law in 2004, the funds had not been appropriated for its implementation until very recently (Duban 2006, 50). According to the U.S. State Department, only "[f]our victims of trafficking benefited from the program in 2005."[56] Until at least 2006, there were no state shelters specifically for trafficking victims, even for those who have been deported, and now there are just two, in Karelia and St. Petersburg.[57] There is no law or practice to provide for resident status for a foreign victim, perhaps leading to involuntary deportations. There is no national referral mechanism to coordinate the work of law enforcement and service-providing agencies (Duban 2006, 50), although the U.S. government supported a series of conferences to en-courage cooperation between police and NGOs.[58] Unsurprisingly, in this con-

text, victims have generally been unwilling to cooperate with law enforcement. There are a handful of NGO shelters, but with few spots and few women. For example, in a recent year, the Angel Coalition had eighty-four women temporarily in their shelters.[59] In October of 2006, the IOM in Moscow announced a €4 million program to help women who had been trafficked and then deported to Russia, with a Moscow shelter.[60] But as of 2007 the shelter was relying on a medical model and, while working with some NGOs directly, IOM has not coordinated with existing NGO networks.[61] This lack of engagement has alienated some Russian activists. Located in a private—not a state—hospital, the shelter has no support from Russian authorities. In 2007, the national Public Chamber, a part of the Russian government, gave some small grants to three anti-trafficking NGOs, but most victim assistance is funded by international grants (U.S Department of State 2007).

### Prevention

The government has taken few steps toward a campaign to prevent trafficking. Senior governmental officials participate in meetings on trafficking and talk about trafficking, raising media attention to the trafficking, but there has been no federal program on the prevention of trafficking (Duban 2006, 51). Raising popular awareness of the problem is mostly left to the women's crisis centers, who rely on foreign grants. Locally, women's crisis centers have been able to work with local authorities only when they initiate and take responsibility for implementation. Only small reforms have been initiated, such as the Ministry of Foreign Affairs placing warnings on consular affairs websites for those wishing to travel or work abroad (U.S Department of State 2005). "Overall, victim protection and assistance is the weakest component of the Russian antitrafficking strategy" (Tiuriukanova 2006, 92).

### Regional Variation

Despite these widespread problems, some regions have been more active than others. Authorities in Far Eastern Khabarovsk have acknowledged the scale and severity of the problem since 2000, initiating antitrafficking measures such as closing down businesses that recruit women, and initiating a multi-agency working group to facilitate cooperation since 2000 (Erokhina 2005, 90–92). Other active regions include Yaroslavl (where there has been coordination between government and NGO to create a referral procedure), Karelia (with the longest EU border), and the Primorskii region (in the Far East). In the Tatar Republic, the Public Initiative Fund received support from the Tatar government, the Russian president's administration and the chief of the Tatar Migration Inspection. In June 2004, after dozens of prosecutions using the preexisting laws, the first major prosecution under the new antitrafficking legislation took place in the Far Eastern city of Vladivostok. On the whole, the most reform-oriented regions are in the Far East or northern regions, reflecting both the extent of the problem and international attention to the problem.

In sum, of the three interventions, the state preemption of the trafficking issue achieved the most dramatic policy reform, but not without risking the long-term global feminist goals of transforming the sex/gender hierarchies that regulate people's lives. As with sexual assault and domestic violence, there were global feminist norms, albeit in this case, with some serious contention between camps about the desired policy reform (i.e., whether to criminalize prostitution or not). As with domestic violence, a significant amount of funding went to activism and raising public awareness. More so than for other issues, there was significant foreign financial support for legislative reform. Distinct from intervention into the other forms of gender violence was the extent of state-on-state pressure, such as diplomatic pressure and U.S. threats of economic sanctions. According to Tiuriukanova, the leading Russian expert on trafficking, Russia passed an antitrafficking law "because of the support of the [U.S.] State Dept, other international organizations, the U.S. Embassy, and [the American legal advisor] Tom Firestone."[62]

Together, all pressures were somewhat effective—more activism, more media coverage, new laws—but not in the ways that global feminists from either camp would have liked, as prosecution has been increased, but not protection and prevention. This omission reflects different thinking. Instead of seeing women's rights as being violated, both Russian and American officials tend to see trafficked women as inherently vulnerable, disregarding the multiple layers of gender, globalization, and neoliberalism that have constituted the conditions that facilitate the trafficking in women. Instead of a comprehensive feminism in which critiques of the sex/gender system are institutionalized, the intervention resulted in pseudofeminism, in which, at best, there is a new responsiveness to the problems that some women face. Domestic violence policies, especially when directed as protecting mothers and families, can also be pseudofeminist, but in the new Russia, activists have managed to keep at least some of the more radical critique of sex/gender hierarchies.

This kind of intervention is not likely to meet global feminist goals in the long term. Because the interest from states was not about empowering women but about protecting borders and markets, state preemption legitimated more state coercion and reinscribed gender neotraditionalism, where men are responsible for violently protecting "their" women (even while, paradoxically, domestic violence rates remain high). Although the intervention initiated a new conversation about gender violence in Russia, feminist approaches and/or feminists are not likely to be included, not just as a result of Putin's new politics of controlling NGOs and legal formal debate. At the March 2006 Second All-Russian NGO assembly on trafficking, there were fewer NGOs invited than at the previous one, and no real dialogue between the state officials and the NGOs. There were no new plans to expand the Russian approach, either to improve victim services, to consider reorienting the process with the victims' needs as center, or to foster the coordination of the state with the NGOs. If anything, the women's crisis centers were more excluded from the process, and the convener, when offered U.S. support for a second day just for the NGOs, declined.

The nationalistic reaction to the heavy-handed trafficking intervention in Russia has been expanded to other, related issues. Since 2005, the Russian government has effectively banned U.S. adoption of Russian children instead of directly addressing the concerns that had arisen about some dramatic and horrific stories of the abuse of Russian children in the United States by a few adoptive parents. (Rather than help some quarter of a million children in Russia who are potentially available for adoption, the Russian government would prefer to virtually halt any foreign adoptions.) In 2007, the Russian government decreed that only Russian citizens could sell in Russia's 5,200 markets, where one-fifth of all trade takes place.[63] Instead of addressing the corruption, crime, and coercion of these markets directly, the new policy is "farmers for the fatherland," in which even legal immigrants cannot sell fruits and vegetables and illegal immigrants are being arrested and deported. While Russia appears to take some trafficking cases more seriously, "[w]hen French police briefly detained Russian billionaire Mikhail Prokhorov . . . on suspicion of 'illegal trafficking of young girls,' public officials in Moscow condemned the action as evidence of an 'anti-Russian campaign.'"[64]

More so than for the other interventions, the antitrafficking intervention circumvented the domestic policy process. Instead of what Keck and Sikkink (1998) call the "boomerang pattern," in which domestic movements frustrated by the state bypass the state by finding international allies who then bring pressure against the state, antitrafficking politics in Russia was shaped by a foreign strong state. Foreign ministries replaced human rights advocates as the international leverage; embassy staff, especially from the United States, replaced transnational feminists and human rights lawyers as the central policy entrepreneurs.

The intervention most closely resembled that of smart sanctions and suggests that smart sanctions can work in a limited way on a not-high-priority issue (for states), especially when there is a clearly articulated global norm for reform. But such sanctions work better at attaining stated policy reform than getting the reforms to penetrate deep into practice. For global feminists, this intervention is not the worst-case scenario—global feminist norms penetrated enough that the United States advocated the inclusion of local women's groups who played an unusually prominent role in the drafting of legislation—but state preemption of issues is not likely to achieve feminist results until there are states that are truly feminist.

# CHAPTER SEVEN

# Conclusion: Recommendations for Future Interventions

O VER THE LAST TWO decades, strong states, intergovernmental agencies, and large donors have increasingly justified their interventions as helping women. Their claims are given legitimacy by a new consensus among international women's activists and human rights advocates that women's rights are human rights. Central to this global feminist consensus are new claims that gender-based violence—such as rape, domestic violence, and trafficking in women—constitutes a violation of women's human rights. For those activists committed to protecting women's rights and those policymakers concerned with the impact of their decisions, it is essential to shed light on these interventions' consequences for women and for the broader structures of sex and gender that organize the social order. Although several studies consider the impact of specific types of interventions—international norms (e.g., Thomas 2001; Merry 2006a), transnational advocacy networks (e.g., Keck and Sikkink 1998; Moghadam 2005), democracy assistance (e.g., Wedel 2001; Henderson 2003; Sundstrom 2006), and economic sanctions (e.g., Pape 1997)—this is the first to compare systematically the effects of the various interventions. Drawing upon extensive fieldwork as well as some quantitative indicators, the previous chapters show how profoundly such interventions can impact gender and women's lives even in a relatively short time. The in-depth case study of such a critical case as Russia, where global feminism was unlikely to take root, also permits the examination of the processes through which global initiatives penetrate into a diverse and expansive polity.

What does this analysis tell us about interventions and global feminist reform? How does the Russian case stand in comparison to other cases? What does this comparison suggest about why certain interventions work better than others? What does this study show about how social scientists should study gender violence and other policies? Finally, what does this analysis offer to those concerned with fostering gender justice?

## BRIEF REVIEW OF THE FINDINGS

The new global feminist consensus on violence against women suggests three general objectives for intervention upon which to assess interventions' success. On the first objective, the mobilization of local activism, the Russian case shows the weakness of the least intrusive form of intervention, transnational feminist networking. Despite activists' hopes and scholars' assertions, the impact of this new form of more egalitarian transnational organizing was mostly symbolic. As in most countries where resources for broad-based progressive social organizing are scarce, transnational networking among feminists reached Russian feminists only in global cities such as Moscow and St. Petersburg. With only small grants, these local activists could appropriate the international model, the women's crisis center in which volunteers staff a crisis hotline, but they could neither create a broader movement nor become successful advocates for societal or policy change.

Similarly, such minimally intrusive interventions are likely to have little impact on the second and third indicators of intervention success, raising awareness and increasing state responsiveness in policy and practice (see table 7.1). In the intervention on the issue of sexual assault in Russia, transnational feminists' joining forces with human rights advocates to try to enforce new global norms led to virtually no changes: no measurable shift in the awareness of sexual assault as a violation of women's rights and no state reform. Although the Russian government now acknowledges violence against women in its reports for various international women's rights processes, such as CEDAW, the commitments remain empty promises without the imposition of additional incentives. The "Helsinki effect"—the impact of the acceptance of human rights norms by legitimacy-seeking repressive states (Thomas 2001)—was minuscule, if anything. For those concerned about re-enacting imperialism—who therefore shun more invasive interventions—the results are frustrating. In countries such as Russia, minimally intrusive interventions are not sufficient to foster the realization of new global norms.

On the other hand, the most aggressive interventions are likely to provoke only superficial reform and risk reinforcing the sex/gender system that feminists seek to undermine. As illustrated in the U.S.'s intervention on the issue of trafficking in women, when another state issues economic (or military) threats—even if ac-

**TABLE 7.1.** *Foreign Intervention into Russia's Gender Violence Politics*

| ISSUE | INTERVENTION | IMPACT ON RAISING AWARENESS & INCREASING RESPONSIVENESS |
|---|---|---|
| Sexual assault | global feminist alliances with international human rights advocates (blame & shame) | little change |
| Domestic violence | global feminist alliances with donors (blame & shame + assistance) | increased awareness and some reforms of policy and practice |
| Trafficking in women | state preemption (blame & shame + assistance + state pressure) | pseudofeminist legal reform |

companied by lavish funding of local organizing and reform initiatives—the interests of the intervening state overwhelm the concerns of women on the ground. The funding of women's organizing in Russia was refracted through the U.S.'s evangelical politics and exploited global feminist disagreements over how best to tackle trafficking in women. The Bush administration's requirement that funding recipients be antiprostitution, in a context where this debate does not make much sense, led to the institutionalization of conflicts within the Russian movement and the de-funding of the robust feminist crisis centers. In the post–9/11 era of preemptive foreign policy, U.S. threats of economic sanctions spurred the Russian parliament to adopt national legislation criminalizing human trafficking, attracting a great deal of media coverage in the process. However, the reforms include no assistance for victims and nothing to prevent future trafficking, and in a state where police wield arbitrary authority, criminalization may put women in more precarious positions.

More broadly, with the inhibition of local feminist activism, the increased coverage of the issue and the reforms were predicated only on remilitarized visions of the global order mixed with resurgent nationalism characteristic of both the Bush and Putin administrations. Trafficking in women mattered to the Russian media and Russian politicians because they understood that the bodies of Russian women were being exploited by foreigners and because the solution involved strengthening Russia's coercive forces. Once again casting men as the protectors of women, the reform contained no critique of the use of violence by men against the women they are assigned to protect. While some women may benefit from the arrest and prosecution of their traffickers, the aggressive intervention reinforced the gender neotraditionalism with which all women in Russia must contend. States, all of which remain dominated by elite male interests, do not preempt a comprehensive global feminism, but only a kind of pseudofeminism in which they claim to want to protect women, but do nothing to enforce women's rights or transform gender. For those policymakers imagining aggressive campaigns to help women globally, be wary of relying on even well-intentioned states.

What proves most effective at achieving all three global feminist objectives, as well as the larger goal of undermining the sex/gender system, are alliances between global feminists and large donors. In terms of supporting local activism in Russia, the women's crisis center movement developed only with the addition of substantial funding from international development agencies and large charitable foundations that made new commitments to global feminism, including hiring and otherwise including global feminists. Likewise, as demonstrated for the issue of domestic violence in Russia, these alliances were effective at fostering new awareness and state reform. Within a decade, these alliances led to multiple, widespread public awareness campaigns and collaborations with local activists who successfully translated global norms into the Russian vernacular. Unlike the alliance between global feminist and human rights advocates without the addition of substantial funding, these campaigns resulted in increased coverage of the issue in the media, sometimes even reflecting feminist ways of thinking about domestic violence. In turn, opinion leaders such as journalists and local politicians as well as the general population have grown less tolerant of domestic violence. In response to the international attention, several of Russia's regions passed new domestic violence laws, others opened shelters, and yet others developed innovative cross-institutional relationships, such as between the local crisis center and the police. Although awareness and reform are incomplete, this kind of funded intervention has led to significant steps toward the global feminist objectives of mobilization, broader awareness, and policy reform as well as the end goal of undermining the sex/gender hierarchy.

Such funding of NGOs and of other democratizing reforms has come under a lot of criticism by academics recently. The most biting criticism from those concerned about progressive reform is that such funding may contribute to welfare state retrenchment; the new NGOs, especially those providing services that were previously responsibilities of the state, may legitimate less government intervention. The activism and impact of the women's crisis centers in postcommunist Russia demonstrates how foreign-funded NGOs can become much more than instruments of neoliberalism. Although perhaps not the mass-based women's movement imagined by nostalgic Western feminists, the women's crisis center movement represents a successful combination of organization and activism, the kind of organizations that build civil society and deepen democracy. Most activists were not ready to absolve the state of responsibility to address gender violence; instead, they were making powerful arguments for the resumption of some previous state responsibility and the addition of new responsibilities. Especially considering their critique of economic domestic violence, these organizations were charting a middle way between state and market. Moreover, while the international funding had strings attached and perhaps heightened suspicions within the movement, it also provided essential economic resources for a society undergoing massive economic and social dislocation.

Comparing foreign financial assistance to both more and less intrusive interventions illustrates that critics of democracy assistance have overstated their case. Such large-scale funding initiatives can indeed cause all sorts of problems, but supporting democratic and justice-oriented NGOs is the best option available if activists want to promote global change. The essential question to investigate, to which I will return, is how to make these funded interventions successful.

## RUSSIA'S REFORMS IN COMPARISON
## TO THE UNITED STATES

The achievements of global feminist alliances with donors and the Russian women's crisis center movement stand in clearer relief when contrasted with the United States. In the mid-1990s, a common refrain of the Russian activists was that Russia was some twenty to thirty years behind the United States in terms of activism, awareness, and policy responsiveness. They were right in that U.S. gender violence activism began by the early 1970s, and certainly Russia has a long way to go to provide even the level of responsiveness in the United States. However, it took the United States more than two decades to pass national legislation addressing violence against women, the 1994 Violence Against Women Act. Although the act has now been reauthorized twice, in 2000 and 2005, the most radical element, the allowance of a federal civil remedy, was quickly struck down by the Supreme Court. The Supreme Court also denies that there exists constitutional responsibility to protect women (and even children) from family violence, even if there is a protection order in place (Jones 2000).[1] Further, concern about domestic violence has become de-radicalized, an issue of protecting the neotraditional family for conservatives and a reputation booster for companies such as Philip Morris/Altria. Many U.S. activists have also grown concerned about the consequences, especially for women of color, of requiring arrest and of depending on the criminal justice system. High-profile rape cases reveal that the United States too has lingering beliefs about certain men's entitlement to sex and lingering skepticism about actual claims of gender violence. Even on the issue of trafficking, controlling for population differences, U.S. law enforcement has been prosecuting approximately only the same number of cases as in Russia, where the criminal justice system remains, by and large, corrupt and ineffective (Tiuriukanova 2006, 79).[2]

At a time of prosperity and stability, the U.S. government made no other significant domestic institutional or policy reforms, instead focusing its attention only on women abroad. With no domestically focused, high-level women's agencies within the federal government, the State Department's Office of International Women's Issues has monopolized claims to be helping (foreign) women. In late 2007, the International Violence Against Women Act was introduced into Congress to provide billions of dollars to address gender violence globally and to create new offices in the State Department and USAID. Although this legislation, if passed, may provide some useful assistance, the insertion of the U.S. interest abroad is undermined by its recent history of the "global gag rule" (banning foreign NGOs from receiving U.S. funds if they also perform or discuss abortion), the antiprostitution pledge (a similar ban for those foreign NGOs who consider the option of legalizing prostitution), and the denunciation of contraception in the otherwise generous global donation to address HIV infections. These interventions asserting gender neo-traditionalism come on top of a U.S. war in Iraq seen by many in the world as an unlawful use of U.S. force.

## WHY ISSUE DIFFERENCES ARE NOT IMPORTANT HERE

The book's argument also rests on an assumption that the issues of sexual assault, domestic violence, and trafficking in women have similar enough politics that the differences are not causally important. Perhaps they are different. Perhaps women who have been battered make more appealing claimants to donors and human rights advocates than victims of sexual violence, especially the ones who have chosen to travel abroad to engage in the sex industry but end up coerced. Granting women the right and the economic and social support to opt out of violent intimate relationships may be more easily incorporated into societal norms than addressing sexual violence. Interest in funding anti-domestic violence initiatives, in a world where activists have succeeded in transforming battery from a private to a public concern, might also reflect the new trend of targeted consumerism as activism and might leave donors and human rights advocates less interested in sexual assault. In the specific context of Russia, Sundstrom (2006, ch. 3) argues that foreign assistance was more successful on the issue of domestic violence than employment discrimination and sexual harassment precisely because domestic violence could be framed in terms of bodily harm. In the language of social movement theorists, this framing was more resonant with Russian culture and society because it was universal.

Moreover, perhaps fully remedying sexual assault is a more radical undertaking than eliminating domestic violence as a systemic problem. It would require constituting a system and culture that recognizes women's sexual autonomy and validates women's rights to sexual pleasure. This is a monumental shift as even societies often seen as most progressive on this issue, including the United States, resist giving women the right and the opportunity to choose freely whether and when to be sexually intimate with another person (Schulhofer 1998; Zippel 2006). Finally, trafficking in women in some ways is such a different kind of issue because it invokes more directly notions of state sovereignty and security, especially in the post–9/11 world.

Though I acknowledge these differences in the issues at a theoretical level, there is little evidence of their importance here. Sexual assault was the first issue that interveners took up in Russia and, despite some flux in global interest, remains a central component of the global critique of gender violence, for example as illustrated in a recent U.N. report on violence against women (see U.N. Secretary General 2006). Other forms of sexual violence, especially female genital mutilation and sex trafficking, have captured much international attention and resources in the 1990s and 2000s. Much like the campaign against domestic violence, all these campaigns, at one time or another, have been driven by concerns other than realizing women's full sexual autonomy.

More significantly, Russia's gender violence politics is not at the stage of granting women's full autonomy, but at an earlier stage of recognizing that gender violence constitutes bodily harm, a violation of women's right to bodily integrity. The politics of institutionalizing a norm of bodily integrity for these gender violence issues is mostly the same. In contrast to Sundstrom (2006), the analysis in chapter 4 shows that sexual harassment too is primarily cast by activists as an issue of bodily harm because of Russia's history of regulating sexual harassment as a violent crime. Overall, since these gender violence issues operate in mostly the same way in this period of Russia's history, the assumption of similarity is warranted.

## HOW AND WHEN FUNDING CAN WORK

A brief comparative analysis of other similar interventions on the issue of domestic violence in formerly communist countries in East and Central Europe and the former Soviet Union highlights how and why funding of gender violence activism worked in Russia. Most states in the region had experienced some intervention, and by 2006, most had passed some kind of domestic violence reform (Johnson and Brunell 2006; Brunell and Johnson 2007).

First, funding was targeted to an issue in which there was local interest, not just interest among international organizations and donors. Even before the direct interventions, several key Russian feminists in several large cities had been growing concerned about gender violence, and other activists were quickly mobilized because the problem of domestic violence was conspicuous in early post-Soviet Russia. In Armenia, Ukraine, and Moldova, by contrast, interest in the domestic violence issue was mostly an external imposition embraced by strategic women's organizations who had little commitment to global feminist objectives (Hrycak 2006; Johnson 2007b). Funding to these organizations, like other civil society funding going into post-Soviet states, bolstered already existing patronage networks.

Second, both transnational and local activists were included in the design and implementation of the intervention into Russia's domestic violence politics. The same was true of Bulgaria, which, as of 2006, was the first to adopt the region's most progressive reform, a protection order (Johnson and Brunell 2006).[3] Although the opportunity for reform was created by Bulgaria's desire to meet requirements for EU membership, the extensiveness of the reform was a result of tireless local activism, the appropriation and translation of a Minnesota law, and support from the Minnesota Advocates for Human Rights (MAHR). As in

Russia, the distribution of funding to combat domestic violence in Russia was bolstered by an unusually inclusive relationship with local activists, the result of MAHR's commitment to inclusion. In Russia, the relationship between transnational and local was perhaps more balanced (vis-à-vis the West) than elsewhere because activists could benefit from Russia's former superpower status. The norms of inclusivity that fostered the transnational movement against gender violence (Weldon 2006) were successfully translated by transnational feminists into the intervention process.

Third, interest and funding into Russia's domestic violence politics was sustained over more than a decade. The relationships built between some women's crisis center leaders and donors meant, in essence, multiyear and predictable funding for some key organizations until recently. Funding allowed these organizations to grow in ways that many other women's organizations could not. In the Czech Republic, activism was also stimulated by global feminist interest in gender violence combined with an infusion of financial support, leading to the creation of at least five crisis centers networked into WAVE, the European transnational feminist network (Johnson and Brunell 2006). Reforms, consisting of a national training program for police officers and a law reclassifying violence in the home as a criminal offense, were passed in 2002 and 2003 after a campaign facilitated by the Women's Network Program of the Open Society Institute. However, as the Czech Republic improved its economy and as donor interest shifted elsewhere, Czech organizations lost the financial support essential to pursuing more substantial reforms and activism waned. Even this wealthier society, where per capita income is two times more than in Russia,[4] lacked the necessary infrastructure, wealth, and cultural commitments to nourish feminist mobilization.

Fourth, Russia retained enough sovereignty that it did not give in to international pressure to pass symbolic legislation on domestic violence. In contrast, in those countries hoping to gain EU membership in 2004 or 2007, new policies on domestic violence were an easy signal of the requested gender-equality commitments. Yet, the EU's new gender-mainstreaming approach—and the lower status of gender issues in the process of harmonization of local laws with EU law—has meant that superficial changes were often sufficient for real change (Krizsan, Paantjens, and van Lamoen 2005). Although described in English as about "domestic violence," most initiatives employ native-language equivalents of "violence in the family" and—in practice—usually mean only child abuse. Post-Soviet states hoping to establish themselves as civilized, such as Ukraine and Kyrgyz Republic, also passed laws designed to signal commitments to international norms. As in the Global South (Luciano, Esim, and Dubbury 2005), many reforms in the region represent only promises, without the necessary funds to support real change. On the other hand, Russia's sovereignty, allowing it to resist international pressure, meant that there has not been national legislation on domestic violence. Delaying reform in Russia, paradoxically, preserved international and local interest, providing some fodder for continued activism and creating the possibility for meaningful reform. On the issue of trafficking, the more aggressive intervention from the United States' threats of sanctions had the same effect as EU pressure on potential members: leading to mostly symbolic reform but little, if anything, to undermine the sex/gender hierarchy.

## THE ARGUMENT FOR GLOBAL-LOCAL STRUCTURAL FRAMEWORK

In terms of theory, this study demonstrates the analytical power of a global-local structural framework (see table 1.1). These chapters demonstrate that, following the emergence of the global feminist consensus, it is not correct to assume that gender politics is only a domestic process. Russia is a country more sovereign than most and thus not necessarily likely to be influenced by global processes. If even Russia was influenced by foreign intervention, this suggests that, by the mid-1990s, international ideas, organizations, and institutions might also shape the national gender politics in most countries. Domestically centered gender policy analyses, such as feminist comparative policy studies, would do well to make sure to consider the potential impact of extranational institutions.

The global-local framework requires potentially influential structures at all levels, the mechanisms between them, and the direction of impact to be held up for observation. In this Russian study, the primary relationship is one of foreign intervention in which the global has more impact on the local than vice versa. Russia's gender violence politics was not in the shape of Keck and Sikkink's (1998) boomerang, where local organizations draw in international organizations to end-run the state. The pattern was also not the ping pong model found in the EU gender violence policy, where activism and initiatives bounce back and forth between the EU level and the member states (Zippel 2006, 120). At this point, Russia's gender violence politics was more like a game of catch. Global actors (donors, transnational activists, and governments) tossed the ball (funds, norms, diplomacy) at Russia (activists, policymakers, social workers, and law enforcement officials) and waited to see whether Russia would catch or drop the ball or step out of the way. (Sometimes, as in the case of U.S. intervention on the issue of trafficking, the ball was thrown at the catcher's head.) This variation shows that all three of these models are context-, time-, and issue-specific. The global-local structural framework is a reminder to consider the possibility of such variation.

Finally, the framework requires the inclusion of the impact of gender on the process and of the process on gender as a composite of norms, rules, institutions. When policy analyses do not foreground gender as a structural variable, they will miss potentially unsettling consequences and well as mischaracterize the causal mechanisms. In this Russian case, such focus on gender is essential to understanding how and why the Russian polity both resists and accepts some global feminists arguments. It is also essential to recognizing the long-term costs of the antitrafficking intervention predicated on neotraditional notions of gender relations. As this study shows, the assertion of social movement theory that success occurs when norms and models resonate with the local culture is not quite right. The new antitrafficking ideas resonate so much with Russia's resurgent nationalism and gender neotraditionalism that they issue no critique of the underlying problems of gender inequality. As proposed in chapter 2 (see table 2.1), gender analysis should also consider whether initiatives contain any comprehensive feminism opposing sex/gender hierarchies. Many initiatives that are cloaked in feminist language are parafeminist (where gender is not seen as socially constructed) or pseudofeminist (where the initiative is simply designed to address problems typically faced by women).

## RECOMMENDATIONS

The findings of this study lead to the following recommendations for those activists and scholars committed to the ideas of global feminism:

*Global feminists should stay involved.* It is understandable that some Western feminists would prefer to keep their hands clean by not involving themselves with interventions from strong states or even international development agencies. Unfortunately, the costs of this approach can be high for women in the rest of the world. A century after the British claimed to be helping women through colonization, the world is in the midst of a new wave of foreign intervention ostensibly to help women. When global feminists are not included in the process of designing and implementing interventions, the results are likely to be much worse.

*Feminist involvement is especially important for the United States and for anti-trafficking efforts.* It is especially important that those committed to global feminism stay involved in the U.S.'s foreign policy and work to hold the U.S. administration accountable for its claims to promote women's rights, not just protect women. This will be crucial if the U.S. Congress decides to pursue more legislation similar to the Trafficking Victims Protection Act or the International Violence Against Women Act. One strategy would be to call for institutional reform so that independent women's groups have some institutionalized input into the U.S. State Department's Office of International Women's Issues. On the issue of trafficking, in the United States and beyond, it is important that feminists from all sides be involved in the process—and that they allow for disagreement on the issue of prostitution—in order to create an environment for local organizations to consider the options they see best to address the problem. Although some activists will probably balk at this pragmatic approach, this case study suggests the huge costs to feminist activism of imposing this ideological conflict. The messy conflicts between global feminists on trafficking in persons have given states more room to preempt the issue of trafficking.

*Sustained, flexible, and responsive funding can work.* Likewise, although there have been problems with NGO funding, feminist alliances with charitable donors, human rights activists, and intergovernmental organizations can work. Although some observers have been critical of the hierarchies created by long-term funding, such funding, this case shows, can promote change. Women's activists in the postconflict regions, such as the Balkans and the South Caucuses, have been particularly impressed with the Swedish foundation Kvinna till Kvinna. They provide long-term financial support across ethnic, religious, and national affiliations, through partnership with local women's organizations, from the viewpoint that local women's organizations know their own problems best. Until gender violence is eliminated—or at least until postcommunist states and society take full responsibility for eliminating violence against women—support should also available for everyday existence, not just projects.

*The language of human rights has limits.* The language of human rights has become a powerful tool for combating gender injustice and gender violence, especially in industrialized and urban societies such as Russia, where there are no other good alternatives to countering Russian myths about gender violence. However, the language of human rights can be preempted by strong states in the service of "security" and "order," especially when it leans toward discussions of safety and violence. This has become a bigger risk since the September 11, 2001, attacks on the United States. A more democratic approach would be to engage in the language of responsibility, not just rights. Women have rights to live free from violence, and states, men, and other women have responsibilities to prevent violence. The language of women's human rights has the greatest limitations when used to address trafficking in women (Ucarer 1999). This focus has downplayed what appears to be the growing problem of the trafficking in men for labor. The focus also can help hide the global economic inequality that shapes the problem. In more community-based societies, other strategies than human rights, such as collectively shaming abusers, may be more effective. The human rights approach should be seen as one among many strategies for pursuing change.

*Statutory reform is not the be-all and end-all.* There has been much global feminist attention to passing new laws against domestic violence, and many countries have passed legislation. Pushing laws without sufficient mobilization and transformation in the awareness of opinion leaders means that the resulting legislation is often toothless at best. As in Russia, laws on the books do not translate easily into changes in state practice in most countries, a lesson that should have been learned from the unfulfilled promise of Soviet-era commitments to address the woman question. New laws are only a small part of a larger process of reform that activists hope will lead to improved lives for women. States that pass symbolic legislation should not be off the hook, and global feminist resources may be more effective when focused on increasing local mobilization and shifting the public awareness.

*There is a need for more thinking about interventions' impact on marginalized groups.* Perhaps the most underdeveloped aspect of the comparative study of gender politics continues to be the theorizing of marginalized groups such as ethnic, disabled, or queer women, but including these groups is an essential part of the new global feminist consensus's intention to respect autonomous self-organizing (Weldon 2002; 2006). I urge my comparative social scientist colleagues to create more innovative ways to keep in mind all the multiple and intersecting hierarchies across cases and levels of politics. Without this kind of analysis, progressive donors who attempt to reach such groups may, as happened with an EU project on domestic violence among ethnic minorities in Russia, undermine feminist projects and exacerbate racism.

More broadly, this study is a call for detailed empirical study of policy issues with gendered impact. By systematically comparing the impact of interventions, this book demonstrates how such feminist social science can be done. It also shows that this kind of research can produce insights into what initiatives might make things better for women.

# APPENDICES

# WOMEN'S HUMAN RIGHTS AND GENDER VIOLENCE

Documents that are in **boldface** have the status of international law.

| KEY U.N. DOCUMENTS ON WOMEN'S RIGHTS (DATE ADOPTED) | REFERENCES TO | |
|---|---|---|
| | **VIOLENCE AGAINST WOMEN (VAW) OR GENDER VIOLENCE** | **RAPE** |
| **Convention on the Elimination of All Forms of Discrimination against Women (1979)** | — | — |
| Nairobi Forward Looking Strategies for the Advancement of Women (1985) | makes VAW a priority, calls for legal measures and national machineries to address VAW | includes rape as part of VAW |

| SEXUAL HARASSMENT | DOMESTIC VIOLENCE | TRAFFICKING IN WOMEN (OR FORCED PROSTITUTION) |
|---|---|---|
| — | — | **calls for measures "to suppress all forms of traffic in women and exploitation of prostitution of women" (Art. 6)** |
| requires "appropriate measures to prevent sexual harassment on the job or sexual exploitation in specific jobs, such as domestic service" (para. 139, also 287) | calls for<br><br>(1) "domestic violence" to be a priority<br><br>(2) the establishment of "national machinery . . . prevention policies . . . assistance and protection . . . [and the strengthening of] legislative measures [including the provision of] legal aid"<br><br>(3) the mobilization of "community resources to identify, prevent and eliminate . . . family violence . . . and to provide shelter, support, and reorientation services for abused women"<br><br>(4) "measures . . . aimed at making women conscious that maltreatment is . . . a blow to their physical and moral integrity" (paras. 231, 245, 271) | condemns "trafficking in women for the purposes of prostitution" and "involuntary prostitution" understood to result from "economic degradation that alienates women's labour through processes of rapid urbanization and migration resulting in underemployment and unemployment. It also stems from women's dependence on men." (para. 290)<br><br>calls for state and international measures, including (para. 291)<br><br>(1) the provision of "[r]esources for the prevention of prostitution and assistance in the professional, personal and social reintegration of prostitutes . . . providing economic opportunities, including training, employment, self-employment and health facilities for women and children."<br><br>(2) cooperation between governments and NGOs "to create wider employment possibilities for women."<br><br>(3) "[s]trict enforcement provisions . . . to stem the rising tide of violence, drug abuse and crime related to prostitution" (para 291) |

| KEY U.N. DOCUMENTS ON WOMEN'S RIGHTS (DATE ADOPTED) | REFERENCES TO | |
|---|---|---|
| | VIOLENCE AGAINST WOMEN (VAW) OR GENDER VIOLENCE | RAPE |
| CEDAW Committee General Recommendation 12 (1989) | calls for states to include VAW in their CEDAW reports | references "sexual violence" |
| CEDAW Committee General Recommendation 19 (1992) | elaborates on how VAW violates the articles of CEDAW | includes "sexual assault" |
| Vienna Declaration and Programme for Action (1993) | establishes VAW as a violation of human rights and calls for legal measures, national action, and international coordination to eliminate VAW | highlights the "systematic rape of women in war" (sec. I, para. 38) |
| U.N. Declaration on the Elimination of Violence against Women (1993) | as the first U.N. document to do so, elaborates a frame of violence against women: rooted in unequal power between women and men and a key mechanism for subordinating women (preamble) | includes a broad frame of sexual violence, including marital rape |
| Beijing Platform for Action (1995) | established VAW as one of the 12 areas of central concern<br><br>defines VAW as "any act of gender-based violence that results in, or is likely to result in, physical, sexual or psychological harm or suffering to women" (113) | one mention of rape |
| Beijing Declaration on Women (1995) | reaffirms a commitment to VAW and the Declaration on the Elimination of VAW<br><br>first time governments agreed to include VAW as a crucial issue | — |

| SEXUAL HARASSMENT | DOMESTIC VIOLENCE | TRAFFICKING IN WOMEN (OR FORCED PROSTITUTION) |
|---|---|---|
| includes "sexual harassment at the workplace" | includes "abuses in the family" | — |
| includes "sexual harassment in the workplace" as undermining "equality in employment" | "Family violence is one of the most insidious forms of violence against women." | includes "trafficking in women," a form of "sexual exploitation" |
| links "gender-based violence" with "all forms of sexual harassment and exploitation" (sec. I, para. 18) | "stresses the importance of working towards the elimination of violence against women in public and private life" (sec. II, para. 38) | considers "international trafficking" as resulting in "gender-based violence" (sec. I, para. 18) |
| defines sexual harassment as part of VAW (art. 2) | advocates research | includes "trafficking in women and forced prostitution" as part of VAW (art. 2) |
| implied in various references to "violence against women" | implied in various references to "violence against women" | expresses concern about "forced prostitution" of the girl-child |
| — | asserts that a "harmonious partnership" between husbands and wives is essential for the "consolidation of democracy" (para. 15) | — |

| KEY U.N. DOCUMENTS ON WOMEN'S RIGHTS (DATE ADOPTED) | REFERENCES TO | |
| --- | --- | --- |
| | VIOLENCE AGAINST WOMEN (VAW) OR GENDER VIOLENCE | RAPE |
| Optional Protocol to CEDAW (1999) | reaffirms Vienna Declaration and Programme of Action, the Beijing Declaration and Platform for Action,<br><br>allows citizens or groups to bring claims to the CEDAW Committee | — |
| Protocol to Prevent, Suppress and Punish Trafficking in Persons, especially Women and Children (2000) | — | — |

*Note:* Russia ratified CEDAW in 1981 (as the Soviet Union), the Optional Protocol to CEDAW in 2004, and the Trafficking Protocol in 2004.

| SEXUAL HARASSMENT | DOMESTIC VIOLENCE | TRAFFICKING IN WOMEN (OR FORCED PROSTITUTION) |
|---|---|---|
| — | — | — |
| — | — | defines "[t]rafficking in persons [as] the recruitment, transportation, transfer, harbouring or receipt of persons, by means of the threat or use of force or other forms of coercion, of abduction, of fraud, of deception, of the abuse of power or of a position of vulnerability or of the giving or receiving of payments or benefits to achieve the consent of a person having control over another person, for the purpose of exploitation. Exploitation shall include, at a minimum, the exploitation of the prostitution of others or other forms of sexual exploitation, forced labour or services, slavery or practices similar to slavery, servitude or the removal of organs." (Art. 3a)

recommends the three Ps: prevention, protection, and prosecution |

# NOTES ON MEASUREMENT AND METHOD

This appendix provides more detail on the measurements and methods used to quantify mobilization against gender violence in chapter 3 and media attention to gender violence in Russia in chapters 4 through 6.

## *Women's Mobilization against Gender Violence*

Measuring the extent of mobilization against gender violence in Russia is a difficult endeavor. As Weldon (2002, 223–24) discusses in detail, measuring women's mobilization is a challenge even in more established and stable democracies. There is a tendency among scholars to count the number of organizations or the number of activists involved with the organizations to approximate mobilization. This kind of data, if available, facilitates the use of statistical methods. The problem is that mobilization refers to the strength and importance of these organizations, which may or may not relate to the numbers of organizations or individuals. For example, one small organization with a few official members may be very powerful. To get around this problem, Costain (1998) suggests coding accounts of organizational activities in the media. Weldon (2002, 224) measures the public support for the movement "as expressed in public opinion polls, newspaper editorials, number of signatures on petitions, size of demonstrations, behavior of public officials, and so on."

Measuring women's mobilization in Russia creates even more difficulties. As I discuss in chapter 3, NGOs in postcommunist countries have a tendency to emerge and disappear quickly, sometimes because the NGO was simply a mechanism to apply for a grant and other times because the environment was inhospitable. Marc Howard (2003) conducted surveys across the region to get a sense of people's involvement in civil society, but his was a question about the strength of civil society as a whole. The number of activists in the women's crisis centers is so small that such a survey would be impractical. Moreover, Russia did not participate in the largest survey of NGOs, the Johns Hopkins Comparative Nonprofit Sector Project (Kaldor, Anheier, and Glasius 2003, 359).

In a study that also looks at foreign intervention into Russia's NGO sector, Sundstrom (2006, appendix 5) uses both the number of officially registered NGOs and estimates by local NGO resource centers. She recognizes that the official estimates include inactive organizations and exclude those that have not officially registered, an onerous process in Russia. She adds the experts from the local NGO resource to provide a more accurate figure and acknowledges that these estimates may vary across region, not just because of different numbers of organizations, but also because of the different degrees of knowledge of these resource centers.

This kind of triangulation and recognition of biases seems the best that is reasonably possible to do in Russia at this time.

My approach here is to give both conservative and generous estimates of the number of organizations working against gender violence (see table 3.1). These estimates are based on fieldwork and third-party lists of gender violence organizations in Russia from donors, transnational feminist networks, human rights advocates, and Russian umbrella organizations concerned about gender violence. The lists I used were the following:

1. Founding members of the Russian Association of Crisis Centers for Women (RACCW), 1994
2. RACCW members, 1995
3. Participants in a Russian lawyer project for women's crisis centers of Women, Law, and Development International, 1997
4. Organizations that self-identified as working on violence against women in a 1998 directory of women's NGOs in Russia (Abubikirova, Klimenkova, Kotchkina, Regentova, and Troinova 1998, 9)
5. Organizations receiving funds from the United States Agency for International Development (USAID) through the International Research and Exchange Board (IREX) project to aid women's crisis centers in Russia, 1999
6. Organizations receiving USAID funds through the IREX project to aid women's crisis centers in Russia, 2000
7. RACCW members, 2000
8. Organizations working with USAID's Trafficking and Information Dissemination Project, 2001–2004
9. Organizations working with USAID's Trafficking Prevention Project in the Russian Far East and Siberia, 2001–2004 (Some organizations on this list were not included because there was incomplete information or because they were U.S. organizations.)
10. Network for Crisis Centres for Women in the Barents Region, 2003
11. Women against Violence Europe, 2003
12. ANNA Information Network, 2004
13. RACCW members, 2004
14. Angel Coalition, 2004
15. Directory of Russian organizations concerned about trafficking in persons from the American Bar Association Central and Eurasian Law Initiative, 2004
16. List of women's crisis centers in Russia from the Open Society Institute, 2007

I rejected lists that did not seem credible, such as a 2004 list from UNIFEM of organizations working as part of its campaign against gender violence. I found that there was almost no overlap with any of the other lists, and when I contacted a random sample, I discovered that the organizations did not really exist or that the organizations had no experience with this kind of activism. With my research assistant, Gulnara Zaynullina, I compiled a master list of all organizations found on these various lists, making note of which and how many lists each organization was on. We also identified the organizations by region, using the eighty-nine regions that existed in Russia up in 2004.

As elaborated in chapter 3, the conservative estimates are based on fieldwork and on several of the lists that I knew from fieldwork included only organizations that were comprehensive women's crisis centers, engaged in providing assistance to individuals and in broader advocacy, that had links to global feminist ideas. The master list of organizations allowed me to gauge the organizations' longevity, links with other organizations, fundability, and issue orientation as well as the movement's geographical distribution. As I describe in chapter 3, I use several of these larger lists for the generous estimates of the number of organizations working against gender violence in Russia. For the full data set, please contact the author.

## Media Coverage of Gender Violence

To provide a quantifiable measure of the impact of the new politics of gender violence on Russian society, I conducted a content analysis of the print media. The Soviet legacy of using the media as mechanisms of propaganda meant not only that Soviet citizens had the literacy to read newspapers and magazines, but that they turned to these media for information. During the height of Gorbachev's glasnost, the communist-era newspapers that had been charged with reporting only the official "truths" were liberated. They began publishing exposés of social problems and discussions of the taboos of Soviet history, greatly expanding their readership as most Russian citizens became engrossed in these newly possible conversations. The inflation of the early 1990s, however, brought an end to the romantic period of print journalism as the price of newspapers, without advertising, became prohibitive. The Russian public, in general, turned to the television for their news. In an era of decreasing circulation of Russian newspapers, newspaper coverage reflects consciousness among intellectual elites and opinion leaders more than widespread public consciousness of the problem.

Content analysis within political science is typically a quantitative analysis that "relies upon the scientific method, including an observance of the standards of objectivity/inter-subjectivity, a priori research design, reliability, validity generalizability (with probability sampling from a defined population of messages), replicability, and hypothesis testing" (Neuendorf 2004, 33). It has become a methodologically sophisticated process, but in this project, I use a simple content analysis, employing the "bread and butter" of content analysis, the counting of manifest characteristics, to bolster the other methods of the book, including ethnography and discourse analysis. In other words, while accepting the primary assumption of discourse analysis—that reality is produced—I sought quantifiable measures for shifts in social reality. This requires a relaxation of the positivist assumptions of content analysis as well as a relaxation in the claims of discourse analysis that words have no stable meaning (Hardy, Harley, and Phillips 2004). Investigating gender politics, which shift reality, but which have increasingly been subject to positivist analysis, requires methodological eclecticism.

The content analysis was conducted using databases available from East View Information Services (www.eastview.com). In specific, I used three databases: (1) Central Newspapers, which includes over fifty daily and weekly newspaper of national importance, (2) Regional Newspapers, which covers papers and editions from across Russia, and (3) Russian/NIS Newswires, which covers the wire service bulletins and includes only one non-Russian newswire (for more details about these databases, see http://online.eastview.com/login_russia/index.jsp). The search, with assistance from Gulnara Zaynullina, was first conducted in June–July of 2004 and then updated in 2006. The raw quantitative data is available upon request from the author.

We took terminology found in use by activists and searched for the number of articles in which the various terms appeared. As Russian declines its nouns, we used wildcards to represent the endings. Since the databases include prominent English-language newspapers, such as the *Moscow Times,* we included English language terminology. This broader search proved somewhat problematic as articles could be republished in different versions of the national newspaper or reprinted in regional newspapers. For the most part, I decided that these represented additional usage, in the sense that the regional newspapers chose to reprint the article. Other times, when the repeat was not meaningful—as when a television listing for the musical *Chicago* including "spousal violence" (search term: супружеск* /1 насили*) ran for two weeks—the repeated publications were eliminated. This analysis gives a sense of the relative frequency of the uses of different terms and a general sense of the salience of the issues.

As these databases added new sources over time, they could not be used to estimate the change over time in the references to gender violence. I turned to the newspaper *Izvestiia* [News] for the data represented in tables 4.2, 4.3, 5.2, and 6.2. This long-running, high-circulation, national daily newspaper had been one of the few included in the databases from the early 1990s. And, although *Izvestiia* had been the mouthpiece of the Soviet government, after being privatized in 1992, the paper emerged as a fairly reliable source of information. Into the new century, the paper stayed somewhat critical of the Putin administration even as most other media had self-censored themselves as a result of his campaign to wield control over the mass media. For example, in 2004, during the hostage crisis in Beslan, which was bungled tragically by the Russian authorities, *Izvestiia* published a controversial photo that contradicted the administration's line. In 2005, state-controlled gas giant Gazprom bought a controlling interest in *Izvestiia*, suggesting that the paper will cease to be credible as an independent source of news. To estimate the amount of media attention to gender violence over time, I used *Izvestiia* from 1994 up through 2005, conducting the same kind of terminological searches described above.

# NOTES

## 1. Introduction

1. Nataliia Ivanovna Abubikirova (executive director, Association of Crisis Centers for Women "Stop Violence"), interview by the author, Moscow, July 23, 2004.
2. In Mazur's (2002, 158) review of several European cases, she argues that extranational institutions were important mostly for getting the problem defined and on the agenda (especially for the issue of trafficking in women), but the case studies themselves do not examine how these international pressures work.
3. U.S. Department of State, "About International Women's Issues," http://www.state.gov/g/wi/c21438.htm (accessed February 6, 2008).
4. Financial resources are especially important in poorer societies such as Russia because there is little money available and often poor financial infrastructure, limiting organizations in doing "basic" things like mailing flyers or soliciting donations (Sperling 1999).
5. Initiated in 1991 by Rutgers University's Women Global Leadership Institute, the annual period of activism symbolically links gender violence with human rights advocacy. Thousands of organizations in hundreds of countries have participated, an illustration of transnational cooperation between different women's groups across the global divides.
6. Note that these distinctions are about the global level, not the local, which is the arena theorized by feminist comparative policy. The original matrix in Stetson (2002) refers to the domestic policy-process.

## 2. The Global Feminist Challenge, Communism, and Postcommunism

1. Personal communication with Debra Liebowitz, April 9, 2007.
2. Minnesota Advocates for Human Rights (hereafter MAHR), "Women's Program," http://www.mnadvocates.org/Women_s_Program.html (accessed June 28, 2006).
3. The English-language website is http://www.stopvaw.org and the Russian http://www.russian.stopvaw.org.

4. MAHR, "Stop Violence Against Women," 2003, http://www.stopvaw.org/Stop _Violence_Against_Women.html (accessed June 28, 2006).

5. Rape was defined as "sexual intercourse with the application of physical force or threats or taking advantage of the helpless state of the victim" (Art. 117 1960 RSFSR CrC). Conviction rates for rape were about 90%, higher than the average for most crimes (Danilenko and Burnham 1999). In 1990, 54% of adult convicted rapists were sentenced to between five and ten years (D'iachenko and Koloskova 1995, 84). Another 33.9% were sentenced to three to five years. The average sentence in 1990 was 7.5 years, slightly higher than the average sentence for imprisonment for all crimes (7.4). From 1990 through 1993, approximately one rapist a year was sentenced to die.

6. A 1923 decree established that it was a crime to take advantage of a woman's dependent position to compel her to have "sexual relations." The 1960 RSFSR CrC made this crime clearly separate from rape, under Article 118. In her genealogy of sexual harassment in Russia, Suchland (2005) shows that behaviors global feminists now consider sexual harassment have been forbidden in Russian law since at least the nineteenth century, initially as "crimes against the honor and chastity of women."

7. Andrei Sinelnikov, *Russia: Inside the Broken Cell,* 2004, Family Violence Prevention Fund, http://www.endabuse.org/programs/display.php3?DocID=106 (accessed May 28, 2004).

8. This way of disaggregating feminism was inspired by Robinson 1995.

9. Iuliia Isaeva, interview with the author, Saratov, Russia, June 24, 1999.

10. Local precincts are encouraged by the Ministry of Internal Affairs to report lower levels of crime and high prosecution rates, creating incentives to reject statements. In addition, corruption proliferates in the institutions of the police and procuracy, the Russian supercharged prosecutor's office (Human Rights Watch 1999). In the 1990s, the problem was so bad that, in many places, Russians did not even consider turning to the police for most problems.

11. See Human Rights Watch (1997, 22). The stats are from liberal Moscow-based weekly *Argumenty i Facty.* Reported in *World Press Review,* the original article was "The Rape Game," February 6, 1996.

12. According to Khodyreva (1996), one of the most prominent popular myths about rape in Russia is that "rape is mostly an act between an assaulter and a victim who were not acquainted before. Marital rape is still a topic absolutely not developed" (34). Another Russian researcher notes that "in public consciousness rape and domestic violence against women are the only crimes in which victims are held responsible for crimes committed against them" (Booklet: Syostri [2002] *Metodicheskoe Posobie: Pomoshch' Perezhivshim seksual'noe nasilie* [Moscow: Syostri]).

13. These numbers are from *Prestupnost' i Pravonarusheniia Statisticheskii Sbornik* [Crime and Delinquency: Statistical Review], Ministry of Internal Affairs of the Russian Federation, Ministry of Justice of the Russian Federation, Inter-governmental Statistical Committee of the Commonwealth of Independent State, Moscow, 1996, 2000, and 2001.

14. Council of Europe, *European Sourcebook of Crime and Criminal Justice Statistics,*

http://www.europeansourcebook.org/esb/index.html 1999 (accessed October 7, 2004).

15. Sophie Lambroschini. March 7, 2001. Russia: Domestic Violence Persists. *RFE/RL Newsline.*

16. Of course, fear of rape does not necessarily reflect the prevalence of rape. Fear of this kind of violent and gang rape was part of the morality-based education on women's bodies and sexuality (Rivkin-Fish 2005).

17. In 1994, it was reported that one new sexual harassment case using Art. 118 of the RSFSR 1960 CrC was being pursued in the Siberian city of Barnaul, but was dropped as part of a general amnesty (Alessandra Stanley, April 16, 1994, "Sexual Harassment Thrives in the New Russian Climate," *New York Times,* p. 1). All activists, scholars, and lawyers with whom I discussed this agreed that the statute had been rarely, if ever, used. In her dissertation on sexual harassment, Jennifer Suchland (2005) comes to a similar conclusion.

18. Tat'iana Maksimova, 1999, "And They Show Our Girls into the Office," *Business Tuesday, Weekly Supplement to Trud,* translated and reprinted in *Current Digest* 51, no. 18: 15.

19. These range from less grievous physical injury (Arts. 115–16 1996, Russian Federation [RF] CrC) to "grave harm to health" (Arts. 111–13), torture (Art. 117), murder (Art. 105), kidnapping (Arts. 126, 127), threats of harm or homicide (Art. 119), and property damage (Art. 167). Other potentially relevant aticles include provisions against private or public insults (Art. 130), sexual violence (Arts. 131, 132), incitement to suicide (Art. 110), self-defense in homicide (e.g. Art. 37, 108), and the establishment of criminal responsibility while intoxicated (Art. 23).

20. "Dwelling quarters are inviolable. No one has the right to enter dwelling quarters against the will of the residents" (Art. 25, 1993 Russian Constitution).

21. This argument is based on a distinction made in the criminal procedural code (RSFSR CrPC Art. 27) between *publicly* and *privately* prosecutable crimes. Less severe assault (Arts. 115 and 116 of the 1996 RF CrC) is only privately prosecutable. They are the only articles that could cover domestic violence that do not stipulate years in prison. The punishments available are fines, obligatory or correctional tasks, or brief arrest. The criminal procedural code also allows the procuracy to terminate the investigation if the victim reconciles with the abuser.

22. The RF Housing Code (Art. 98) allows for the eviction of a tenant of a state-owned apartment when a person continues to behave inhospitably, but it was not typically being used this way. There is no provision for eviction of a tenant from private housing; however, the constitutional provision on housing (Art. 25) suggests that judges could evict for a reasonable cause such as using violence against other residents.

23. According to the law, neither provocation nor being drunk exculpates the accused. Article 113 of 1996 RF CrC establishes punishment for battery even when the batterer is agitated (e.g., living through a long-term stressful situation) or provoked by a victim's mockery, insult, or unlawful or immoral behavior. However, the punishment for battery "in [such] a state of temporary insanity" is less than two years, while if the same act was committed while "sane," the punishment could be up to fifteen years.

24. Art. 6.11 in RF Administrative Code; art. 210 in the 1960 RSFSR Administrative Code.
25. Zoia Khotkina, interview by the author, Moscow, September 27, 2005.
26. See Tiuriukanova and Erokhina 2002 and the yearly U.S. State Department reports on trafficking (from 2001).
27. Zoia Khotkina, interview by the author, Moscow, September 27, 2005.
28. Inter-Parliamentary Union, "Women in Parliaments: World Classification," http://www.ipu.org/wmn-e/classif.htm (accessed August 17, 2006). The United States has 15.2% in its House of Representatives.
29. Women who were wayward or failed to carry out the necessary chores were to be "instructed." For the worst offenses, women were to be lashed on bare skin, albeit "without anger" (Levin 1989, 238). The *Domostroi* also advocated isolating women from social contacts, depriving them even of the moral authority of choosing when to go to church. Nevertheless, only husbands and fathers (not fathers-in-law or brothers-in-law) were allowed to "instruct" women.
30. Yaroslava Krestovskaya, "Condoleezza Rice's Anti-Russian Stance Based on Sexual Problems," *Pravda,* January 11, 2006, http://english.pravda.ru/printed.html?news_id=16724 (accessed January 17, 2006).
31. Alice Lagnado (2002), untitled article, *The Times,* April 6.
32. According to Sperling (1999, 106), the first forum was announced by the popular newspaper *Moskovski komsomolets* as a "gathering of overexcited lesbians," driving the Dubna city officials initially to withdraw permission for the event. See also Racioppi and See (1997, especially ch. 6) and Kay (2000, especially 174–76).
33. Some 31 of the 89 regions included similar entities in 2002–2003 (Duban 2006), 37.

### 3. The Women's Crisis Center Movement

1. This was part of the "Victims of Trafficking and Violence Protection Act of 2000" (114 STAT. 1464 PUBLIC LAW 106–386—October 28, 2000, 106th Congress), http://www.state.gov/documents/organization/10492.pdf (accessed February 3, 2006).
2. In the United States, some feminist groups took the opportunity, creating a "feminist-evangelical alliance" (Nina Shapiro, August 25, 2004, "The New Abolitionists," *Seattle Weekly,* p. 22), but this alliance has become one-sided. For background on this evangelical-feminist alliance, see also Francoise Girard, "Global Implications of U.S. Domestic and International Policies on Sexuality," IWGSSP Working Papers, No. 1, June 2004, Columbia University Mainman School of Public Health, http://www.healthsciences.columbia.edu/dept/sph/cgsh.html (accessed January 5, 2005).
3. In their study of such mobilization in St. Petersburg, Brygalina and Temkina (2004) periodize in the following way: preliminary phase, 1985–91; emergence, 1991–95; institutionalization, 1995–2000; and transformation, 2000–2002.
4. Nadezhda Kuznetsova, interview by the author, Saratov, Russia, June 24, 1999.
5. At this point, RACCW was an informal organization, that is, unregistered with the Ministry of Justice (registration was a politicized and often fraught process). When the RACCW registered in 1999 (with 35 centers), they were compelled to

alter their name. As of 1999, the formal name is the Association Stop Violence, but for the sake of simplicity and continuity with other English-language studies, I use RACCW throughout.

6. RACCW, 1995, "Report to the NGO Forum of the Fourth United Nations World Conference on Women in Beijing: Violence Against Women in Russia: Research, Education, and Advocacy Project," Moscow, Russia.

7. Marina Mironova, interview by the author, Moscow, June 23, 1997.

8. Irina Khaldeeva, interview by the author, Saratov, Russia, June 22, 1999.

9. Marina Aristova (founder of a municipal shelter in St. Petersburg), interview by the author, October 3, 2005.

10. Gabrielle Fitchett, interviews by the author, Moscow, July 7, 1997; March 25, 1999.

11. RACCW, 1995, "Report to the NGO Forum of the Fourth United Nations World Conference on Women in Beijing: Violence Against Women in Russia: Research, Education, and Advocacy Project," Moscow, 14.

12. In 1994, the consortium distributed almost $100,000 for "seed grants" to women's NGOs, including to some women's crisis centers, while others became members (Nechemias 2001). St. Petersburg Crisis Center, Syostri, and Yaroslavna all received support from the consortium.

13. Pashina (2004, 23) argues that a new understanding of violence against women— and of how to respond—emerged "[t]hrough contacts with the activists from the West and learning about women's projects in Germany (Fun Fauen-Anstiftung), the United States (Winrock International), Canada (Vancouver Rape Crisis Centre)." Northwestern Russian scholar-activists wrote simply, "Originally the idea of a crisis centre was taken from the West" (Liapounova and Drachova 2004, 64). A Moscow-based leading academic involved in founding ANNA describes the crisis center in Ventura, Calif., as her model (Rimasheevskaia 2005).

14. Marina Aristova, interview by the author, Moscow, October 3, 2005.

15. Mariia Regentova, interview by the author, Moscow, July 8, 2002.

16. Nataliia Sereda, interview by the author, Barnaul, Russia, July 1, 2002.

17. Elena Shitova [Schitova], 2002, "Women's Alliance," *Bradley Herald,* 1, 7, Washington, D.C.: Bureau of Education and Cultural Affairs, U.S. State Department.

18. When I was there in the summer of 2002, Sereda and her husband worked 14-hour days (even on the day after our red-eye flight from Moscow), meeting with women seeking assistance, supporting other activists, including some women from the region who wanted to found their own crisis center, and cajoling law enforcement agencies to take domestic and sexual violence seriously (and not to blame the victim). In 2002, reflecting her commitment and skills, Sereda was elected vice president of RACCW.

19. The Altai Crisis Center for Men established a parallel, overlapping organization, Men's Conversation, to facilitate this.

20. Nataliia Sereda (interview by the author, Barnaul, Russia, July 1, 2002) argued that the availability of funds greatly facilitated the dialogue she was able to open with local leaders because of the pressure from transnational activism and foreign assistance. As Laurie Essig (1999) found for queer activists in Russia, "relationships of power go both ways and . . . Russians are not just victims of

American colonizing tendencies, but the beneficiaries as well. . . . Russians are appropriated by Westerners, and . . . Russians reappropriate those appropriations for their own purposes" (127).

21. Pam Brunson (program director of Opora), 2005. Telephone conversation, September 26.

22. Svetlana Yakimenko (NIS director of Project Kesher), interview by Elisabeth Duban (ABA-CEELI), Moscow, April 6, 2005. With support from Open Society, Project Kesher took place in the 2002 16 days' campaign against gender violence. This followed a 2000–2002 U.S. State Department–funded project with other Jewish international organizations.

23. Results of the broader survey, including Sweden, Finland, and Norway, are reported on in Saarinen, Liapounova, and Drachova 2003a.

24. For the most part, until 1998, Russian women's organizations were supported by small grants, from individuals or small organizations, mostly short term, and often based on meeting with transnational feminists. For example, the major funders of Syostri through 1997 were the All-World Women's Fund, Women of the Methodist Church, Canadian Embassy in Moscow, International Women's Club in Moscow, a women's shelter in Santa Monica, California, women at a hotline in Berlin, a German television company, and other Western individuals. The funding available in early to mid-1990s from the Consortium of Women's Nongovernmental Organizations was the first sign of what would become available and the potential pitfalls (Hrycak 2002).

25. USAID contracted with the U.S. nonprofit the International Research and Exchanges Board (IREX) to distribute the funds. The 1999 USAID call for proposals identified the program in the following way: "These programs raise awareness of domestic violence issues, at the core targeting law enforcement officials. They bring together social workers, crisis center activists, lawmakers, health workers and law enforcement professionals. The programs are being carried out in different localities in Russia and the U.S. to increase interaction in a multi-disciplinary approach to the problem of domestic violence" (e-mail: Center for Civil Society International ccsi@u.washington.edu; Columbia Law School, "Call for Proposals from U.S. NGOs: Program to Support Crisis Centers for Women in the Russian Federation," February 19, 1999, *Public Interest Law Initiative,* http://www.pili.org/lists/piln/archives/msg00316.html [accessed February 16, 2005]).

26. Other important funders included the Open Society Institute, the British Know How Fund, and the EU's postcommunist transition Tacis program. For more information on Tacis, which required European partners, see European Union, "Tacis: Overview," *External Relations,* http://europa.eu.int/comm/external_relations/ceeca/tacis/ (accessed January 30, 2006).

27. In total, this project (up to 2002) was supported through 15 grants, from various Nordic and EU sources, totaling €363,078 (Saarinen, Liapounova, and Drachova 2003b).

28. According to one Russian observer (Khodyreva 2004), in contrast to the American and British donors, the Nordic interveners understood that Russian centers would work differently than Western ones, but that they also needed start-up support. Transnational feminist networks, with their horizontal

structure, can treat all organizations as the same even though the global system of inequality clearly leads to different kinds and amounts of resources. At the same time, the leaders worked hard to foster a model of horizontal sharing across the region (Saarinen 2004).

29. European Union, "Tacis IBPP 2001: Project overview," *Programs and Projects,* 2001, http://europa.eu.int/comm/europeaid/projects/ibpp/downloads/2001_selected_projects_russia.pdf (accessed February 13, 2006).

30. See Iuliia Kachalova, "Rezul'taty proekta po razvitiiu v Rossii seti podderzhki dlia zhenshchin, postradavshikh ot nasiliia" [Results of the project on the development of a support network for women suffering from violence in Russia], Fund "Focus," http://www.crisis.ipd.ru/articles/manual/conference-7.shtml (accessed February 13, 2006).

31. In 2001, USAID put out an appeal for an intermediary organization to distribute another round of grants to women's crisis centers, and several key players applied; but without much explanation, in 2002 USAID decided to not to fund any, in essence ceasing its work on domestic violence except through other democracy assistance programs. Inna Loukovenko (chief of NGO Support Program Unit, USAID), interview by the author, June 28, 2002.

32. By 2002, some rich Russians and their businesses were donating some of their wealth, but not usually to NGOs (and even less likely to feminist organizations). Because of the NGO boom in the 1990s in which some NGOs deceived their Russian donors, private businesses—even in this time of relative economic prosperity—were replacing financial donations in favor of high-profile one-time donations in kind (e.g., a wheelchair for a disabled person). The exception was the oil baron Khodorkovksy, who set up his version of Georges Soros's Open Society, Open Russia, which did fund some women's organizations, but not crisis centers. In the women's crisis center movement, I heard of some Russian donations, such as to the Moscow-based crisis center Yaroslavna, but these grants came from personal connections and were small. Yaroslavna's grant came from a businessman whose friend had received crisis services from Yaroslavna (Al'bina Pashina, interview by the author, Moscow, July 15, 2004). The new priority of sustainability was also at cross-purposes with a late 1990s attempt to spread funding more fairly across organizations and out into the regions.

33. These funds were distributed by IREX as USAID's subcontractor. IREX, "Trafficking Prevention and Information Dissemination (TPID)," *Civil Society,* 2004, http://www.irex.org/programs/tpid/index.asp (accessed September 15, 2004). The program support was substantial. For example, in 2003, IREX received $235,000 for this project. U.S. Department of State, "The U.S. Government's International Anti-Trafficking Programs: Fiscal Year 2003," 2004, http://www.state.gov/g/tip/rls/rpt/34182.htm#eur (accessed September 15, 2004).

34. The goals of the project were to strengthen these centers' focus on trafficking, offer professional training to women in high-risk areas, offer social services to "victim-returnees," and raise awareness of the problem through NGOs and local leaders. IREX, "Prevention of Trafficking in Women and Girls Program," 2004, http://www.irex.org/programs/completed/anti-trafficking/index.asp (accessed September 23, 2004). See also U.S. Department of State, "The U.S. Government's International Anti-trafficking Programs: Fiscal Year 2002," 2003,

http://www.state.gov/g/tip/rls/rpt/17858.htm#eurasia (accessed October 13, 2006). When I visited Barnaul in 2002, I found that they had published and distributed many pamphlets and brochures on trafficking and were beginning to counsel women on the phone who were considering working abroad.

35. "The activity also includes conducting a baseline research to study the demographics of women at risk and applying research results for designing future trafficking prevention programs" (Winrock International's collaboration with women's organizations, Trafficking Prevention Project, described on U.S. Department of State, "The U.S. Government's International Anti-trafficking Programs: Fiscal Year 2002," 2003, http://www.state.gov/g/tip/rls/rpt/17858.htm# eurasia [accessed October 13, 2006]). A similar USAID program was administered by Winrock International, Trafficking Prevention Project, Russian Far East and Siberia, from 2001 to 2004 (for more information, see the Winrock website at http://www.winrock.org).

36. U.S. Department of State, "The U.S. Government's International Anti-trafficking Programs: Fiscal Year 2002," 2003, http://www.state.gov/g/tip/rls/rpt/34182.htm#eur (accessed October 13, 2006). The grant was $19,930.

37. In 2003, this was to the tune of $794,662, approximately one-third of which went to women's crisis centers. Ibid.

38. Juliette Engel (founding director, MiraMed Institute and Angel Coalition), interview by the author, Moscow, July 27, 2004.

39. Angel Coalition, "Members," http://www.angelcoalition.org/members.html (accessed August 3, 2004).

40. Angel Coalition, "History and Mission," 2004, http://www.angelcoalition.org/history.html (accessed September 16, 2004).

41. Also included is the Moscow Project Kesher.

42. Juliette Engel. 2004. "Report to the Office to Monitor and Combat Trafficking in Persons, International Organization of Migration, Moscow—The Russian Project: Assisting Victims to and from the Russian Federation (Year One Final Report)." MiraMed, Moscow.

43. Donna Hughes, "Prostitution in Russia: Does the U.S. State Department Back the Legalization of Prostitution in Russia?" November 21, 2002, http://www.nationalreview.com (accessed October 1, 2004).

44. Johnson's list, a listserv distributed by David Johnson at the World Security Institute, formerly the Center for Defense Information (http://www.cdi.org/russia/johnson/). Engel described a "pro-prostitution lobby . . . in the US and in the rest of the world who benefit from the billions traffickers earn from buying and selling women and children" (Juliette Engel, December 14, 2002, "Sex work lobby loses fight to exclude 'consensual sex workers' from proposed legislation: Russian anti-trafficking coalition hails proposed Duma law as major step in war to stop the international sexual exploitation of Russian women and children").

45. I could not find copies of these letters, but the stories were told to me by several women's crisis centers and by Tom Firestone. Firestone (U.S. attorney and resident legal adviser at the U.S. embassy in Moscow 2002–2004), interview by the author, Brooklyn, N.Y., 2004.

46. This letter was reprinted on Johnson's list.

47. Anna-Louise Crago, "Unholy Alliance," Rabble (http://www.rabble.ca/), 2003;

reprinted http://www.alternet.org/rights/15947/ (accessed May 21, 2003). See also the 2005 End Demand for Sex Trafficking Act.

48. See the United States Leadership against HIV/AIDS Tuberculosis, and Malaria Act, 22 U.S.C. §§ 7601–7682 (2003), and the 2003 Trafficking Victims Protection Reauthorization Act, 22 U.S.C. sections 113 (g) (1) and (2) (webpage: Center for Health and Gender Equity, 2005, "Application of the 'Prostitution Loyalty Oath' in U.S. Global AIDS Policy," November, online at http://www.genderhealth.org/pubs/ProstitutionOathTimeline.pdf [accessed April 12, 2007]. In May of 2006, two district federal court decisions overturned the antiprostitution pledge for U.S.-based nonprofits working globally, but in 2007, one case was reversed, stating that the antiprostitution pledge did not limit freedom of speech. None of the decisions eliminated the antiprostitution pledge for foreign NGOs receiving U.S. funds, including as subgrantees of U.S. organizations.

49. U.S. Department of State, "Pathbreaking Strategies in the Global Fight against Sex Trafficking: Prevention, Protection, Prosecution," February 23–26, 2003, http://www.state.gov/g/tip/c8628.htm (accessed October 2004).

50. One place that these comments were published was the website of the *Detroit Free Press,* http://www.freep.com/voices/columnists/epowe17_20040617.htm (accessed October 2004).

51. An unaffiliated witness to the 2002 meetings, a U.S. prosecutor, at which this pro-prostitution lobby was alleged to have emerged, denied this accusation: "I never heard a single word in support of legalizing prostitution" from the NGOs (Tom Firestone, interview by the author, Brooklyn, N.Y., 2004). A U.S. off-the-record informant mentioned a late 1990s discussion among funders and activists where legalizing prostitution was discussed. It is also true that some of these organizations rejected the criminalization of prostitution (which is currently only an administrative offense). At a 2000 forum on trafficking cited in the allegations, there was a USAID-funded discussion of the possibility of criminalizing prostitution as a way of addressing the problem, but participants reasoned that criminalization would push the phenomenon more underground and limit women's recourse through the law (Melanie H. Ram, 2000, *Putting an End to the Trafficking of Women in the NIS and CEE* [Washington, D.C.: IREX]).

52. U.S. Department of State, "The U.S. Government's International Anti-Trafficking Programs: Fiscal Year 2004," 2004, http://www.state.gov/g/tip/rls/rpt/51689.htm (accessed October 2004). An additional large grant went to Winrock International, which had in the past worked with feminist women's crisis centers, but now partnered only with nonfeminist organizations that are "experts in communicating with youth and strengthening family values." Winrock International, "About the Program 'Path to Success,'" 2004, http://www.success.winrock.ru/eng/index.htm (accessed February 1, 2006).

53. Marina Regentova (RACCW leader), interview by the author, Moscow, July 8, 2002.

54. While still regularly commuting to Russia, Pisklakova had moved to the United States, giving her new skills and access to American funders.

55. Funding came from the UK development agency, then the EU's European Initiative for Democracy and Human Rights. RACCW leaders even restructured

the network on the model of Women's Aid; day-to-day activities remained under management in Moscow, but leadership was allocated to the regions; the Saratov Crisis Center director was elected as president, and vice presidency (and the next president) went to the director of the Barnaul Women's Alliance.

56. Women's Aid, "Women's Aid International Projects," 2004, http://www .womensaid.org.uk/international_projects/early2004updateinternat.htm (accessed February 1, 2006).

57. Regentova and Abubikirova, discussion with the author, September 26, 2005.

58. For example, Fatima received a grant from the OSCE's Office for Democratic Institutions and Human Rights, to produce training materials on trafficking (published in 2003).

59. Nataliia Sereda, personal communication, June 30, 2005.

60. Since communism's collapse, new feminist groups have often developed within academic contexts since they often had earlier access to feminist writings (Sperling et al. 2001).

61. Olga Liapounova (psychologist at Bridges of Mercy), interview by the author, Arkhangelsk, Russia, September 28, 2005. Also present was Raisa Danilova, founder and director of the center.

62. Conversation at the Bridges of Mercy, Arkhangelsk, Russia, September 29, 2005.

63. During most of the analysis in this book, Russia was a federation of 89 subnational units (with various names signifying different types of authority) recently overlaid with seven federal districts. For simplicity, I use the word "region" to refer to one of these subnational units. By 2006, the number of subnational units had decreased with the consolidation of several regions.

64. Mariia Regentova, interview by the author, Moscow, July 8, 2002.

## 4. Sexual Assault

1. See Section IV of the 2003 report from the Special Rapporteur on violence against women, "Integration of the Human Rights of Women and the Gender Perspective: Violence Against Women" (E/CN.4/2003/75), http://www.unhchr.ch/ Huridocda/Huridoca.nsf/TestFrame/d90c9e2835619e79c1256ce00058c145 ?Opendocument (accessed December 6, 2005). There are exceptions, such as rapes of white women by black men in the U.S. pre–civil rights South.

2. "Cultural practices within the family which are violent toward women" (E/CN.4/2002/83), http://www.ohchr.org/english/issues/women/rapporteur/ issues.htm (accessed December 5, 2005).

3. "Sexual harassment includes such unwelcome sexually determined behaviour as physical contact and advances, sexually coloured remarks, showing pornography and sexual demand, whether by words or actions. Such conduct can be humiliating and may constitute a health and safety problem; it is discriminatory when the woman has reasonable grounds to believe that her objection would disadvantage her in connection with her employment, including recruitment or promotion, or when it creates a hostile working environment" (para 18).

4. Nataliia Abubikirova, "Nasilie protiv zhenshchin" [Violence against women], FEMINF, no. 4, Moscow, April 1994, http://www.owl.ru/win/books/ feminf/04/02.htm (accessed October 13, 2006).

5. They rejected the myth that "men rape because they cannot restrain their passion or strong sexual desires," claiming instead that "rape is a crime against a person. The purpose of the Yrapist is to subjugate the victim and/or to demonstrate his power." Syostri, "Syostri: 5 years!" (bulletin available at the fifth-year anniversary press conference, Moscow, 1999).

6. Marina Mironova, interview by the author, Moscow, June 23, 1997.

7. Natalia Abubikirova (FALTA co-founder, RACCW leader), interview by the author, Moscow, July 23, 2004.

8. There were different-colored brochures for different forms of gender violence, including sexual violence and sexual harassment, and one describing the rights women have in Russia.

9. Feminist academics, such as Valerie Sperling, who later wrote a book on the Russian women's movement, brought their own concerns with sexual violence. Sperling had written an article on rape and sexual violence (Sperling 1990).

10. The most notable collaborations were the English-Russian magazine *Woman Plus* as well as the affiliated website, "Open Women Line" (http://www.owl.ru), "Russian Feminism Resources" (http://www.geocities.com/Athens/2533/russfem.html), and the Russian-language magazine *Vy i My* [You and We]: *The Women's Dialogue* (later *We/My*).

11. The editor of the volume published following the conference explains how she struggled to find the words in Russian to connote the problem, deciding to use "sexual overtures at work" (*seksual'nye domogatel'stva na rabote*) (Khotkina 1996). She had also considered "sexual persecution at work" (*seksual'nyoe presledovanie na rabote*) and "sexual coercion at work" (*seksual'noe prinushdenie na rabote*).

12. Kletsin's study defines the necessary but not sufficient condition for sexual harassment as the "unexpected (unprovoked) sexual activity at work" (26). In his survey, he describes these activities as sexual looks/gestures, obscene jokes/comments, touches/embraces/touches, inclination to sex, sexual letters/phone calls, and distribution of erotic material (28). Calling attention to the fact that these activities are sexual harassment when they are unexpected or unprovoked suggests that when they are expected or provoked, there is no sexual harassment. Under MacKinnon's interpretation, the distinction is whether they are unwanted.

13. M. G. Avidzba, D. A. Mikhailiukov, and L. D. Sinitsyna, 1999, *Seksual'nye Domogatel'stva na rabote: Chto eto takoe i kak sebia zashchitit'*, Tula, Russia: Tul'skii regional'nyi tsentr podderzhki zhenshchin i sem'i "Podruga," Tul'skaia gorodskaia organizatsiia zhenshchin. Dianne Post, from the ABA-CEELI, frustrated by their "misunderstanding," revised the text to reflect the American feminist claim that only the harasser is to blame. T. A. Lopatina, M. G. Avidzba, D. A. Mikhailiukov, and L. D. Sinitsyna, "Seksual'nye Domogatel'stva na rabote: Chto eto takoe i kak sebia zashchitit' s uchetom opyta USA," 1999, http://www.owl.ru/win/books/harassment/ (URL no longer active).

14. Natali'ia Abubikirova, "Nasilie protiv zhenshchin" [Violence against women], *FEMINF*, no. 4, Moscow, April 1994, http://www.owl.ru/win/books/feminf/04/02.htm (accessed October 13, 2006). A. A. Denisova, ed., *Slovar' Gendernykh Terminov*, Moscow: East-West Women's Initiative Project and Canadian Fund for the Support of Russian Women, 2002, http://www.owl.ru/gender/index.htm (accessed October 5, 2006).

15. I witnessed this kind of resistance at a 1999 Kaluga conference on gender violence at which an invited guest, a local Orthodox priest, spewed forth for almost an hour. In an illogical miasma of blame, he claimed that gender violence is rooted in the breakdown in society's morals and traditional gender roles, Russian women's reliance on abortion, and the rise in pornography, all instigated by the West. Condemning women's sexuality, he flatly rejected the language of rights, calling it dangerous.

16. Lilya Askhatovna Shatrova (director of the laboratory for gender studies "Bink"), interview by the author, Kazan, Russia, July 13–14, 2004. Shatrova was affiliated with the local women's crisis center through a bond of friendship and shared feminism. The impetus for addressing sexual harassment came out of Shatrova's own experience with sexual harassment in academia, but was facilitated by contact with the women's crisis center ANNA, which passed on a translated booklet describing what rights are violated by sexual harassment.

17. Some of these articles appear to discuss the concept (for example, using the term "sexual coercion" (*seksual'noe prinuzhdenie*), but "sexual coercion" was used to refer to lots of different kinds of gender violence (domestic violence, sexual harassment) and prostitution.

18. On the issue of sexual harassment, Russian activists wanted to introduce an American-like concept of sexual harassment that would include not hiring women who refused to provide sexual services. This shift could manifest as using the English term "sexual harassment" or Russians terms such as "sexual overtures" (*seksual'nye domogatel'stva*), "sexual encroachment" (*seksual'noe posiagatel'stvo*), or the more literal translation of "sexual harassment" (*seksual'noe presledovanie*).

19. Alessandra Stanley, April 16, 1994, "Sexual Harassment Thrives in the New Russian Climate," *New York Times,* p. 1.

20. The Institute for Urban Economics is a well-connected Moscow affiliate of the U.S. Urban Institute, and the project was part of a multi-country project of the U.S.-based women's rights organization Women, Law, and Development International, funded by USAID.

21. Zabelina (2002) used a stratified sample of both rural and urban residents, from eighteen to thirty years of age, men (38%) and women, in thirteen of the eighty-nine Russian regions.

22. Only one-fifth of the men agreed (Zabelina 2002), 44.

23. In my review of the articles on the case in English and Russian, on the Internet and on East View Publications' databases, I found only one article (from http://www.strana.ru) that referenced a women's crisis center (ANNA), as well as Amnesty International, which was running an anti-gender violence campaign at the time. I found no references to Syostri.

24. There were no reforms elsewhere on sexual harassment. There are also no legal requirements that employers take measures to prevent sexual harassment and no guidelines within the Ministry of Education and Science or university charters articulating a policy on sexual harassment (Duban 2006, 74, 79).

25. Russian Association of Crisis Centers for Women, 1995, "Report to the NGO Forum of the Fourth United Nations World Conference on Women in Beijing:

Violence against Women in Russia: Research, Education, and Advocacy Project," Moscow. Received June 30, 1997.

26. Under the Soviet criminal code, "simple rape" was defined as "sexual intercourse by use of force or threats or by taking advantage of the helpless state of the victim" (1960 RSFSR CrC).

27. In the commentaries on the codes, documents from esteemed legal scholars that elaborate on the law for lawyers and judges, the language was often about "natural" sexual intercourse, which is "perverted" by violence (see Severin 1984, Art. 117, comment 3).

28. Nadezhda Kuznetsova, 1997, unpublished chapter: "Violence against Women," Saratov, Russia.

29. Article 133 of the 1996 Criminal Code criminalizes "compelling a person to sexual intercourse, sodomy, a lesbian act or the commission of any other act of a sexual character by means of blackmail, threat of destruction, damaging, or seizures of property or by taking advantage of the material or other dependence of the victim."

30. As Suchland (2005, 156) explains, the previous version

recognized [compulsion] as a non-violent sex crime that affected only women [because it was] rooted in economic and sexual understandings of women's sexual difference. Because women are no longer classified in this way, the economic and moral harm addressed in the old statute is erased. As a result, only the sexual behavior component is left. And, in relationship to the surrounding statutes on sex crimes, compulsion is now in effect . . . a non-violent form of improper forced sex. But, the core meaning and evidence for the crime is gone, which makes compulsion practically impossible to prosecute.

31. The new rape article defines rape as "sexual intercourse with the application or threat of the application of force against the victim or other persons or by taking advantage of the helpless state of the victim" (1996 Russian Federation Criminal Code, Art. 131), and the punishments, from 3–6 years' imprisonment for simple rape to 8–15 years for the most grave rape, remained approximately the same. Legal theorists continued to reflect Ignatov's kind of thought and suggested that psychological pressure is even less likely to be seen as coercion (Naumov 1997). Whereas the Soviet code considered "psychological violence" (physical threats against a woman that are immediately actionable, in Article 117) as sufficient to establish the lack of consent (Severin 1984), the post-Soviet commentary requires the "application of force."

32. Mariia Mokhova (Syostri director), interview by the author, Moscow, June 29, 2002.

33. In her reflection on her experience, Post (2002) describes fourteen months of such trips to more than two dozen Russian cities, some more than once, in Russia's west, north, south, and center, and in western Siberia. I attended workshops with Post in March 1999 in the cities of Orel and Kaluga, not far from Moscow.

34. Post assessed that not just the views of those in the helping professions and NGOs, but also judges' views, were transformed. A November 1998 seminar

was so engaging that the judges did not leave until more than an hour after the scheduled closing time because they were so engaged in a debate about provocation. After getting the judges to agree that getting robbed after walking down a street wearing expensive clothing and jewelry was not provoking assault, Post had posed a similar scenario about sexual assault: a woman wearing a short skirt and tight blouse.

35. Report on the development of social services by the Russian Ministry of Health and Social Development, January 1, 2005, http://www.mzsrrf.ru/mon_ainfo/256.html.

36. CEDAW Committee, "Committee Is Generally 'Encouraged' by Russian Federation Report, but Concerned over Chechnya, Women's Access to Senior Positions," January 25, 2002, http://www.un.org/News/Press/docs/2002/WOM1314.doc.htm (accessed October 13, 2006).

37. Syostri found that 10% of women who had been raped went to the police, and only one of five of those who attempted got the police to officially registered their compliant ("Metodicheskoe Posobie: Pomoshch' Perezhivshim seksual'noe nasilie" [Methodological study aids: assistance to survivors of sexual violence], a book received by the author in 2002).

38. This skepticism remains constant and widespread, as illustrated at a 1999 ABA-CEELI conference in Chelyabinsk conducted by Post (2002). The widely respected police chief explained that violence in society is the fault of mothers who have brought up their children so badly and, simultaneously (paradoxically), part of men's biological instincts. He also saw sexual pleasure where Post saw harassment and violence, such as in rampant sexual relations between employers and employees and make-up sex after domestic battery. Other police officers explained that one of their responsibilities is to assess the character of a woman before they accept a complaint of rape (i.e., whether she is a "whore," drunk, psychologically ill, or an illegal alien). In other seminars conducted by Post, police routinely rejected a date-rape scenario as not rape and argued that most rape claims are set-ups in which a woman cries rape so that she can blackmail the alleged rapist.

39. Mariia Mokhova, interview by the author, Moscow, June 29, 2002.

40. Steven Lee Myers, "Putin's Flippant Comments on Israeli Scandal Are Heard," *New York Times,* October 20, 2006, p. A8.

## 5. Domestic Violence

1. "Recommendation Rec(2002)5 of the Committee of Ministers to Member States on the Protection of Women against Violence and Explanatory Memorandum," adopted April 30, 2002. For more information, see Minnesota Advocates for Human Rights (MAHR), "Council of Europe," November 3, 2003, http://www.stopvaw.org/Council_of_Europe11.html (accessed April 4, 2006).

2. MAHR, "What Is Domestic Violence," September 10, 2003, http://www.stopvaw.org/What_Is_Domestic_Violence_.html (accessed February 28, 2006).

3. TFNs, such as UNIFEM, Open Society's Network Women's Program, and MAHR, have adopted the norm about raising awareness for domestic violence.

For example, see MAHR, "United Nations Model Legislation," September 10, 2003, http://www.stopvaw.org/United_Nations_Model_Legislation.html (accessed February 28, 2006).

4. MAHR, "Coordinated Community Response," February 1, 2006, http://www.stopvaw.org/Coordinated_Community_Response.html (accessed April 7, 2006).

5. While in 1974 only Canada has passed legislation addressing violence against women, by 1994 thirty-two of thirty-six continuously democratic states had enacted legislation, most of which was targeted to domestic violence (Weldon 2002), 31. For example, after decades of activism, in 1994, the United States finally passed national legislation, the Violence Against Women Act. Although it included provisions against rape, the bulk of the $1.6 billion that was allocated (over three years) was for programs for abused women and improving the criminal justice system response to domestic violence (Elman 1996), 50.

6. Organisation for Economic Co-operation and Development, "Aid Statistics," 2006, http://www.oecd.org/dac/stats/regioncharts (accessed April 6, 2006).

7. Ritu R. Sharma, "Women and Development Aid," http://www.ciaonet.org/pbei/fpif/shr01/index.html (accessed March 2, 2006). Although the Gender Plan of Action was not well implemented in general by USAID, Sharma found that the Eastern Europe and Eurasia division received high marks for its shift in priorities.

8. The shift to domestic violence is evident even though they stated an interest in funding violence-against-women projects more broadly. For example, UNIFEM's list of trust fund grantees, from 1997 to 2004, includes only 16 grants out of 170 grants (or 9%) that were explicitly targeted toward sexual violence and/or harassment. Twenty percent went to projects explicitly about domestic violence, but many more simply stated that they were addressing "violence against women" or "gender-based violence." See United Nations Development Fund for Women, "Trust Fund to Eliminate VAW," http://www.unifem.org/gender_issues/violence_against_women/trust_fund.php (accessed December 6, 2005).

9. In 1999, Philip Morris spent $2 million on domestic violence programs in the U.S., and $108 million advertising this and their other charitable donations (totaling $60 million). Lori Dorfman, "Philip Morris Puts Up Good Citizen Smokescreen," November 27, 2000, http://www.alternet.org/story/10129/ (accessed February 28, 2006): Independent Media Institute.

10. Tania Sidrenkova (associate at the Inform Center of the Independent Women's Forum), interview by the author, Moscow, June 20, 1997. Also Julie Kachalova, 1996, "Violence against Women in the New Russia," *WIN News* (reprinted from *Woman Plus*), issue 22–23 (Summer): 43.

11. Marina Pisklakova (founder of ANNA), interview by the author, Moscow, June 21, 2002. The term sounds strange in Russian—as it does in English (Jones 2000)—because there is little domestic about the level of violence in many of the incidents in domestic violence.

12. Nadezhda Nadezhdina, 16 January 1998, "SOS against a Background of Love," *Trud,* 7.

13. This is from the MCGS website: "MCGS activity is inspired by the universal human values set forth in the Universal Declaration on Human Rights (United

Nations, 1948), the Convention on Elimination of All Forms of Discrimination Against Women (United Nations, 1979), the Nairobi Forward Looking Strategies on Improving the Status of Women (United Nations, 1985) and the Beijing Platform of Actions (United Nations, 1995)." MCGS, "History of Moscow Center for Gender Studies," http://www.gender.ru/english/about/history.shtml (accessed March 1, 2004).

14. Tatiana Klimenkova (philosopher at MCGS, a founder of ANNA), interview by the author, Moscow, June 25, 1997.

15. "Violence and Women," *Vy and My [You and We]: The Women's Dialogue,* Fall 1993.

16. Simultaneous with this campaign, the Moscow crisis centers, with the International Women's Club, held a Moscow campaign titled "Stop Violence Against Women," which was centered around an art competition, at the Radisson-Slavianaskaia Hotel, by professional artists and those familiar with violence. The event was covered by the national television news.

17. In Russian, *"Domashnemu nasiliiu net opravdanii."* In 1995, the ANNA leadership had decided that they wanted to "appropriate the model for a campaign and conduct something similar in Russia" (Andrei Sinel'nikov, 2000, "Nasilie v sem'e i obrazovanie naceleniia: Ot osoznaniia—k deistviiu" [Violence in the family and the education of the population: from awareness to action], *Nasilie i Sotsial'nye Izmeneniia: Teoriia, Praktika, Issledovaniia [Violence and social changes: theory, practice, research],* Center ANNA [Moscow: TACIS/CARITAS]). The first use of this slogan I found was in Scotland.

18. Personal communication with Nadezhda Khvorova (director of the campaign), July 15, 2002. Also Inna Loukavenko, personal communication with the author, June 10, 2003.

19. Such as ORT's *Dobroe Utro,* RTR's *Semeinye Novosti,* and TV-6's *Ya Sama.* Personal communication with Nadezhda Khvorova (director of the campaign), July 15, 2002.

20. For example, LaCrosse, Wisconsin–Dubna, Minneapolis-Novosibirsk (through Connect/US-Russia), and Appleton, Wisconsin–Kurgan.

21. As noted in the first English-language book on the Russian women's movement, even formerly communist-related women's groups (e.g., a *zhensoviet* in Toitsk, a town near Moscow) were beginning to talk about the issue in the early 1990s, but with no clear terminology (Racioppi and See 1997, 111).

22. For example, before 1999, movement leaders were skeptical of the third women's crisis center in Moscow, Yaroslavna. The center's name, an archaic given name for a Russian woman (indicating the daughter of a man named Yaroslavl), signaled a link to Russian history. Leaders also worried that the center's location within a university psychology department might mean a psychological approach to domestic violence that downplayed the perpetrator's criminal responsibility. Their skepticism was alleviated through ABA-CEELI facilitated contact.

23. A 2001 poll conducted among women's organizations in St. Petersburg found leaders becoming more skeptical of such global appropriation (Balibalova, Glushchenko, and Tikhomirova 2001, 124). To the question, "Is it possible to use the experience of foreign countries in Russia," 50% of those polled said "yes," and

50% said "partially." Women's organizations were still more open than a control group of students, 35% of whom said "no."

24. Irina Khaldeeva, interview by the author, Saratov, Russia, June 22, 1999.

25. From the 1998 "Stop Violence Against Women" campaign booklet. For Balibalova, Glushchenko, and Tikhomirova 2001, "domestic violence is a real act or a threat of physical, sexual, psychological or economical insult and violence of one individual against another one, with whom an offender has or had intimate relationships or other close contacts" (117).

26. As described by social movement theorists (Benford and Snow 2000), frame amplification "involves the idealization, embellishment, clarification, or invigoration of existing values or beliefs" and has proven especially important "to movements that have been stigmatized because their beliefs and/or values contradict the dominant culture's core values" (624).

27. ANNA's proficiency at modifying the U.S. campaign to fit Russian society was appreciated by FVPF, who then used some of the Russian-made materials to target Russian-immigrant populations in the United States. The USAID-funded Internews campaign purposely left much discretion to the regional crisis centers because the director's goals included fostering the regional crisis centers, not just raising awareness of domestic violence (Khvorova personal communication). Illustrating the alliance with transnational feminist networks and the ideas of global feminism, the campaign was coordinated with the global 16 Days of Activism against Gender Violence, and one of the conditions of the production grants was the inclusion of women's crisis centers in all stages of the program production. At least for USAID, the project was so successful that they extended funding to 2002 (Inna Loukavenko, personal communication with the author, June 10, 2003).

28. When the crisis centers were more solvent, there had even been a couple of public demonstrations, a rare occurrence for women's organizations in Russia (Sperling 2005). For example, a St. Petersburg crisis center had held a 1999 protest; the Women's Alliance had held a 2002 march (169).

29. During 2003–2004, RACCW activists made "64 media appearances, publications and interviews." Women's Aid, "Women's Aid International Projects," 2004, http://www.womensaid.org.uk/international_projects/early2004updateinternat.htm (accessed February 1, 2006).

30. English-language articles covering domestic violence and/or the crisis centers appeared in the *Moscow Tribune* (September 1, 1995), the *Moscow Times* (July 18, 1997; January 15, 1997; May 28, 1997; October 8, 1997; January 13, 1998), and *St. Petersburg Times* (October 13, 1997). Russian-language articles were published in *Komsomolskaia Pravda* (March 28, 1995), *Izvestiia* (July 29, 1995), *Rossiskaia Gazeta* (May 31, 1996), *Vechernaya Moskva* (October 18, 1997), *Nezavisimaia Gazeta* (October 20, 1997), *Argumenty i Fakty* (March 11, 1997), and *Trud-7* (January 16, 1998). Talk shows, such as the women's show *Ya Sama* and a more obviously political program with pundit Vladimir Posner, also discussed domestic violence.

31. Zabelina (2002, ch. 5) conducted a content analysis of central and regional (Irkutsk and the Komi republic) newspapers in 2000 and 2001. They also found

that battery and femicide were the most common forms of gender violence discussed.

32. The men, more so than the women, were concerned about the consequences of domestic violence on women's reproductive and maternal capacity (Zabelina 2002, 46). Views about domestic violence were gendered: when asked specifically what constituted violence, women consistently had a broader understanding, including such things as scolding, swearing, intimidation ("verbal violence"), and compelling someone to drink alcohol or take drugs, whereas men were much more likely to include only physical violence (battering) (42–43).

33. As in the first study, this survey employed a stratified sampling technique, but in this case targeted 2,100 married people in seven regions (and fifty localities) in Russia. Illustrating the breadth of the Russian movement's concept of domestic violence, the study covers "psychological violence" (severe criticism, insults, prohibitions, threats, or "humiliating remarks"), "economic violence" (enforced dependence on husbands for money, prohibitions against studying or working, and threats of economic abandonment), "physical violence" (such as hitting, beating, shoving, twisting arms, or threats of such physical harm, often justified as a response to a wife's "bad" behavior), and "sexual violence" (wife rape, not considering a wife's sexual desires). Not all of this data is presented disaggregated, but, for example, 65% of the husbands and 85% of the wives thought physical abuse of wives constituted a crime (Gorshkova and Shurygina 2003), 37.

34. A 2006 survey conducted by Levada's polling agency, Public Verdict, found that only 3% of Russians understood themselves to be protected from arbitrary and illegal actions of the police or other law enforcement organs; only 2% thought the prosecutor's office and judicial system protected their rights if the police violated them. Women were even more skeptical than men. "Zhenshchiny chuvstvuiut sebia nezashchishchennymi ot proizvola militsii" [Women feel less safe from arbitrary police actions], March 10, 2006, http://www.hro.org/editions/wom/2006/03/10.php (accessed March 14, 2006). The Moscow Helsinki Group argued that most women suffering from domestic violence will not turn to the police because they do not trust them (Lukshevskii 2003).

35. The difference between men's and women's views is striking. Whereas 56% of husbands thought domestic violence was a private matter, only 31% of wives agreed (Gorshkova and Shurygina 2003), 37. Whereas 42% of husbands thought they had a right to punish their wife, only 22% of wives concurred. Whereas 30% of husbands thought that they had a right to beat their wife if she committed adultery, only 12% of wives thought so.

36. See also Russian Association of Crisis Centers for Women, 1995, "Report to the NGO Forum of the Fourth United Nations World Conference on Women in Beijing: Violence against Women in Russia: Research, Education, and Advocacy Project," Moscow, Russia.

37. My interpretation of this data differs somewhat from Gorshkova and Shurygina (2003) on this question. Part of the difficulty with examining this study is the inexactness of the questions. For example, for the stem "Do you agree that . . . ," one of the possible answers was "a husband has a right to beat his wife if he punishes her for something." More younger women thought that men had

the right to beat their wives than any other age cohort, but this could reflect a critique, a recognition that in practice husbands have this right. (Other possible answers indicated less tolerance.) A much more useful question would have been whether people saw domestic violence as a violation of women's rights.

38. On the question of whether people agreed that violence against women in the family existed in Russia, they found a slightly lower agreement (Zabelina et al. 2007, 78). The authors interpreted this as a sign of decreasing awareness, but the question changed slightly (to ask whether respondents agreed there was "problem of violence in the family") and the shift does not appear statistically significant, especially considering the different populations and methods.

39. As recorded by East View Universal regional and national newspaper databases, when the survey was released in 2003, there were three articles published on the survey in national or regional newspapers, four the next year, and three in 2006. These articles were published in *Komersant Daily, Izvestiia, Moskovskie Novosti, Rossiiskaia Gazeta, Komsomol'skaia Pravda,* and the *Moscow Times.*

40. For the view of Russian activists, see Balibalova, Glushchenko, and Tikhomirova (2001), Rimasheevskaia (2005), and the Institute for Social and Gender Policy (2004). MAHR, "Russian Federation," June 10, 2004, http://www.stopvaw.org/Russian_Federation.html (accessed March 20, 2006). Balibalova, Glushchenko, and Tikhomirova (2001) found that 100% of women's activists in St. Petersburg were in agreement that there is a need for legislation on domestic violence. For human rights approaches, see Lukshevskii (2003), Amnesty International (2005), and Benninger-Budel and O'Hanlon (2004). The latter explains, "Specific legislation criminalizing domestic violence is important, recognizing the special relationship and interdependence between the victim and the perpetrator, which gives rise to the necessity for specially designed laws to combat this form of violence" (307).

41. Galina Sillaste (consultant on the legislation), interview by the author, Moscow, July 7, 1997.

42. The final version was titled "On the Fundamentals of the Social-Legal Defense from Violence in the Family" [Ob osnovakh sotsial'no-pravovi zashchity ot nasiliia v sem'e]. The Russian text of the bill that I have is the variant offered in May 1997, which was given to me by the Inform Center of the Independent Women's Forum, Moscow, in June 1997.

43. The preamble calls for the establishment of "social services to solve difficult life situations in the family, created by the danger of the perpetration of violence in the family or evoked by perpetration [of violence]." The bill claims that social services are key, not just to treat the medical and psychological pains of domestic violence, but to prevent violence in the family.

44. Galina Sillaste, 1998, "Zakon v Tupike: Sem'ia dolzhna byt' zashchishchena ot nasilii" [Legislation at a dead end: the family should be protected from violence]. *Obosrevatel'* [Observer] 2 (January): 52–54. Also, Sillaste, interview by the author, Moscow, July 26, 1999.

45. If anything, the articles have become more limited. Although in the past, law enforcement might "catch" some domestic violence under the net of hooliganism, many apartments have been privatized, and police are more reluctant to intervene, making the postcommunist article (Art. 213)—or its less severe version

in the Administrative Code—much less effective for domestic violence (Johnson 2001). The 2001 Administrative Code (Art. 20.1) regulates "minor hooliganism." Police, if they observe violence, may request the batterer give a statement, but cannot arrest (Duban 2006), 90.

46. There has been a hopeful sign more recently. In 2005, the Constitutional Court declared that the lack of involvement by state investigators and prosecutors in the process is unconstitutional (Duban 2006). It cast private prosecution as a victim's additional right, to initiate or dismiss the case. Constitutional Court rulings, in this state where rule of law remains weak, may be ignored, but they also may, if there is political will, create avenues for meaningful change.

47. For example, their 1996 "Conception on the Improvement of the Status of Women in the Russian Federation" barely mentions domestic violence in the section on violence against women (calling it "everyday violence").

48. The resolution was given to me by Liudmila Nikolaevna Kiselova (director of the department of socioeconomic position of women and the problem of the national population at the Ministry of Labor and Social Development), Moscow, July 30, 1999.

49. More than just ideological alliances, many of these old-style feminists also had links to transnational feminists. Lakhova, for example, when head of the Women of Russia party attracted a lot of global feminist attention and had staff who were directly connected to transnational feminist networks, such as the Network of East-West Women (Richter 2002). These links made them even more responsive to global feminists' pressures, such as from the Beijing conference on women. Lakhova also chaired the 1997 women's crisis center conference on the domestic violence bill.

50. Open Women Line, "Informatsiia o deiatel'nosti Departamenta po delam detei, zhenshchin i sem'i i Ministerstva truda i sotsial'nogo razvitiia RF v 2003 godu" [Information about the programs of the Department of Children, Women, and the Family in the Ministry of Labor and Social Development of the Russian Federation in 2003], April 1, 2004, http://www.owl.ru/content/docs/rus/p54202.shtml (accessed February 27, 2006).

51. The failure to pass domestic violence legislation meant that the decree required regional governments to provide the resources out of their social service budgets. As many regions were financially impoverished, the ministry advocated joint projects with nongovernmental organizations, leading to some successful women's crisis centers. In addition to the state-supported crisis centers, approximately one hundred other institutions operated separate "crisis departments for women." Ministry of Health and Social Development, "Informational Material on Social Policy on the Family, Women, and Children," November 2, 2005, http://www.mzsrrf.ru/inf_soc_pol_wom_cild/64.htm (accessed March 22, 2006]). These centers tend not to serve rural or Roma women. They cannot assist most migrants, even internal migrants who move to the city from elsewhere, as these migrants tend not to have the legal residency permits required to access state services (Duban 2006, 119).

52. Russia has a complex federal system, in which some of the regions act more independently than others. By law, legal authority is reserved to the central government for some issues, the regional government for others; for another

set of issues, authority is shared between the central government and regional governments (RF Constitution, Arts. 71–73). Gender violence, in so much as it is an issue of human rights, healthcare, family, and/or housing, is one of the latter. Regional governments have the right to draft legislation as long as the legislation does not contravene federal law, meaning that policy on domestic violence may also be drafted at the regional level.

53. From material on Interfax "Vremia," no. 31 (473) from July 28, 2004, I "Stolitsa S," no. 615.

54. Arkhangel'skoe oblastnoe sobranie deputatov [Arkhangelsk regional assembly of deputies], Oblastnoi zakon: O sotsialno-pravovoi zashchite i reabilitatsii lits, podvergshikhsia nailiiu v sem'e [Regional law: On the social-legal defense and rehabilitation of persons suffering from violence in the family], June 3, 2003. Given to me by crisis center staff.

55. Activists from the very active crisis center in Arkhangelsk told me that they had heard of the law only in 2005.

56. Marina Vadimovna Aristova (former director and founder of the St. Petersburg City Center for Social Assistance for Women in Danger, 95–98), interview by the author, Moscow, October 3, 2005.

57. There are also Committees on Issues of Women, Children, and the Family founded in all 89 regions in the years between 1996 and 2000 (Duban 2006), 34.

58. Albina Pashina, interview by the author, Moscow, June 13, 2002.

59. Marina Nikolaevna Nikitina (director), telephone conversation, Moscow, July 22, 2004. See also Nikitina in Rimasheevskaia 2005.

60. Dianne Post, interview by the author, Moscow, February 23, 1999.

61. Post explicitly aligned herself with global feminism by highlighting the universalizing claim of women's human rights and arguing the similarities between Russian and American experiences (Post 2000). For example, when a Russian would argue the Russian specificity of the problem because in Russia there is a proverb "If he beats you, he loves you," she would argue that she heard the same thing in her life or work in the United States. In trips to Kaluga and Orel in March of 1999, in which I participated and observed, Post highlighted issues crucial in the American experience of domestic violence, such as provocation, post-traumatic stress disorder, and the ways that battered women tend to behave.

62. Liudmila Nikolaevna Kiselova (at the Ministry of Labor and Social Development), interview by the author, Moscow, July 30, 1999; Larisa Ponarina (director of ANNA), interview by the author, Moscow, July 26, 2004. Funding came from the Canadian International Development Agency.

63. Ministry of Health and Social Development, "Informational Material on Social Policy on the Family, Women, and Children," November 2, 2005, http://www.mzsrrf.ru/inf_soc_pol_wom_cild/64.htm (accessed March 22, 2006).

64. Project Harmony, "Domestic Violence Community Partnership: Project Overview," 2002, http://www.projectharmony.org/programs/comm/past/dvcp/ (accessed March 28, 2006).

65. The pairings are: Vermont-Karelia; Maine-Arkhangelsk; Maryland–Leningrad region; Western New York–Novgorod; New Hampshire–Vologda;

Massachusetts-Tomsk; Connecticut-Pskov; Alaska-Sakhalin; and Oregon-Khabarovsk; For more information, see the organization's website: http://www.rarolc.net.

66. Archangel Committee, "History of the Maine-Archangel Rule of Law Project," Portland, Maine, 2003, http://www.arkhangelsk.org/rule_of_law.htm (accessed April 3, 2006).

67. In contrast, the American mock court gave the apartment and primary custody to the wife and ordered the husband to pay child support (while also giving him liberal visitation rights).

68. Faye Luppi, personal communication with the author, January 4, 2006. See also Russian American Rule of Law Consortium (hereafter RAROLC), "Maine-Arkhangelsk," http://www.rarolc.net/partnerships/me-arkhangelsk.php (accessed April 3, 2006).

69. Tatiana Zykina (professor of law, chief of Civil Law Department, vice dean of international affairs, Arkhangelsk State Technical University Faculty of Law), interview by the author, Arkhangelsk, Russia, September 29, 2005. I also interviewed staff at one of the legal clinics.

70. Olga Liapounova, interview by the author, Arkhangelsk, Russia, September 28, October 1, 2005.

71. RAROLC, "Massachusetts to Tomsk," June 1–3, 2004, http://www.rarolc.net/events/detail.php?cid=60 (accessed April 3, 2006).

72. Ministry of Health and Social Development, "Informational Material on Social Policy on the Family, Women, and Children," November 2, 2005, http://www.mzsrrf.ru/inf_soc_pol_wom_cild/64.htm (accessed March 22, 2006).

73. Amnesty International (2005, 17) found that data was being collected "on the ground" and passed off to the ministry, but this data was not being aggregated, analyzed, or published. Zabelina (2007, 10) argues that, although as of 2005 these statistics are being gathered and are available upon request, no statistics or analysis have been publicly released.

74. Marina Vadimovna Aristova (former director and founder of the St. Petersburg City Center for Social Assistance for Women in Danger), interview by the author, Moscow, October 3, 2005.

75. Nataliia Sereda (founder of the Women's Alliance), interview with the author, Barnaul, Russia, July 1, 2002.

76. Ol'ga Pol'shchikova, 2004, "Mir na semle nachinaetsia doma" [Peace on earth begins at home], *Altaiskaiia Pravda*, May 24, available online through East View Universal Databases [accessed June 28, 2004].


### 6. Trafficking in Women

1. *The Trafficking of NIS Women Abroad: An International Conference in Moscow 3–5 November 1997 Conference Report*, 1998, Global Survival Network in collaboration with the International League for Human Rights (Washington, D.C.: Global Survival Network).

2. The Trafficking of NIS Women Abroad: An International Conference in Moscow 3–5 November 1997, 1998, Conference Report.

3. Article 3 appears to allow for the possibility that consensual prostitution could,

at times, be regulated under the protocol ("The consent of a victim of trafficking in persons to the intended exploitation . . . shall be irrelevant") (Sullivan 2003). In 2006, the special rapporteur on the human rights aspects of the victims of trafficking in persons, especially women and children, reargued that the protocol represented a compromise, trying to clarify that trafficking required some type of coercion or fraud, but not the abolition of all forms of (adult) prostitution, although many forms, in practice, do meet some of the standards of trafficking (Huda 2006). The rapporteur recommended the criminalization of the use of prostituted persons, such as the law enacted in Sweden, to discourage the demand side of trafficking.

4. Russia is not a member, but an observer (see website, "IOM Member States," updated through December 2005, http://www.iom.int/en/who/main_members. shtml [accessed April 17, 2006]).

5. Council of Europe Committee of the Ministers, Recommendation R (2000) 11, "Action against Trafficking in Human Beings for the Purposes of Sexual Exploitation," http://cm.coe.int/ta/rec/2000/2000r11.htm (accessed April 17, 2006).

6. Nina Shapiro, "The New Abolitionists," *Seattle Weekly,* August 2004, p. 22.

7. Anna-Louise Crago, 2003, "Unholy Alliance," *Rabble,* reprinted online at http://www.alternet.org/rights/15947/ (accessed May 21, 2003). See also the 2005 End Demand for Sex Trafficking Act.

8. See the U.S. report prepared for the 10-year anniversary of the Beijing conference, *Working for Women Worldwide: US Commitment* (2005). The report highlights the U.S. antitrafficking efforts, including the "success story" of "fighting human trafficking in Europe and Eurasia."

9. Association of Crisis Centers "Stop Violence," 2004, *Protivodeistvie torgovle liud'mi* [Actions against human trafficking] (brochure) (Moscow: TACIS).

10. The conference was "The Trafficking of Newly Independent States Women Abroad" (Problema vyvoza zhenshchin iz stran SNG dlia seks-torgovli za rubezhom) and reported in Caldwell, Galster, and Steinzor 1997.

11. Participants included Russian, Ukrainian, Dutch, and Thai activists as well as representatives from international NGOs, the U.S. State Department, and the Russian government. The speakers from the Russian government were Liudmila Zavadskaya, deputy minister of justice, and Olga Samarina, deputy director of the Department of Family, Women and Children of the Ministry of Labor.

12. For example, several women's crisis center leaders participated in a 1998 conference in Budapest sponsored by the Network Women's Program and the Global Survival Network. The conference included speakers from the sex-work feminist groups, Network of Sex Works Project, and GAATW, but no participants from the antiprostitution feminist CATW, although there were many questions raised by the participants from postcommunist societies. International Movement against All Forms of Discrimination and Racism, *Transnational Training Seminar on Trafficking in Women,* June 20–24, 1998, Budapest, Hungary, Network Women's Program of the Open Society Institute in collaboration with the Global Survival Network; Network Women's Program, New York, http://www.imadr.org/project/petw/budapest.pdf (accessed October 5, 2006).

13. For a copy of the articles in English, see http://www.we-myi.org/issues/34/INDEX.HTM.

14. Elena Schitova [Shitova], personal communication with the author, August 11, 2005.

15. USAID, "Path to Success" with Winrock International, March 11, 2005, http://www.usaid.ru/en/main/documents/index.shtml?lang=en&id=1653 (accessed April 20, 2006).

16. Juliette Engel (founding director, MiraMed Institute and Angel Coalition), interview by the author, Moscow, June 27, 2004.

17. ABA-CEELI, 2004, *Directory of Organizations Working Against Human Trafficking in the Russian Federation* (Moscow: ABA-CEELI).

18. The book was then translated, updated, and re-edited into Stoecker and Shelley 2005a. The project was funded by a grant from the U.S. State Department's Bureau of Educational and Cultural Affairs.

19. In 1998, the Duma passed an amendment, the 1996 Criminal Code (Art. 152.2e), which prohibited the sexual trafficking of minors by criminal groups (Shelley and Orttung 2005). But even this reflected little change in practice or recognition of the broader problem of trafficking in women. No system was created for preventing or combating trafficking in minors or in women. The legal changes simply created a way to prosecute the sex trafficking of minors if law enforcement stumbled upon it.

20. See various official government public documents from the State Duma (1997–2000) available from East-View's Russian Government Publication database. Ultranationalist Vladimir Zhirinovsky even proposed legislation on this problem.

21. Elena Tiuriukanova (leading research at the Institute for Socio-Economic Population Studies at the Russian Academy of Sciences), interview by the author, Moscow, July 26, 2004.

22. U.S. Department of State, "Trafficking in Persons Report," July 2001, http://www.state.gov/g/tip/rls/tiprpt/2001/3937.htm.

23. U.S. Department of State, "Release of 2002 Trafficking in Persons Report," June 5, 2002, http://www.state.gov/g/tip/rls/rm/2002/10781.htm.

24. Statement to international press by Russian labor minister Alexander Pochinok, Moscow, April 3, 2002, Angel Coalition site, http://www.angelcoalition.org/PDF/RussiaResponse.pdf (accessed September 8, 2004).

25. The draft legislation bill was titled Federal Law: On Countering Trafficking in Persons and Measures To Protect Victims of Trafficking in Persons 2003) [Federal'nyi zakon: O protivodeistvii torgovle liud'mi 2003]. The working group was under the auspices of the Committee on Legislation and the Committee on Women, Family, and Youth. The group included Elena Mizulina from the Union of Right Forces; several nongovernmental organizations: representatives from two women's crisis centers, Syostri, and the Perm Center against Violence and Human Trafficking; as well as Elena Tiuriukanova, a member of the MCGS. Also included were representatives from two TraCCC-affiliated centers in Irkustk and Vladivostok, the MIA, Ministry of Foreign Affairs, the General Procuracy, and the Ministry of Labor.

26. The bill called for "social partnership and cooperation with public associations and non-governmental organizations" (Art. 5 draft law):

1. Whenever asylums or centers as provided for by Articles 24 and 25 above are established, the federal commission and regional commissions shall be obliged to invite for cooperation public associations and non-governmental organizations working in the area of countering trafficking in persons.
2. The Federal Commission and regional commissions shall be obliged to offer organizational, material and other assistance in the activities of non-governmental organizations aiming to prevent trafficking in persons and help victims of trafficking in persons.
3. Financial support may be granted to a public association or a non-governmental organization with the funds allocated from the federal budget, if in accordance with an open tender which was held, the program of events and measures to counter trafficking in persons or to create an asylum or a center proposed by the public association or non-governmental organization has been included into the federal program to counter trafficking in persons or other federal programs. (Art. 26) (Federal Law: On Countering Trafficking in Persons and Measures To Protect Victims of Trafficking in Persons 2003)

27. Tom Firestone (assistant U.S. attorney and resident legal adviser at the U.S. embassy in Moscow 2002–2004), interview by the author, Brooklyn, N.Y., September 18, 2004. Also U.S. Department of State, "Trafficking in Persons Report," June 11, 2003, http://www.state.gov/g/tip/rls/tiprpt/2003/21262.htm# tiers.

28. Excerpts from Federal Law No. 162-FZ, "On Introducing Changes and Amendments to the Criminal Code of the Russian Federation," passed by the State Duma. The relevant changes were Article 1271 Trafficking in Persons, Article 1272 Use of Slave Labor, and some changes to Article 241.

29. The 2004 legislation, which specifically referred to victims of "trafficking in persons," provided for some legal protection for trafficked women who bear witness against their traffickers. Mizulina, http://www.mizulina.ru/index.php?in_do=show_art&in_id=565 (accessed May 15, 2005). There was also specific legislation on witness protection for trafficked victims; this legislation was scrapped for the broader legislation.

30. The deputy was Aleksandr Baranikov from the West-leaning Union of Right Forces.

31. Elena Tiuriukanova, interview by the author, Moscow, July 26, 2004; trafficking in persons was translated as *torgolvia liud'mi*, protection as *zashchita*.

32. Putin's October 2003 declaration that Russia would deal with trafficking justified this decision as part of Russia's continuing desire to be a part of the international community. This is also the way the story told in the media. According to an article in the long-established and generally well-regarded newspaper *Izvestiia*, the passage of the legislation illustrated that "the legal climate in Russia is again changing under the influence of international society" (Vladimir Perekrest, "Radi zhenshchin i detei. Prezident vnes popravki, uzhetochaiushchie otvetstvennost' za torgolviu liud'mi," *Izvestiia (Rossiia)*, October 28, 2003, p. 8).

33. Juliette Engel, 2002, "Sex work lobby loses fight to exclude 'consensual sex workers' from proposed legislation: Russian anti-trafficking coalition hails proposed Duma law as major step in war to stop the international sexual exploitation of Russian women and children." in David Johnson, *Johnson's Russia List*, http://www.cdi.org/russia/johnson, Center for Defense Information.

34. Tom Firestone (assistant U.S. attorney and resident legal adviser at the U.S. embassy in Moscow 2002–2004), interview by the author, Brooklyn, N.Y., September 18, 2004.

35. There were many differences, even from the limited version of the legislation that Mizulina handed to the administration. For example, this draft eliminated the criminalization of prostitution and the criminalization of the dissemination of information about trafficking victims. Most importantly, it included no criminalization of the recruitment (*verbovka*) of persons, the primary part of the problem that takes place on Russian soil when people are trafficked abroad. Paleev appeared to have taken the quite limited Criminal Code article on the trafficking of children (Art. 152) that had passed in 1998 and added adults.

36. A provision was added that allowed for the prosecution of corrupt officials involved in facilitating trafficking (Art. 127$^1$.2.c 2003 Criminal Code). A second provision allows prosecution for the falsification and seizure of documents (Art. 127.$^1$2.e 2003 Criminal Code). A third facilitates the prosecution of pimps (Art. 127, Explanatory Note 2). Explanatory note 2 was also changed so that a person who voluntary releases his victim and assists authorities can be excused from criminal liability. The previous draft read "or." Tom Firestone (assistant U.S. attorney and resident legal adviser at the U.S. embassy in Moscow 2002–2004), interview by the author, Brooklyn, N.Y., September 18, 2004.

37. When President Putin announced the reintroduction of antitrafficking legislation in the fall of 2003, accepting the Bush argument, he declared, "Trafficking in persons is a part of international organized crime."

38. State Department, 2007, "Country Reports on Human Rights Practices 2006: Russia," Bureau of Democracy, Human Rights, and Labor, March 6, http://www.state.gov/g/drl/rls/hrrpt/2006/78835.htm (accessed April 23, 2007).

39. Maria Mokhova, interview by the author, Moscow, July 23, 2004.

40. As illustrated in the case of domestic violence legislation (chapter 4), "it is not common to have NGOs involved in legislation" (Tiuriukanova 2004). According to Maria Mokhova, the director of Syostry, "Tom Firestone was the reason that the NGOs were included in the working group, that [the Russian government] had to listen to us a little" (interview by the author, Moscow, July 23, 2004). Mizulina did have the working group under the auspices of the Committee on Women, Family, and Youth along with the Committee on Legislation as the proposed legislated targeted women.

41. There were a small uptick in 2000, but this was due to the release and discussion of the Steven Soderbergh film *Traffic*. This pattern of coverage contrasts with what trafficking experts see as the height of the problem in the late 1990s (Khodyreva 2004).

42. Angel Coalition, "Trafficking Surveys," http://www.angelcoalition.org/surveys.html (accessed August 30, 2004).

43. Association of Crisis Centers for Women "Stop Violence," 2004, *Preduprezhdenie*

*i presechenie torgovli liudmi: Sbornik materialiov mezhdunarodnogo seminara [Prevention and elimination of trafficking in persons: collection of materials from the international seminar]* (Moscow: Association of Crisis Centers for Women "Stop Violence").

44. U.S. law draws careful distinctions between paying fees for adoption or surrogacy and the creation of a market, but the Russians, with a history of Marxist-Leninist critiques of commodification, are more keenly aware that there is economic inequality and perhaps exploitation at play when residents from richer countries pay money for children from poorer countries. In this way, the Russian conception of human trafficking resembles the sex-work feminist approach as it includes a broader understanding of exploitation than just sexual exploitation. There are some Russian feminist arguments that also draw upon these broader ideas about economic violence. See, for example, Tiuriukanova (2005b).

45. Igor' Nekhames, "Chelovek. Bol'naia tema. Seks-rabyni na vyvoz" [Person. Painful subject. Sex-slave woman for export], *Literaturnaia Gazeta*, April 14, 2004.

46. Stories from the women's crisis center contradict this assertion. Many trafficked victims appear to prefer returning to Europe—in what they hope will be better circumstances, at least less coercive prostitution/sex work—to staying in Russia.

47. Syostri produced 2004 *Training Portfolio* with the IOM; Fatima for the RACCW produced a 2003 booklet providing *Informational Materials for Educational Activities on the Prevention of Trafficking in Persons,* with OSCE.

48. As of 2006, the UN has also begun to release worldwide reports on trafficking. See United Nations Office on Drugs and Crime, "Trafficking in Human Beings," April 2006, http://www.unodc.org/unodc/trafficking_human_beings. html (accessed July 16, 2006).

49. Engel, 2006, comments at the NGO forum for the 2006 Commission on the Status of Women.

50. State Department, 2007, "Country Reports on Human Rights Practices 2006: Russia," Bureau of Democracy, Human Rights, and Labor, March 6, http:// www.state.gov/g/drl/rls/hrrpt/2006/78835.htm (accessed April 23, 2007).

51. Michael Schwirtz, "Russia: Human Trafficking Ring Broken," *New York Times,* March 16, 2007.

52. State Department, 2007, "Country Reports on Human Rights Practices 2006: Russia," Bureau of Democracy, Human Rights, and Labor, March 6, http:// www.state.gov/g/drl/rls/hrrpt/2006/78835.htm (accessed April 23, 2007).

53. Tom Firestone, interview by the author, Brooklyn, N.Y., 2004.

54. Vladimir Golubovskii in Association of Crisis Centers for Women "Stop Violence," 2004, *Preduprezhdenie i presechenie torgovli liudmi: Sbornik materialiov mezhdunarodnogo seminara [Prevention and elimination of trafficking in persons: collection of materials from the international seminar]* (Moscow: Association of Crisis Centers for Women "Stop Violence").

55. Larisa Ponarina, ANNA National Center for the Prevention of Violence, Moscow Open Society Institute, 2006, "Violence against Women: Does the Government Care in Russia?" Fact Sheet: Open Society Institute, http://www.stopvaw.org/

sites/3f6d15f4-c12d-4515-8544-26b7a3a5a41e/uploads/RUSSIA_VAW_FACT_
SHEET_2006_2.pdf (accessed April 24, 2007).

56. State Department, 2007, "Country Reports on Human Rights Practices 2006: Russia," Bureau of Democracy, Human Rights, and Labor, March 6, http://www.state.gov/g/drl/rls/hrrpt/2006/78835.htm (accessed April 23, 2007).
57. Larisa Ponarina, ANNA National Center for the Prevention of Violence, Moscow Open Society Institute, 2006, "Violence against Women: Does the Government Care in Russia?" Fact Sheet: Open Society Institute, http://www.stopvaw.org/sites/3f6d15f4-c12d-4515-8544-26b7a3a5a41e/uploads/RUSSIA_VAW_FACT_SHEET_2006_2.pdf (accessed April 24, 2007).
58. State Department, 2007, "Country Reports on Human Rights Practices 2006: Russia," Bureau of Democracy, Human Rights, and Labor, March 6, http://www.state.gov/g/drl/rls/hrrpt/2006/78835.htm (accessed April 23, 2007). The U.S. State Department stated that this resulted in written agreements between police and NGOs in two cities. Some activists have told me that this U.S. pressure has provoked more nationalist resistance.
59. This estimate was for January 2005 to February 2006. Angel Coalition 2006 Presentation on trafficking in Russia, an event parallel to the Commission on the Status of Women, U.N. Church Center, New York, March 2, 2006.
60. "The new initiative is part of the on-going IOM project 'Prevention of Human Trafficking in the Russian Federation' that is financed by the European Commission Delegation in Russia with co-funding from the governments of Switzerland and the United States." MAHR website, "Reintegration Assistance for Victims of Trafficking," http://www.stopvaw.org/Reintegration_IOM_for_Trafficking_Victims.html (accessed April 23, 2007).
61. Elisabeth Duban (former gender expert at ABA-CEELI Moscow), personal communication, January 14, 2008.
62. Elena Tiuriukanova (leading research at the Institute for Socio-Economic Population Studies at the Russian Academy of Sciences), interview by the author, Moscow, July 26, 2004.
63. Andrew E. Kramer, "Markets Suffers after Russian Bans Immigrant Venders," *New York Times,* April 14, 2007, p. A3.
64. Victor Yasmann, 2007, "Russia: Re-branding the Nation," *RFE/RL,* February 6, http://www.rferl.org/featuresarticle/2007/02/01743cd3-2f57-49d6-91d0-15d2e62cc15f.html (accessed December 19, 2007).

## 7. Conclusion

1. See also *Castle Rock v. Gonzalez* (545 U.S. 748 (2005)).
2. Russia prosecuted some 25 cases over the last couple of years, whereas in the United States, with almost twice the population, approximately 20 cases per year are opened, albeit with more defendants per case than in Russia. See Tiuriukanova 2006 (79) and U.S. Department of Justice press release, "Justice Department Highlights Five Years of Unprecedented Success Fighting Human Trafficking," March 15, 2006, http://www.usdoj.gov/opa/pr/2006/March/06_crt_144.html (accessed May 22, 2006).

3. G. Tisheva, MAHR, "The Law on Protection against Domestic Violence in Bulgaria: Insights and History," *Stop Violence Against Women,* May 31, 2005, http://www.stopvaw.org/31May2005.html (accessed October 21, 2006).

4. See CIA, "Rank Order Pages," *The World Factbook,* April 4, 2006, https:// www.cia.gov/cia/publications/factbook/docs/rankorderguide.html (accessed August 3, 2006). As of 2004–2005, Russia's GDP per capita is about average for all countries in the world. It is also about average for formerly communist countries.

# WORKS CITED

Abubikirova, Nataliia. 1994. "Nasilie protiv zhenshchin" [Violence against women]. Moscow.

———. 2002. "Russia: The Main Goal Is to Protect the Victims." *We/Myi: The Women's Dialogue,* no. 18.

Abubikirova, N. I., T. A. Klimenkova, E. V. Kotchkina, M. A. Regentova, and T. G. Troinova. 1998. *Directory of Women's Non-Governmental Organizations in Russia and the NIS.* I. Savelieva. Moscow: Aslan Publishers.

Abubikirova, N. I., M. A. Regentova, E. V. Morozova, and T. G. Poddubnaiia, eds. 1999. *FemInf: Transnatsional'nyi Biznes ili Svoboda Peredvizheniia* [FemInf: Transnational Business or Freedom of Movement]. Vol. 5. Moscow: Fal'ta/ Women's Network Program of the Open Society Institute.

Al-Ali, Nadje. 2003. "Gender and Civil Society in the Middle East." *International Feminist Journal of Politics* 5, no. 2: 216–32.

Alvarez, Sonia E. 1999. "The Latin American Feminist NGO 'Boom.'" *International Feminist Journal of Politics* 1, no. 2: 181–209.

Amnesty International. 2005. *Rossiiskaia Federatsiia: Ne kuda bezhat'—domashnee nasilie nad zhenshchinami* [Russian Federation: Nowhere to turn to—Violence against women in the family], EUR 46/056/2005. London: Amnesty International.

Anderson, Benedict. 1983. *The Imagined Community: Reflections on the Origin and Spread of Nationalism.* New York: Verso.

Attwood, Lynne. 1996. "The Post-Soviet Woman in the Move to the Market: A Return to Domesticity and Dependence?" In *Women in Russia and Ukraine,* ed. Rosalind Marsh, 255–66. New York: Cambridge University Press.

———. 1997. "'She Was Asking for It': Rape and Domestic Violence against Women." In *Post-Soviet Women: From the Baltic to Central Asia,* ed. Mary Buckley, 99–118. Cambridge: Cambridge University Press.

Azhgikhina, Nadezhda. 2002. Editor's introduction. Special issue on the Trafficking of Women, *We/Myi, The Women's Dialogue,* no. 18.

Balibalova, D. I., P. P. Glushchenko, and E. M. Tikhomirova. 2001. *Sotsial'no-provavovaia zashchita zhenshchin: Predotvrashchenie nasiliia v otnoshenii zhenshchin i detei* [Social-legal defense of women: The prevention of violence against women and children]. Saint Petersburg: CPB: NII Khimmii SPBGU.

Basu, Amrita. 1995. *The Challenge of Local Feminisms: Women's Movements in Global Perspective.* Boulder: Westview Press.

Beck, Adrian, and Annette Roberston. 2005. "Policing in Post-Soviet Russia." In *Ruling Russia: Law, Crime, and Justice in a Changing Society,* ed. William Pridemore, 247–81. Lanham, Md.: Rowman and Littlefield.

Benford, Robert D., and David A. Snow. 2000. "Framing Processes and Social Movements: An Overview and Assessment." *Annual Review of Sociology* 26, no. 1: 611–39.

Benninger-Budel, Carin, and Lucinda O'Hanlon. 2004. "Violence against Women in Russia: A Report to the Committee on Economic, Social and Cultural Rights." *Violence against Women: 10 Reports/Year 2003: For the Protection and Promotion of the Human Rights of Women.* Geneva: World Organisation against Torture.

Bobylev, Sergei N., and Anastassia L. Alexandrova. 2005. *Human Development Report 2005 Russian Federation: Russia in 2015; Development Goals and Politics Priorities.* Moscow: UNDP.

Boichenko, L. D. 2004. *Problemy nasiliia i treffika: Vozniknovenie i preduprezhednie* [The problems of violence and trafficking: Origin and prevention]. Petrozavodsk: Petrozavodsk State University.

Bridger, Sue, ed. 1999. *Women and Political Change: Perspectives from East-Central Europe.* New York: St. Martin's Press.

Brunell, Laura, and Janet Elise Johnson. 2007. "The New WAVE: How Transnational Feminist Networks Promote Domestic Violence Reform in Postcommunist Europe." Unpublished manuscript.

Brygalina, Julia, and Anna Temkina. 2004. "The Development of Feminist Organisations in St. Petersburg 1985–2003." In *Between Sociology and History,* ed. Anna-Maija Castren et al., 207–26. Helsinki: SKS/Finnish Literature Society.

Buckley, Mary. 1985. "Soviet Interpretations of the Woman Question." In *Soviet Sisterhood,* ed. Barbara Holland, 24–53. Bloomington: Indiana University Press.

———. 1999. "From Faction Not to Party: 'Women of Russia.'" In *Women and Political Change: Perspectives from East-Central Europe,* ed. Sue Bridger, 151–67. New York: St. Martin's Press.

Bunch, Charlotte. 1995. "Transforming Human Rights from a Feminist Perspective." In *Women's Rights, Human Rights: International Feminist Perspectives,* ed. Julie Peters and Andrea Wolper, 11–17. New York: Routledge.

Bush, Diane Mitsch. 1992. "Women's Movements and State Policy Reform Aimed at Domestic Violence against Women: A Comparison of the Consequences of Movement Mobilization in the United States and India." *Gender and Society* 6, no. 4: 587–608.

Caiazza, Amy. 2002. *Mothers and Soldiers: Gender, Citizenship, and Civil Society in Contemporary Russia.* New York: Routledge.

Caldwell, Gillian, Steven Galster, and Nadia Steinzor. 1997. *Crime and Servitude: An Expose of the Traffic in Women for Prostitution from the Newly Independent States.* Washington, D.C.: Global Survival Network.

Chapkis, Wendy. 2005. "Soft Glove, Punishing Fist: The Trafficking Victims Protection Act of 2000." In *Regulating Sex: The Politics of Intimacy and Identity,* ed. Elizabeth Bernstein and Laurie Schafner, 51–65. New York: Routledge.

Checkel, Jeffrey T. 1998. "The Constructivist Turn in International Relations Theory." *World Politics* 50, no. 2: 324–48.

Clark, Cindy, et al. 2006. *Where Is the Money for Women's Rights? Assessing Resources and the Role of Donors in the Promotion of Women's Rights and the Support of Women's Organizations.* Toronto: Association of Women's Rights in Development; Just Associates.

Coker, Donna. 2004. "Race, Poverty, and the Crime-Centered Response to Domestic Violence." *Violence Against Women* 10, no. 11: 1331–53.

Colonomos, Ariel. 2004. "Civil Norms and 'Unjust" Embargoes." *Journal of Human Rights* 3, no. 2: 194–201.

Coomaraswamy, Radhika. 1996. *Report of the Special Rapporteur on Violence against Women, Its Causes and Consequences, in Accordance with Commission on Human Rights Resolution 1995/85 (United Nations E/CN.4/1996/53), A Framework for Model Legislation on Domestic Violence,* E/CN.4/1996/53/Add.2.

Corrin, Chris, ed. 1996. *Women in a Violent World: Feminist Analyses and Resistance across 'Europe.'* Edinburgh: Edinburgh University Press.

Costain, Anne N. 1998. "Women Lobby Congress." In *Social Movements and American Political Institutions,* ed. Anne N. Costain and Andrew S. McFarland. Lanham, Md.: Rowman and Littlefield.

Danilenko, Gennady M., and William Burnham. 1999. *Law and Legal System of the Russian Federation.* Yonkers, N.Y.: Juris Publishing.

Davis, Lance, and Stanley Engerman. 2003. "History Lessons: Sanctions: Neither War nor Peace." *Journal of Economic Perspectives* 17, no. 2: 187–97.

D'iachenko, A., and I. Koloskova. 1995. "Iznasilovaniia: Statisticheskii aspect" [Rape: Statistical aspect]. *Voprosy Statistiki* [Questions of statistics], no. 2: 81–84.

Dobash, R. Emerson, and Russell P. Dobash. 1992. *Women, Violence, and Social Change.* New York: Routledge.

Drakulic, Slavenka. 1993. "A Letter from the United States—The Critical Theory Approach." In *How We Survived Communism and Even Laughed,* 123–32. London: Vantage.

Duban, Elisabeth. 2006. *CEDAW Assessment Tool Report for the Russian Federation.* Moscow: ABA-CEELI.

Einhorn, Barbara. 1993. *Cinderella Goes to Market: Citizenship, Gender and Women's Movements in East Central Europe.* New York: Verso.

Elman, R. Amy. 1996. *Sexual Subordination and State Intervention: Comparing Sweden and the United States.* Providence, R.I.: Berghahn Books.

Enloe, Cynthia. 1993. *The Morning After: Sexual Politics at the End of the Cold War.* Berkeley and Los Angeles: University of California Press.

Erokhina, Liudmila D. 2002. "Torgovlia zhenshchinami: Fenomen real'nyi ili nadumannyi?" In *Torgovliia liud'mi: Sotsiokriminologicheskii analiz* [Human trafficking: Social-criminological analysis], ed. E. B. Tiuriukanova, and L. D. Erokhina, 35–58. Moscow: Academia.

———. 2005. "Trafficking in Women in the Russian Far East: A Real or Imaginary Phenomenon?" In *Human Traffic and Transnational Crime: Eurasian and American Perspectives,* ed. Sally Stoecker and Louise Shelley, 79–94. New York: Rowman and Littlefield.

Erturk, Yakin. 2006. *Integration of the Human Rights of Women and a Gender*

*Perspective: Violence against Women: Report of the Special Rapporteur on Violence against Women, Its Causes and Consequences: Mission to the Russian Federation,* E/CN.4/2006/61/Add.2.

Essig, Laurie. 1999. *Queer in Russia: A Story of Sex, Self, and the Other.* Durham, N.C.: Duke University Press.

Estrich, Susan. 1987. *Real Rape.* Cambridge, Mass.: Harvard University Press.

*European Sourcebook of Crime and Criminal Justice Statistics.* 1999. Council of Europe. Available online http://www.europeansourcebook.org/esb/index.html (accessed October 7, 2004).

Ferree, Myra Marx. 2003. "Resonance and Radicalism: Feminist Framing in the Abortion Debate of the United States and Germany." *American Journal of Sociology* 109, no. 2 (September): 304–44.

Fish, M. Steven. 1998. "The Determinants of Economic Reform in the Post-Communist World." *East European Politics and Societies* 12, no. 1: 31–78.

Fraser, Arvonne S. 1987. *The U.N. Decade for Women: Documents and Dialogue.* Boulder, Colo.: Westview Press.

Fraser, Nancy. 1990. "Struggle over Needs: Outline of a Socialist-Feminist Critical Theory of Late-Capitalist Political Culture." In *Women, the State, and Welfare,* ed. Linda Gordon, 199–225. Madison: University of Wisconsin Press.

Friedman, Elisabeth. 1995. "Women's Human Rights: The Emergence of a Movement." In *Women's Rights, Human Rights: International Feminist Perspectives,* ed. Julie Peters and Andrea Wolper, 18–35. New York: Routledge.

Funk, Nanette. 1993. "Feminism East and West." In *Gender Politics and Post-Communism: Reflections from Eastern Europe and the Former Soviet Union,* ed. Nanette Funk and Magda Mueller, 318–30. New York: Routledge.

———. 2006. "Women's NGOs in Central and Eastern Europe and the Former Soviet Union: The Imperialist Criticism." In *Women and Citizenship in Central and Eastern Europe,* ed. Lukić, Jasmina, Joanna Regulska, and Darja Zaviršek. Hampshire, Great Britain: Ashgate.

———. 2007. "Fifteen Years of the East-West Women's Dialogue." In *Living Gender after Communism,* ed. Janet Elise Johnson and Jean C. Robinson, 203–26. Bloomington: Indiana University Press.

Geertz, Clifford. 1973. *The Interpretation of Cultures.* New York: Basic Books.

Ghodsee, Kristen. 2004. "Feminism-by-Design: Emerging Capitalisms, Cultural Feminism, and Women's Nongovernmental Organizations in Postsocialist Eastern Europe." *Signs: Journal of Women in Culture and Society* 29, no. 3: 728–53.

Gondolf, Edward W., and Dmitri Shestakov. 1997. "Spousal Homicide in Russia versus the United States: Preliminary Findings and Implications." *Journal of Family Violence* 12, no. 1: 63–74.

Goodey, Jo. 2004. "Sex Trafficking in Women from Central and East European Countries: Promoting a 'Victim-Centered' and 'Woman-Centered' Approach to Criminal Justice Intervention." *Feminist Review* 76: 26–45.

Gorshkova, I. D., and I. I. Shurygina. 2003. *Nasilie nad zhenami v sovremennykh rossiiskikh sem'iakh* [Violence against women in contemporary Russian families]. Moscow: Moscow State University Women's Committee.

Goscilo, Helena. 1996. *Dehexing Sex: Russian Womanhood during and after Glasnost.* Ann Arbor: University of Michigan Press.

Granik, Lisa. 1997. "The Trials of the Proletarka: Sexual Harassment Claims in the 1920s." In *Reforming Justice in Russia, 1864–1996: Power, Culture, and the Limits of Legal Order,* ed. Peter H. Jr. Solomon, 131–67. Armonk, N.Y.: M. E. Sharpe.

Hardy, Cynthia, Bill Harley, and Nelson Phillips. 2004. "Discourse Analysis and Content Analysis: Two Solitudes?" *Qualitative Methods* 2, no. 1: 19–22.

Hawkesworth, Mary E. 2006. *Globalization and Feminist Activism.* Lanham, Md.: Rowman and Littlefield.

Heise, Lori, et al. 1994. Violence against Women: A Neglected Public Health Issue in Less Developed Countries. *Social Science and Medicine* 39: 1165–79.

Hemment, Julie. 1999. "Gendered Violence in Crisis: Russian NGOs Help Themselves to Liberal Feminist Discourse." *Anthropology of East Europe Review* 17, no. 1 (Spring): 35–38.

———. 2004a. "Global Civil Society and the Local Costs of Belonging: Defining 'Violence against Women' in Russia." *Signs* 29, no. 3: 815–40.

———. 2004b. "Strategizing Gender and Development: Action Research and Ethnographic Responsibility in the Russian Provinces." In *Post-Soviet Women Encountering Transition: Nation-Building, Economic Survival, and Civic Activism,* ed. Kathleen Kuenhast and Carol Nechemias, 313–33. Washington, D.C.: Woodrow Wilson Center Press; Baltimore: Johns Hopkins University Press.

———. 2007. *Empowering Women in Russia: Activism, Aid, and NGOs.* Bloomington: Indiana University Press.

Henderson, Sarah L. 2000. "Importing Civil Society." *Democratizatsia* 8, no. 1: 65–82.

———. 2001. "Association of Crisis Centers for Women." In *Encyclopedia of Russian Women's Movements,* ed. Norma Corigliano Noon and Carol Nechemias, 224–26. Westport, Conn.: Praeger.

———. 2002. "Selling Civil Society: Western Aid and Nongovernmental Organization Sector in Russia." *Comparative Political Studies* 35, no. 2: 139–67.

———. 2003. *Building Democracy in Contemporary Russia: Western Support for Grassroots Organizations.* Ithaca, N.Y.: Cornell University Press.

Hester, Marianne. 2005. "Transnational Influences on Domestic Violence Policy and Action—Exploring Developments in China and England." *Social Policy and Society* 4, no. 4: 447–56.

Highlights from the Duma Roundtable on Trafficking. 1999. *Organized Crime Watch—Russia* 1, no. 2. Center for the Study of Transnational Crime and Corruption at American University, Washington, D.C.

Howard, Marc Morje. 2003. *The Weakness of Civil Society in Post-Communist Europe.* Cambridge: Cambridge University Press.

Hrycak, Alexandra. 2002. "From Mothers' Rights to Equal Rights: Post-Soviet Grassroots Women's Associations." In *Women's Activism and Globalization: Linking Local Struggles and Transnational Politics,* ed. Nancy A. Naples and Manisha Desai, 64–82. New York: Routledge.

———. 2006. "Foundation Feminism and the Articulation of Hybrid Feminisms in Post-Socialist Ukraine." *East European Politics and Societies* 20, no. 1: 69–100.

Huda, Sigma. 2006. *Integration of the Human Rights of Women and a Gender Perspective: Report of the Special Rapporteur on the Human Rights Aspects of the Victims of Trafficking in Persons, Especially Women and Children,* E/CN.4/

2006/62. UN Commission on Human Rights, Sixty-second session, Item 12 of the provisional agenda, available at http://www.ohchr.org/english/bodies/chr/docs/62chr/ecn4-2006-62.doc (accessed May 11, 2006).

Hughes, Donna. 2002. "The Corruption of Civil Society: Maintaining the Flow of Women to the Sex Industries." Paper presented at the conference, Encuentro Internacional Sobre Trafico De Mujeres y Explotacion [International Meeting about the Trafficking of Women and Exploitation], Sept. 23, in Malaga, Spain.

Human Rights Watch. 1995. *The Human Rights Watch Global Report on Women's Human Rights.* New York: Human Rights Watch.

———. 1997. "Russia—Too Little, Too Late: State Response to Violence against Women." *Human Rights Watch* 9, no. 13 (December): 1–51.

———. 1999. *Confessions at Any Cost: Police Torture in Russia.* New York: Human Rights Watch.

Ignatov, Aleksei. 1996. Voprosy razvitiia ugolovnogo zakonadatel'stva ob otvetstvennosti za prestupleniia na seksual'noi pochve [Questions on the development of criminal legislation on the responsibility for crime of a sexual basis]. Zoia Khotkina. Moscow: American Bar Association Central and Eastern European Law Initiative, the Women's Consortium, Moscow Center for Gender Studies.

Ishkanian, Armine. 2004. "Working at the Local-Global Intersection: The Challenges Facing Women in Armenia's Nongovernmental Sector." In *Post-Soviet Women Encountering Transition: Nation-Building, Economic Survival, and Civic Activism,* ed. Kathleen Kuenhast and Carol Nechemias, 262–78. Washington, D.C.: Woodrow Wilson Center Press; Baltimore: Johns Hopkins University Press.

Israelian, E. B., and T. Iu. Zabelina. 1995. *Kak sozdat' krizisnyi tsentr dlia zhenshchin* [How to start a crisis center for women]. Moscow: Press-Solo.

Johnson, Janet Elise. 2001. "Privatizing Pain: The Problem of Woman Battery in Russia." *NWSA Journal* 13, no. 3 (Fall): 153–68.

———. 2004. "Sisterhood vs. the 'Moral' Russian State: The Postcommunist Politics of Rape." In *Post-Soviet Women Encountering Transition: Nation-Building, Economic Survival, and Civic Activism,* ed. Kathleen Kuenhast and Carol Nechemias, 217–38. Washington, D.C.: Woodrow Wilson Center Press; Baltimore: Johns Hopkins University Press.

———. 2005. "Violence against Women in Russia." In *Ruling Russia: Law, Crime, and Justice in a Changing Society,* ed. William Pridemore, 147–66. Lanham, Md.: Rowman and Littlefield.

———. 2006. "Public-Private Permutations: Domestic Violence Crisis Centers in Barnaul." In *Russian Civil Society: A Critical Assessment,* ed. Al Evans, Laura Henry, and Lisa McIntosh Sundstrom, 266–83. Armonk, N.Y.: M. E. Sharpe.

———. 2007a. "Contesting Violence, Contesting Gender: Crisis Centers Encountering Local Governments in Barnaul, Russia." In *Living Gender after Communism,* ed. Janet Elise Johnson and Jean C. Robinson, 40–57. Bloomington: Indiana University Press.

———. 2007b. "Domestic Violence Politics in Post-Soviet States." *Social Politics: International Studies in Gender, State, and Society* 14, no. 3: 1–26.

Johnson, Janet Elise, and Laura Brunell. 2006. "The Emergence of Contrasting Domestic Violence Regimes in Postcommunist Europe." *Policy and Politics* 34, no. 4: 578–98.

Johnson, Janet Elise, and Jean C. Robinson, eds. 2007. *Living Gender after Communism.* Bloomington: Indiana University Press.

Jones, Ann. 2000. *Next Time She'll Be Dead: Battering and How to Stop It.* Boston: Beacon Press.

Juviler, Peter H. 1977. "Women and Sex in Soviet Law." In *Women in Russia,* ed. Dorothy Atkinson, Alexander Dallin, and Gail Warshofsky Lapidus, 243–65. Stanford, Calif.: Stanford University Press.

Kaldor, Mary. 2003. *Global Civil Society: An Answer to War.* Cambridge: Blackwell Publishing.

Kaldor, Mary, Helmut Anheier, and Marlies Glasius, eds. 2003. *Global Civil Society 2003.* New York: Oxford University Press.

Kantola, Johanna. 2006. *Feminists Theorize the State.* New York: Palgrave Macmillan.

Katzenstein, Peter J., ed. 1996. *The Culture of National Security: Norms and Identity in World Politics.* New York: Columbia University Press.

Kay, Rebecca. 2000. *Russian Women and Their Organizations.* New York: St. Martin's Press.

————. 2004. "Meeting the Challenge Together? Russian Grassroots Women's Organizations and the Shortcomings of Western Aid." In *Post-Soviet Women Encountering Transition: Nation-Building, Economic Survival, and Civic Activism,* ed. Kathleen Kuenhast and Carol Nechemias, 241–61. Washington, D.C.: Woodrow Wilson Center Press; Baltimore: Johns Hopkins University Press.

Keck, Margaret, and Kathryn Sikkink. 1998. *Activists beyond Borders: Transnational Advocacy Networks in International Politics.* Ithaca, N.Y.: Cornell University Press.

Khodyreva, Natalia. 1996. "Sexism and Sexual Abuse in Russia." In *Women in a Violent World: Feminist Analyses and Resistance Across 'Europe,'* ed. Chris Corrin, 27–40. Edinburgh: Edinburgh University Press.

————. 2004. "The Problem of Trafficking in Women at the Transnational and National Levels: With the Example of Russia and the NIS." In *Crossing Borders: Re-mapping Women's Movements at the Turn of the 21st Century,* ed. Hilda Romer Christensen, Beatrice Halsaa, and Aino Saarinen, 239–53. Odense, Denmark: University Press of Southern Denmark.

————. 2005. "Sexuality for Whom? Paid Sex and Patriarchy in Russia." In *Sexuality and Gender in Postcommunist Eastern Europe and Russi,* ed. Aleksandar Stulhofer and Theo Sandfort, 243–63. New York: Haworth Press.

Khotkina, Zoia, ed. 1996. *Seksual'nye Domogatel'stva na Rabote* [Sexual harassment]. Moscow: American Bar Association Central and Eastern European Law Initiative, the Women's Consortium, Moscow Center for Gender Studies.

Kleimenov, Mikhail, and Stanislov Shamkov. 2005. "Criminal Transportation of Persons: Trends and Recommendations." In *Human Traffic and Transnational Crime: Eurasian and American Perspectives,* ed. Sally Stoecker and Louise Shelley, 29–46. New York: Rowman and Littlefield.

Kletsin, Alexandr. 1998. *Sotsiologicheskii analiz seksual'nykh domogatel'stv na rabote (na primere Sankt-Peterburga)* [Sociological analysis of sexual harassment in the workplace (for example St. Petersburg)]. St. Petersburg: Trudy SPB filial Instituta sotsiologii RAN.

Klotz, Audie. 1995. *Norms in International Relations: The Struggle against Apartheid.* Ithaca, N.Y.: Cornell University Press.

Kon, Igor S. 1995. "Sex as a Mirror of the Russian Revolution." *Demokratizatsiya* 3: 233–42.

———. 2005. "Sexual Culture and Politics in Contemporary Russia." In *Sexuality and Gender in Postcommunist Eastern Europe and Russi,* ed. Aleksandar Stulhofer and Theo Sandfort, 111–23. New York: Haworth Press.

Kostenko, Maksim. 2003. "Work with Batterers in the Altay Regional Centre for Men." In *NCRB: A Network for Crisis Centres for Women in the Barents Region (Report of the Nordic-Russian Development Project, 1999–2002),* ed. Aino Saarinen, Olga Liapounova, and Irina Drachova [Dracheva], 5:1–248. Arkhangelsk, Russia: Pomor State University named after M. V. Lomonosov.

Krizsan, Andrea, Marjolein Paantjens, and Ilse van Lamoen. 2005. "Domestic Violence: Whose Problem? Policies Addressing Domestic Violence in Hungary, the Netherlands, and the EU." *Greek Review of Social Research* 117, no. B: 63–92.

Kuenhast, Kathleen, and Carol Nechemias, eds. 2004. *Post-Soviet Women Encountering Transition: Nation-Building, Economic Survival, and Civic Activism.* Washington, D.C.: Woodrow Wilson Center Press; Baltimore: Johns Hopkins University Press.

Kuznetsova, Nadezhda. 1997. "Prava zhenshchin: Real'nost' i perspektivy." *Vy i My: Dialog Rossiiskikh i Amerikanskikh Zhenshchin* [You and we: Dialogue of Russian and American women] 1, no. 13: 16–18.

Lapidus, Gail Warshofsky. 1977. "Sexual Equality in Soviet Policy: A Developmental Perspective." In *Women in Russia,* ed. Dorothy Atkinson, Alexander Dallin, and Gail Warshofsky Lapidus. Stanford, Calif.: Stanford University Press.

Levin, Eve. 1989. *Sex and Society of the Orthodox Slavs, 900–1700.* Ithaca, N.Y.: Cornell University Press.

Liapounova, Olga, and Irina Drachova [Dracheva]. 2004. "Crisis Centres for Women in North West Russia: Ideology, Management and Practice." In *Crisis Centres and Violence against Women: Dialogue in the Barents Region,* ed. Aino Saarinen and Elaine Carey-Belanger, 39–68. Oulu, Finland: Oulu University Press.

Liapounova, Olga, and Irina Dracheva [Drachova].2005. "Present-Day Situation of Crisis Centres for Women in Northwest Russia (Results of the Research)." Paper given at the NCRB related workshop, Crisis Centres and Violence against Women, at the Nordic conference, "Gender and Violence: Power, Resistance and Challenges for the Future," in Gothenburg, Sweden, June 10–12.

Liborakina, Marina. 1999. *Zhenshchiny i privatizatsiia* [Women and privatization]. Moscow: Institute for Urban Economics; Femina; Women, Law and Development International; USAID.

Lissyutkina, Larissa. 1999. "Emancipation without Feminism." In *Women and Political Change: Perspectives from East-Central Europe,* ed. Sue Bridger, 168–87. New York: St. Martin's Press.

Luciano, Dinys, Simel Esim, and Nata Dubbury. 2005. "How to Make the Law Work? Budgetary Implications of Domestic Violence Laws in Latin America, Central American, and the Caribbean." *Women, Politics, and Policy* 27, no. 1/2: 123–33.

Lukshevskii, S. 2003. *Diskriminatsiia zhenshchin v sovremennoi Rossii* [Discrimination against women in contemporary Russia]. Moscow: Moscow Helsinki Group.

Lyon, Tania Rands. 2003. "Changing Family-State Boundaries: Who Raises the Children in Post-Soviet Russia." Ph.D. diss., Sociology, Princeton University.

———. 2007. "Housewife Fantasies, Family Realities in the New Russia." In *Living Gender after Communism,* ed. Janet Elise Johnson and Jean C. Robinson, 25–39. Bloomington: Indiana University Press.

Matthews, Nancy. 1994. *Confronting Rape: The Feminist Anti-Rape Movement and the State.* New York: Routledge.

Mazur, Amy G. 2002. *Theorizing Feminist Policy.* Oxford: Oxford University Press.

McCarthy, John D., and Mayer N. Zald. 1975. "Resource Mobilization and Social Movements: A Partial Theory." *American Journal of Sociology* 82: 1212–41.

McMahon, Patrice. 2001. "Building Civil Societies in East Central Europe: The Effect of American Non-governmental Organizations on Women's Groups." *Democratization* 8, no. 2: 45–68.

Mendelson, Sarah E., and John K. Glenn, eds. 2002. *The Power and Limits of NGOs: A Critical Look at Building Democracy in Eastern Europe and Eurasia.* New York: Columbia University Press.

Merry, Sally Engle. 2006a. *Human Rights and Gender Violence: Translating International Law into Local Justice.* Chicago: University of Chicago Press.

———. 2006b. "Transnational Human Rights and Local Activism: Mapping the Middle." *American Anthropologist* 108, no. 1: 38–51.

Mertus, Julie. 2004. *Bait and Switch: Human Rights and U.S. Foreign Policy.* New York: Routledge.

Merzova, Elena. 2004. "Development of Crisis Centres—Social Partnership: The Experience of the Crisis Centre Maja (Petrozavodsk)." In *NCRB: A Network for Crisis Centres for Women in the Barents Region (Report of the Nordic-Russian Development Project, 1999–2002),* ed. Aino Saarinen, Olga Liapounova, and Irina Drachova, 129–35. Arkhangelsk, Russia: Pomor State University named after M. V. Lomonosov.

Moghadam, Valentine M. 2005. *Globalizing Women: Transnational Feminist Networks.* Baltimore: Johns Hopkins University Press.

Mohanty, Chandra Talpade. 1991. "Under Western Eyes: Feminist Scholarship and Colonial Discourses." In *Third World Women and the Politics of Feminism,* ed. Chandra Talpade Mohanty, Ann Russo, and Lourdes Torres, 51–80. Bloomington: Indiana University Press.

Mukhin, A. A. 2002. *Rossiiskaia organizovannaia prestupnost' i vlast': Istoriia vzaimootnoshenii* [Russian organized crime and the state: History of mutual relations]. Moscow: Center for Political Information.

Nalla, Mahesh K., and Graeme R. Newman. 1994. "Crime in the U.S. and the Former U.S.S.R.: A Comparison of Crime Trends from the Third United Nations World Survey." *International Journal of Comparative and Applied Criminal Justice* 18, no. 1: 85–94.

Naples, Nancy A. 2002. "Changing the Terms: Community Activism, Globalization, and the Dilemmas of Transnational Feminist Praxis." In *Women's Activism and Globalization: Linking Local Struggles and Transnational Politics,* ed. Nancy A. Naples and Manisha Desai, 3–14. New York: Routledge.

Naumov, A. V. 1997. *Kommentarii k ugolovnomu kodeksu Rossiiskoi Federatsii* [Commentary on the criminal code of the Russian Federation]. Moscow: Iurist'.

Nechemias, Carol. 1991. "The Prospects for a Soviet Women's Movement: Opportunities and Obstacles." In *Perestroika from Below: Social Movements in the Soviet Union,* ed. Judith B. Sedaitis and Jim Butterfield, 73–95. Boulder, Colo.: Westview Press.

———. 2000. "Politics in Post-Soviet Russia: Where Are the Women?" *Demokratizatsiya* 8, no. Spring: 199–218.

———. 2001. "Independent Women's Forum in Dubna." In *Encyclopedia of Russian Women's Movements,* ed. Nomra Corigliano Noon and Carol Nechemias, 261–63. Westport, Conn.: Praeger.

Neuendorf, Kimberly A. 2004. "Content Analysis: A Contrast and Complement to Discourse Analysis." *Qualitative Methods* 2, no. 1: 33–39.

Noonan, Norma Corigliano, and Carol Nechemias, eds. 2001. *Encyclopedia of Russian Women's Movements.* Westport, Conn.: Praeger.

Open Society Institute/Network Women's Program/Violence Against Women Monitoring Program. 2007. *Violence against Women: Does the Government Care in Russia?* Budapest, Hungary: Open Society Institute.

Outshoorn, Joyce. 2004. *The Politics of Prostitution: Women's Movements, Democratic States and the Globalisation of Sex Commerce.* Cambridge: Cambridge University Press.

Pape, Robert A. 1997. "Why Economic Sanctions Do Not Work." *International Security* 22, no. 2: 90–136.

Pashina, Albina [Al'bina]. 2004. "The Crisis Centre Movement in Russia: Characteristics, Successes and Problems." In *Crisis Centres and Violence against Women: Dialogue in the Barents Region,* ed. Aino Saarinen and Elaine Carey-Belanger, 19–38. Oulu, Finland: Oulu University Press.

Pateman, Carole. 1988. *The Sexual Contract.* Stanford, Calif.: Stanford University Press.

Peters, Julie, and Andrea Wolper, eds. 1995. *Women's Rights, Human Rights: International Feminist Perspectives.* New York: Routledge.

Pisklakova, Marina. 1996. "Opyt raboty moskovskogo krizisnogo tsentra s zhertvami seksual'nykh presledovanii" [The experience of working with victims of sexual harassment at the Moscow crisis center]. In *Seksual'nye Domogatel'stva na Rabote [Sexual Harassment],* ed. Zoia Khotkina, 40–42. Moscow: American Bar Association Central and Eastern European Law Initiative, the Women's Consortium, Moscow Center for Gender Studies.

Post, Dianne. 2000. "Domestic Violence in Russia." *Journal of Gender Studies* 9, no. 1: 81–83.

———. 2001. "Women's Rights in Russia: Training Non-lawyers to Represent Victims of Domestic Violence." *Yale Human Rights and Development Law Journal* 4: 135–47.

———. 2002. "Russian Women, American Eyes: The Rebirth of Feminism in Russia" (Draft manuscript prepared for the Kennan Workshop on Women in the Former Soviet Union).

Putnam, Robert D. 1988. "Diplomacy and Domestic Politics: The Logic of 2-Level Games." *International Organization* 42, no. 3: 427–69.

Racioppi, Linda, and Katherine O'Sullivan See. 1995. "Organizing Women before

and after the Fall: Women's Politics in the Soviet Union and Post-Soviet Russia."
*Signs* 20, no. 41 (Summer): 818–50.

———. 1997. *Women's Activism in Contemporary Russia*. Philadelphia: Temple.

Richard, Amy O'Neill. 1999. *International Trafficking in Women to the United States: A Contemporary Manifestation of Slavery and Organized Crime*. Washington, D.C.: Center for the Study of Intelligence.

Richter, James. 2002. "Evaluating Western Assistance to Russian Women's Organizations." In *The Power and Limits of NGOs: A Critical Look at Building Democracy in Eastern Europe and Eurasia*, ed. Sarah E. Mendelson and John K. Glenn, 54–90. New York: Columbia University Press.

Rimasheevskaia, N. M., ed. 2005. *Razorvat' krug molchaniia: O nasilii v otnoshenii zhenshchin* [To break the circle of silence: On violence against women]. Moscow: URSS.

Rivkin-Fish, Michele. 2004. "Gender and Democracy: Strategies for Engagement and Dialogue on Women's Issues after Socialism in St. Petersburg." In *Post-Soviet Women Encounter Transition: Nation-Building, Economic Survival, and Civil Activism*, ed. Kathleen Keuhnast and Carol Nechemias, 288–312. Washington, D.C.: Wilson Center Press.

———. 2005. *Women's Health in Post-Soviet Russia: The Politics of Intervention*. Bloomington: Indiana University Press.

Robinson, Jean. 1995. "Women, the State, and the Need for Civil Society: The Liga Kobiet in Poland." In *Comparative State Feminism*, ed. Dorothy McBride Stetson, and Amy G. Mazur, 203–20. Thousand Oaks: Sage Publications.

Russian Federation. 1999. *Fifth Periodic Reports of States Parties to the Committee on the Elimination of Discrimination Against Women*, CEDAW/C/USR/5. United Nations Division for the Advancement of Women. Available online at http://www.un.org/womenwatch/daw/cedaw/cedaw26/usr5.pdf (accessed June 23, 2008).

———. 2004. *Replies to the Questionnaire of the United Nations Secretariat on the Implementation of the Beijing Platform for Action Adopted by the Fourth World Conference on the Status of Women (Beijing, 1995), and the Final Documents of the 23rd Special Session of the United Nations General Assembly (New York, 2000)*. United Nations Division for the Advancement of Women, http://www.un.org/womenwatch/daw/Review/responses/RUSSIAN-FEDERATION-English.pdf (accessed March 12, 2006).

Saarinen, Aino. 2004. "Exercises in Transversalism: Reflections on a Nordic and NW-Russian Network for Crisis Centres in Barents." In *Crossing Borders: Re-mapping Women's Movements at the Turn of the 21st Century*, ed. Hilda Romer Christensen, Beatrice Halsaa, and Aino Saarinen, 271–87. Odense, Denmark: University Press of Southern Denmark.

Saarinen, Aino, Olga Liapounova, and Irina Drachova [Dracheva]. 2003a. "Crisis Centres in the Barents Region—Questionnaire Report." *NCRB: A Network for Crisis Centres for Women in the Barents Region (Report of the Nordic-Russian Development Project, 1999–2002)*, ed. Aino Saarinen, Olga Liapounova, and Irina Drachova [Dracheva], 161–95. Arkhangelsk, Russia: Pomor State University named after M. V. Lomonosov.

———, eds. 2003b. *NCRB: A Network for Crisis Centres for Women in the Barents*

Region (Report of the Nordic-Russian Development Project, 1999–2002). 1–248. Arkhangelsk, Russia: Pomor State University named after M. V. Lomonosov.

Saguy, Abigail. 2002. "International Crossways: Traffic in Sexual Harassment Policy." *European Journal of Women's Studies* 9, no. 3: 249–67.

Salmenniemi, Suvi. 2005. "Civic Activity—Feminine Activity? Gender, Civil Society, and Citizenship in Post-Soviet Russia." *Sociology* 39, no. 4: 735–53.

Sandoval, Chela. 2000. *Methodology of the Oppressed*. Minneapolis: University of Minnesota Press.

Schneider, Elizabeth M. 2002. *Battered Women and Feminist Lawmaking*. New Haven, Conn.: Yale University Press.

Schulhofer, Stephen J. 1998. *Unwanted Sex: The Culture of Intimidation and the Failure of Law*. Cambridge, Mass.: Harvard University Press.

Severin, Iu. D. 1984. *Kommentarii k ugolovnomu kodeksu RSFSR* [Commentary on the Criminal Code of the RSFSR]. Moscow: Iurisdicheskaia Literatura.

Shelley, Louise. 1987. "Inter-personal Violence in the USSR." *Violence, Aggression and Terrorism* 1, no. 2: 41–67.

———. 2005. "Russia's Laws against Trade in Persons: A Response to International Pressure and Domestic Coalitions." In *Public Policy and Law in Russia: In Search of a Unified Legal and Political Space*, ed. Ferdinand Feldbrugge and Robert Sharlet, 291–305. Leiden, Netherlands: Martinus Nijhoff Publishers.

Shelley, Louise I., and Robert W. Orttung. 2005. "Russia's Efforts to Combat Human Trafficking: Efficient Crime Groups versus Irresolute Societies and Uncoordinated States." In *Ruling Russia: Law, Crime, and Justice in a Changing Society*, ed. William Pridemore, 167–82. Lanham, Md.: Rowman and Littlefield.

Shevchenko, Iulia. 2007. "Does the Gender of MPs Matter in Postcommunist Politics? The Case of the Russian Duma, 1995–2001." In *Living Gender after Communism*, ed. Janet Elise Johnson and Jean C. Robinson, 128–46. Bloomington: Indiana University Press.

Shtyleva, Lubov. 2003. "Gender Education Programme for Volunteers Improved the Work of the Crisis Centre in Murmansk (Prijut)." In *NCRB: A Network for Crisis Centres for Women in the Barents Region (Report of the Nordic-Russian Development Project, 1999–2002)*, ed. Aino Saarinen, Olga Liapounova, and Irina Drachova [Dracheva], 106–15. Arkhangelsk, Russia: Pomor State University.

Snajdr, Edward. 2005. "Gender, Power, and the Performance of Justice: Muslim Women's Response to Domestic Violence in Kazakhstan." *American Ethnologist* 32, no. 2 (May): 294–311.

Snitow, Ann. 1999. "Cautionary Tales." *American Society of International Law, Proceedings of the Annual Meeting*: 35–42.

Solomon, Peter H. 2005. "The Criminal Procedure Code of 2001: Will It Make Russian Justice More Fair?" In *Ruling Russia: Law, Crime, and Justice in a Changing Society*, ed. William Pridemore, 77–98. Lanham, Md.: Rowman and Littlefield.

Sperling, Valerie. 1990. "Rape and domestic violence in the USSR." *Response to the Victimization of Women and Children: Journal of the Center for Women Policy Studies* 13, no. 3: 16–22.

———. 1999. *Organizing Women in Contemporary Russia: Engendering Transition*. Cambridge: Cambridge University Press.

———. 2005. "Women's Organizations: Institutionalized Interest Groups or Vulnerable Dissidents?" In *Russian Civil Society: A Critical Assessment,* ed. Al Evans, Laura Henry, and Lisa McIntosh Sundstrom, 161–77. Armonk, N.Y.: M. E. Sharpe.

Sperling, Valerie, Myra Marx Ferree, and Barbara Risman. 2001. "Constructing Global Feminism: Transnational Advocacy Networks and Russian Women's Activism." *Signs: Journal of Women in Culture and Society* 26, no. 4: 1155–86.

Staggenborg, Suzanne. 1989. "Organizational and Environmental Influence on the Development of the Pro-Choice Movement." *Social Forces* 68: 204–40.

Stetson, Dorothy McBride, ed. 2002. *Abortion Politics, Women's Movements, and the Democratic State: A Comparative Study of State Feminism.* Oxford: Oxford University Press.

Stetson, Dorothy McBride, and Amy Mazur, eds. 1995. *Comparative State Feminism.* Thousand Oaks: Sage Publications.

Stoecker, Sally. 2005. "Human Trafficking: A New Challenge for Russia and the United States." In *Human Traffic and Transnational Crime: Eurasian and American Perspectives,* ed. Sally Stoecker and Louise Shelley, 13–28. New York: Rowman and Littlefield.

Stoecker, Sally, and Louise Shelley. 2005. *Human Traffic and Transnational Crime: Eurasian and American Perspectives.* New York: Rowman and Littlefield.

Suchland, Jennifer Anne. 2005. "On the Transnational Trouble with Gender: The Politics of Sexual Harassment in Russia." Ph.D. diss., Political Science, University of Texas.

Sullivan, Barbara. 2003. "Trafficking in Women: Feminism and New International Law." *International Feminist Journal of Politics* 5, no. 1 (March): 67–91.

Sundstrom, Lisa McIntosh. 2002. "Women's NGOs in Russia: Struggling from the Margins." *Demokratizatsiya* 10, no. 2 (Spring): 207–29.

———. 2006. *Funding Civil Society: Foreign Assistance and NGO Development in Russia.* Stanford, Calif.: Stanford University Press.

Tarrow, Sidney. 1994. *Power in Movement: Social Movements, Collective Action and Politics.* Cambridge: Cambridge University Press.

———. 2001. "Transnational Politics: Contention and Institution in International Politics." *Annual Review of Political Science* 4: 1–20.

Thomas, Daniel C. 2001. *The Helsinki Effect: International Norms, Human Rights, and the Demise of Communism.* Princeton, N.J.: Princeton University Press.

Tilly, Charles. 1984. *Big Structures, Large Process, Huge Comparisons.* New York: Russell Sage Foundation.

Tiuriukanova, E. V. 2005a. "Female Labor Migration Trends." In *Human Traffic and Transnational Crime: Eurasian and American Perspectives,* ed. Sally Stoecker and Louise Shelley, 95–113. New York: Rowman and Littlefield.

———. 2005b. "Zhenskaia migratsiia i torgavlia liud'mi" [Female migration and trafficking in persons]. In *Razorvat' krug molchaniia: O nasilii v otnoshenii zhenshchin [To break the circle of silence: On violence against women],* ed. N. M. Rimasheevskaia, 65–77. Moscow: URSS.

———. 2006. *Human Trafficking in the Russian Federation: Inventory and Analysis of the Current Situation and Responses* (report for the UN/IOM Working Group on Trafficking Human Beings). Moscow: UNICEF, ILO, CIDA.

Tiuriukanova, E. V., and L. D. Erokhina, eds. 2002. *Torgovliia liud'mi: Sotsio-kriminologicheskii analiz* [Trafficking in persons: Socio-criminalogical analysis]. Moscow: Academia.

———. 2004. *Prinuditel'nyi trud v sovremennoi Rossii: Nereguliruemaia migratsiia i torgovlia liud'mi.* Moscow: International Labour Organization.

Tohidi, Nayereh. 2004. "Women, Building Civil Society, and Democratization in Post-Soviet Azerbaijan." In *Post-Soviet Women Encountering Transition: Nation-Building, Economic Survival, and Civic Activism,* ed. Kathleen Kuenhast and Carol Nechemias, 149–71. Washington, D.C.: Woodrow Wilson Center Press; Baltimore: Johns Hopkins University Press.

True, Jacqui. 2003. *Gender, Globalization and Postsocialism: The Czech Republic after Communism.* New York: Columbia University Press.

Ucarer, Emek M. 1999. "Trafficking in Women: Alternate Migration or Modern Slave Trade?" In *Gender Politics in Global Governance,* ed. Mary K. Meyer and Elisabeth Prugl, 230–44. New York: Rowman and Littlefield.

UNIFEM. 2003. *Not a Minute More: Ending Violence against Women.* New York: United Nations Development Fund for Women.

United Nations. 2000. Protocol to Prevent, Suppress, and Punish Trafficking in Person, Especially Women and Children, Supplementary to the United Nations Convention against Transnational Organized Crime. New York: United Nations.

United Nations Secretary General Report. 2006. "In-depth Study on All Forms of Violence against Women." General Assembly, United Nations. A/61/122/Add.1. Available online at http://www.un.org/womenwatch/daw/vaw/SGstudyvaw.htm#more (accessed February 12, 2007).

U.S. Department of State. 1997. "Russia Country Report on Human Rights Practices for 1996." Bureau of Democracy, Human Rights, and Labor. Washington, D.C.

———. 2005. *Victims of Trafficking and Violence Protection Act of 2000: Trafficking in Persons Report.* Washington, D.C.

———. 2007. *Victims of Trafficking and Violence Protection Act of 2000: Trafficking in Persons Report.* Washington, D.C.

Vannoy, Dana, et al. 1999. *Marriages in Russia: Couples during the Economic Transition.* Westport, Conn.: Praeger.

Varbanova, Asya. 2006. *The Story behind the Numbers: Women and Employment in Central and Eastern Europe and the Western Commonwealth of Independent States.* Bratislava, Slovakia: UNIFEM.

Vargas, Virginia, and Saskia Wieringa. 1998. "The Triangle of Empowerment: Processes and Actors in the Making of Public Policy for Women." In *Women's Movements and Public Policy in Europe, Latin America, and the Caribbean,* ed. Geertje Lycklama a Nijeholt, Virginia Vargas, and Saskia Wieringa, 3–23. New York: Garland.

Watson, Peggy. 1993. "Eastern Europe's Silent Revolution: Gender." *Sociology* 27, no. 3 (Aug.): 471–87.

Wedel, Janine R. 2001. *Collision and Collusion: The Strange Case of Western Aid to Eastern Europe.* New York: St. Martin's Press.

Weldon, S. Laurel. 2002. *Protest, Policy, and the Problem of Violence against Women: A Cross-National Comparison.* Pittsburgh: University of Pittsburgh Press.

———. 2006. "Inclusion, Solidarity, and Social Movements: The Global Movement against Gender Violence." *Perspectives on Politics* 4, no. 1: 55–74.

Williams, Andrew. 2004. *EU Human Rights Policies: A Study in Irony.* Oxford: Oxford University Press.

Yuval-Davis, Nira. 1991. "The Citizenship Debate: Women, Ethnic Processes, and the State." *Feminist Review* 39: 58–68.

Zabelina, T. Iu. 1995. "Rossiiskie budni" [Russian experience]. In *Kak sozdat' krizisnyi tsentr dlia zhenshchin* [How to start a crisis center for women], ed. E. B. Israelian and T. Iu. Zabelina, 19–27. Moscow: Press-Solo.

———, ed. 2002. *Rossiia: Nasilie v sem'e—nasilie v obshchestve* [Russia: Violence in the family, violence in society]. Moscow: UNIFEM, UNFPA.

Zabelina, T. Iu., et al. 2007. *Nasilie v sem'e—nasilie v obshchestve* [Violence in the family, violence in Society]. Moscow: UNFPA.

Zippel, Kathrin S. 2006. *The Politics of Sexual Harassment: A Comparative Study of the United States, the European Union, and Germany.* New York: Cambridge University Press.

Zvinkliene, Alina. 1999. "Neo-Conservatism in Family Ideology in Lithuania: Between the West and the Former USSR." In *Women and Political Change: Perspectives from East-Central Europe,* ed. Sue Bridger. New York: St. Martin's Press.

# INDEX

of, 58, 60; geographical distribution of, *51*, 56, 67–68; global feminism and, 52–54; global-local structural framework and, *7;* hotline counseling and, 67, 148; mobilization and, 57, 68, 148; operation/organization of, 30, 50, 67; organizational autonomy and, 56–57, 65; professional vs. sister-to-sister activism, 44–45, 53–54, 56; services offered by, 56; state crisis centers, 107–108; U.S. antiprostitution initiative and, 62–63; women's crisis center movement, 49–52, *50. See also* domestic violence; shelters

Cuba, 125

cult of domesticity, 38

culture: global norms and, 74–75; as repertoires of ideas/practices, 18; violence as cultural practice, 71

Czech Republic, 34, 154

date rape, 70–71, 74, 80, *80*

debt bondage, 33

deliberative disagreements, 11

democracy assistance: crisis center movement and, 57–58, 61; effect on civil society, 6; feminist mobilization and, 68; global intervention and, 147, 150–51; overview of, 45–46

Department on the Affairs of Women, Family, and Youth, 40–41

Department on Women, Family, and Children, 108

deterritorialized ethnography, xiii

Diana center, 77, 79

Dodolev, Yevgeny, 33

Domestic Abuse Intervention Project (Duluth, Minnesota), 96

domestic rowdyism, 108

domestic violence: coordinated community projects, 111–12; criminal justice role in, 151; "domestic violence" term, xiii, 94, 97–98, 100, 101–102; effect of intervention on, *149*, 152; global norms against, 95–100; human rights monitoring of, 110; male power and, 94; media coverage of, 98–99,

101–105, *102;* in postcommunist Russia, 30–32; prosecution for rape and, 88; public awareness and, 103–105, *149;* references in U.N. documents, *160–165;* statutory reform and, 105–107, 157; U.N. condemnation of, 94; verbal violence, 103; "violence in the family" and other terms, 98, 100, *102*, 102, 107, 108–109, 154. *See also* crisis centers

donors. *See* funding

double consciousness, 100–101

Drachova, Irina, 57

Drakulic, Slavenka, 44

drinking/drunkedness, 29

economic violence: domestic violence laws and, xiii, 95; economic conditions for trafficking/prostitution, 9, 33–35, 127–28; economic empowerment programs, 129–30; poverty as influence on experience of violence, 9

ECPAT International (End Child Prostitution, Child Pornography and Trafficking of Children for Sexual Purposes), 34

Egypt, 34

Ekaterinburg, 50, 61, 112

Elman, R. Amy, 4

emotional abuse, 32

End Child Prostitution, Child Pornography and Trafficking of Children for Sexual Purposes (ECPAT International), 34

Engel, Juliette, 61–62

Engels, Friedrich, 27

Ershova, Elena, 41

ethnic groups (Russia): aversion to state/NGO resources, 64; childbearing incentive programs and, 37; Ivannikova case and, 84; Kazan antitrafficking efforts and, 65; RACCW–Women's Aid domestic violence project and, 101; unintended consequences of intervention, 157–58

European Convention on Human Rights, 77

European Union: antitrafficking initiatives, 124, 130; crisis center funding from, 61; democracy assistance study and, 6; domestic violence reform as membership requirements, 153–55; European Union Conference on Russian Civil Society, ix–x, xiii–xiv; human rights policy and, 70; sexual harassment norms and, 72

European Union Russia Center, x

Expert Council on Equal Rights and Opportunities of Men and Women, 41

FALTA, 75

familiar rape, 74, *80,* 80

Family Violence Prevention Fund (FVPF), 98

Fatima, 65–66

femicide, 32, 98. *See also* spousal homicide

Femina Borealis, 58

feminism (general): antiprostitution vs. sex-work feminism, 120–22, 128; centralized vs. decentralized states and, 4; effect of NGOs on, 46; range of de facto feminisms, *27*

feminism (Russia): accomplishments, xi–xii; antitrafficking initiatives and, 129, 134, 138–39; early post-Soviet Western activism and, 1–2; effect of financial donations, 2–3; gender neotraditionalism and, 39; marginalization of feminist discourses, 138–39; postcommunist women's movement, 40–41; professional vs. sister-to-sister activism, 53–54, 56; Soviet feminism, 26–27; support for transnational activism, 9–10; U.S. feminism compared with, 151–52; women's rights beliefs in, xii

feminism (transnational): development of transnational feminism, 18–19; status of "feminist" term, 11; women's rights beliefs in, xii. *See also* global feminist consensus

feminism (U.S.): gender violence policy and, 4; global feminist consensus and, 3; imperialism and, xii; importance to U.S. policy, 156; influence on crisis center model, 53; neoimperialist effects of, 9; Russian feminism compared with, 151–52; view of gender violence in Russia, ix

feminist comparative policy theory, 4–5, 14

feminist entrepreneurs, 94–95, *97*

feminization of poverty, 35–36

Finland, 58

Firestone, Tom, 134, 143, 145

flex organizing, 46

Focus, 58, 61

forced marriage, 32, 71

Ford Foundation: antitrafficking operations and, 128; crisis center funding by, 57–58, 61, 64; domestic violence project funding, 96, 98, 103; as global-local structural framework component, *7;* grants to gender violence activism in Russia, *59;* as postcommunist donor agency, 2

foundations: crisis center funding by, 57–58, *59;* democracy industry initiatives, 45–46; as global-local structural framework component, 7

France, 72

Franco, Marc, x

funding: antitrafficking and, 61, 68; de-funding feminism, 60–61, 149; domestic violence as effective issue for, 96; donor-feminist alliance, 43, 45, 93–94, 150, 153–54, 156–57; Fatima case study, 65–66; feminist mobilization and, 68; global feminist consensus and, 13; as global-local structural framework component, *7;* RACCW case study, 64–65; university funding, 66–67. *See also* democracy assistance; foundations; states

Funk, Nanette, 9

FVPF (Family Violence Prevention Fund), 98

GAATW (Global Alliance Against Trafficking), 121

"game" (two-level) approach, 7

gender: antitrafficking interventions and, 120, 124, 149; civil society and, 46–47; de facto feminisms and, 27; feminization of poverty, 35–36; postcommunist gender roles, 31; public/private spheres and, 20, 35; as social structure, 6–7; Soviet gender roles, 25–26. See also neotraditional gender ideology

gender neotraditionalism. See neotraditional gender ideology

Gender Plan of Action (GPA), 96

gender violence (general): culture and, 18; "gender violence" term, xiii; human rights movement recognition of, 13; as individual vs. gender issue, 17; public/private spheres and, 20; references in U.N. documents, 160–165; scholarship on, 4–5; scope/types of, 14–15; spousal homicide, 24; state responsiveness as global feminist objective, 12–13; "violence against women" term, xiii, 3, 19. See also domestic violence; rape; sexual assault

gender violence (Russia): eroticized violence in pornography, 37; statistics, 29, 32; types of violence recognized, 13

gendered global institutions, 7–8

Georgia, 34

Germany, 34

glasnost, 27

Global Alliance Against Trafficking (GAATW), 121

global feminist consensus: overview, 3–4; antitrafficking initiatives and, 121, 122–23, 127–28, 135, 138–39, 145, 156; formulation of new norms, 13–14; inclusivity as unifying theme, 19; intervention and, 145–46, 147–49, 156; mobilization as goal of, 11; stance against rape in war, 71; standards

for measurement and, 9–10; transnational networking and, 43–45; women's economic concerns and, 9

global norms. See global feminist consensus; norms

Global Survival Network, 127, 130

global-local structural framework: defined, 6–7, 7; as analytical device, 155; boomerang model, 5, 74, 146, 155; game-of-catch model, 155; inclusivity and, 19–20; MAHR "best practices" for, 22–23; multiple global/local feminisms and, 11; ping-pong model, 74, 155; political culture and, 18; unintended consequences of activism, 8, 107

Goodey, Jo, 123

Gorbachev, Mikhail, 27, 29, 40, 100

Gorshkova, I. D., 103–104

GPA (Gender Plan of Action), 96

Great Britain, 70, 76. See also Women's Aid

Greece, 34

G/TIP (Office to Monitor and Combat Trafficking in Persons), 42, 48–49, 61, 63, 124–25, 132

Helsinki effect, 148

Hemmet, Julie, 53, 54

Henderson, Sarah, 58, 60

homosexuality, 36–37, 87

honor killing, 32, 71

hooliganism, 23–24, 30, 108

How to Start a Crisis Center for Women (Kak sozdat' krizisnyi tsentr dlia zhenshchin), 53

Hughes, Donna, 62–63

human rights movement: blame-and-shame model and, 97; effectiveness of monitoring initiatives, 90–91; gender violence as concern, 13, 88–89; as global-local structural framework component, 7; Helsinki effect, 148; imperialism and, xii; International Human Rights Day, 12; legal reform and, 88; prostitution and, 121;

Optional Protocol (CEDAW), 73
Orel, xiv, 89–90
organ donation, 137
Organization for Security and Cooperation in Europe (OSCE): antitrafficking initiatives and, 123, 128, 131,
140–41; condemnation of violence
against women, 23; as global-local
structural framework component, 7
organizational membership, 46
OSCE. *See* Organization for Security
and Cooperation in Europe
OSI. *See* Open Society Institute

Paleev, Mikhail, 134
Pamfilova, Ella, 37
parafeminism, 25–27, *27*, 58, 94, 107–108,
156
Pashina, Albina, 53
patriarchy, 18
peacekeeping forces, 8
Perm, *51*, 130
Permanent Roundtable of Women's
NGOs, 41
Petrozavodsk, *51*, 61
Philip Morris Corp. (Altria), 96
ping-pong effect, 74, 155
Pisklakova, Marina, 64
Poland, 34
political opportunity structure, 6
pornography, 36
Portugal, 34
Post, Dianne, 77, 89–90, 110
postcommunism: Berlin Wall opening,
43; destabilization of leftist feminism and, 9; NGOs role in, 150–51;
privatization of gender violence,
17–18, 27–29, 34, 92; prostitution
relation with, 143; sexual liberation
and, 36–37; trafficking relationship
with, 33–35, 127–28
Powell, Colin, 134
power: "domestic violence" term and,
94; sexual harassment and, 87;
structural difference and, 6–7
power ministries, 48–49
Pozner, Vladimir, 129–30

Presbyterian Church, 56
Priiut Crisis Center (Murmansk), 52
Project Harmony, 111, 115–16
Project Kesher, 56, 130
Prokhorov, Mikhail, 146
prostitution: antiprostitution vs.
sex-work feminism, 120–22, 128;
Bush administration antiprostitution
stance, 63, 149, 152; as individual vs.
gender issue, 34; postcommunist
economy and, 33–35; transnational vs.
Russian perspective, xiii
Protocol to Prevent, Suppress and Punish trafficking in Persons, especially
Women and Children (2000), *164–165*
pseudofeminism, 27, *27*, 124, 135, 145, *149*,
150
Pskov, *51*
Psychological Crisis Center of St.
Petersburg, 62
psychology: crisis centers and, 56; gender
violence as psychological problem, 58
Public Chamber, 16
public/private spheres: domestic violence
as private issue, 104, 106; as gendered
spaces, 20; postcommunist property
laws and, 30; privatization of gender
violence, 17–18, 27–29, 34
Putin, Vladimir: acceptance of sexism,
xi, 79, 92; antitrafficking initiatives
and, 132–35; childbearing incentive
programs of, 37; consolidation of
power by, 4, 15–16, 27–28, 40, 66, 145;
gender neotraditionalism and, 39
Putnam, Robert D., 7

Qatar, 125

RACCW. *See* Russian Association of
Crisis Centers for Women
"Rainbow of Rights" series, 77
rape: crisis centers and, 54; date rape,
70–71, 74, 80, *80;* familiar rape,
74, *80*, 80; as form of violence, 80;
global norms against, 70–71, 74;
Ivannikova case, 83–84; laws on
sexual assault, 85–86, 91–92;

Saratov, xiv, 49, 51, *51,* 61, 100, 112, 130, 137, 140
Saudi Arabia, 125
Schneider, Elizabeth, 100
Security Committee, 131
self-help groups, 56
Serbia, 71
Sereda, Nataliia, 55, 66
"sex worker" term, 120–21
sexual assault: crisis center recognition of, 78–79; effect of intervention on, *149;* global feminist norms and, 69–73; as international rights concern, 88–89, 91–92; media coverage of, 79–81; reform of laws governing, 85–86, 91–92; "sexual assault" term, 70. *See also* gender violence; rape; sexual harassment
sexual autonomy, 152–53
sexual harassment, x, 24; Altai hospital case, 84–85; effect of intervention on, 152; global norms against, 72; laws on sexual compulsion, 78, 86–87, 90; localization of anti-sexual harassment activism, 77–79; media coverage of, 79–81, *80–81,* 85; in postcommunist Russia, 28, 30; references in U.N. documents, *160–165;* Russian cultural norms and, 82; "sexual overtures" term, 86; U.S. views of, 89. *See also* sexual assault
sexually transmitted disease, 87
Sharapova, Guzel', 65
shelters: battered women's movements, 94; difficulty of founding, 52; state-affiliated shelters, 109, 113–15, 143–44
Shitova, Elena, 66
Shurygina, I. I., 103–104
Sikkink, Kathryn: on "accountability politics," 112; *Activists beyond Borders* impact, 69; on the "boomerang effect," 5, 74, 146, 155; on norm implementation, 74, 118; on transnational advocacy networks, 13
simple rape, 71, 88
16 Days of Activism against Gender Violence, 12, 49–50, 76, 95, 99

smart sanctions, 126, 146
social movement theory: amplification of domestic violence norms, 100; antitrafficking norms and, 155–56; crisis centers and, 57; on global norms, 74; political opportunity structure, 6
social responsibility, xii, 157
socialism, 23–24, 43–44
South Caucuses, 157
South Korea, 34
Soviet Union: approach to gender violence, 23–25, 29; early anti-rape activism in, 76; gender roles in, 25–26; labor markets and, 33; legal theory in, 87–88; mothers' rights movement and, 48
spousal homicide, 24, 98. *See also* femicide
St. Petersburg: antitrafficking campaign in, 130; city shelter, 52–53, 109, 113–15, 143; crisis centers, 49, 53, 128; domestic violence as issue for, 98; fieldwork in, xiv; police training by, 90; RACCW affiliate in, 50; sexual assault in, 29–30; St. Petersburg conference on women's organizing (2002), x; St. Petersburg Legal Aid, *59;* transnational activism in, 148; women's organizations in, *51*
St. Petersburg Crisis Center for Women, 49, 128
states: centralized vs. decentralized states, 4–5, 17; diversion of services to NGOs, 46; global feminist norms and, 69, 146; global-local structural framework and, *7;* international law and, 73; neoliberalism and, 9, 150; responsiveness and, 12–13; state feminism, 26; strong state intervention, 119. *See also particular states*
Stop Violence Against Women campaign, 22, 91
Suchland, Jennifer, 78
Sudan, 21
Sundstrom, Lisa McIntosh, 152
Sweden, 4, 58

United Arab Emirates, 34
United Nations: antitrafficking
resolutions, 48, 120, 122–23, 131–32;
consensual documents negotiation
process, 20; gender violence monitoring in Russia, 2; as global-local
structural framework component, 7;
transnational feminism and, 18–19;
treaty compliance regulation, 21; U.S.
opposition to women's initiatives, 9;
violence-against-women stance of, 71
United Nations—Commission on the
Status of Women, xiii–xiv, 18, 21, 122
United Nations—Convention for the
Suppression of the Traffic in Persons
and of the Exploitation of the Prostitution of Others (1949), 24
United Nations—Convention on the
Elimination of All Forms of Discrimination Against Women (CEDAW):
overview, *160–163;* anti-rape activism
and, 77; antitrafficking initiatives
and, 140; compliance assessment
tool, 91; condemnation of trafficking
in, 121; domestic violence stance of,
94; human rights perspective of,
20–22; Optional Protocol to CEDAW
(1999), *164–165;* report of 1999, 90–91;
Russian compliance with, 41, 148;
sexual harassment norms and, 73;
transnational activism and, 88; U.S.
opposition to, 9
United Nations—Decade for Women, 18
United Nations—Declaration on the
Elimination of Violence Against
Women (1993), 21, 72, 77, 121, *162–163*
United Nations—Development Fund
for Women (UNIFEM), 7, 22, 95, 96,
103, 129–30
United Nations—High Commission on
Human Rights, 21, 71
United Nations—Human Rights
Council, 21
United Nations—International Confer-
ences on Women (Mexico City 1975,
Copenhagen 1980, Nairobi 1985),
18–19

United Nations—Millennium Development Goals, 23
United Nations—Security Council, 7–8
United States: antitrafficking initiative,
48, 61–63, 124, 156; First Independent
Women's Forum participation, 76;
human rights policy and, 70; prosecution for rape in, 88; sexual harassment
in, 70, 78, 89; sexual harassment
norms, 72; spousal homicide, 24; as
trafficking destination, 34; Violence
Against Women Act, 96, 151; war on
terror, 124–25
United States—Agency for International
Development (USAID): anti-sexual
violence campaigns and, 79; antitrafficking operations and, 48, 61, 62–63,
128; crisis center funding and, 58, 64,
66; de-funding feminism and, 60;
domestic violence activism and, 96,
99; as global-local structural framework component, 7; human rights
movement and, 89; International
Violence Against Women Act and,
151–52; as postcommunist donor
agency, 2
United States—Department of Justice,
141
United States—Embassy, Law Enforcement Section, 107
United States—State Department: antitrafficking intervention by, 140–41,
145; Bureau of Educational and
Cultural Affairs (ECA), 48; Bureau
of International Narcotics and Law
Enforcement Matters (INL), 111,
130–31; Country Reports on Human
Rights, 132; International Violence
Against Women Act and, 151–52;
Office of International Women's
Issues, 151; Office to Monitor and
Combat Trafficking in Persons
(G/TIP), 42, 48–49, 61, 63, 124–25,
132; as postcommunist donor agency,
2; sexual assault intervention by, 89;
sister-cities partnerships on domestic
violence, 99

university funding, 66–67
Upper Volga region, 130
USAID. *See* United States—Agency for International Development
Uzbekistan, 34

Vandenberg, Martina, 53, 77
Venezuela, 125
vernacularization (of norms): overview, 74–75, 93–98; domestic violence and, 99–101; donor-feminist alliance and, 150, 153–54, 156–57; local collaboration and, 153–54; prior local interest and, 153; trafficking norms and, 127–28
Vershbow, Alexander, 63
victimologiia, 25
Vienna Declaration and Programme for Action (United Nations, 1993), 20–21, 72, *162–163*
Vienna World Conference on Human Rights (1993), 20–21
Vikulov, Valerii, 77
Violence Against Women Act (U.S.), 96, 151
Violence Against Women Monitoring Program (Open Society Institute), 139
"violence against women" term, xiii; global feminist consensus and, 3, 19, 20–21, 70–71
Vladivostok, 130, 144

war crimes against women, 71, 81
WAVE. *See* Women Against Violence Europe
Weldon, S. Laurel, 4–5, 6
"wife beating"/"wife torture" terms, 94
Women, Law, and Development International
Women Against Violence Europe (WAVE), *7*, 57, 154
Women of Russia political movement, 37, 86, 105, 106–107, 108

Women's Aid, 64
Women's Alliance in Barnaul (Zhenskii Al'ians), *51*, 55, 65–66, 84–85, 99, 116–17, 129. *See also* Altai; Barnaul
women's crisis movement. *See* crisis centers
women's provocation theories: crisis center training and, 89–90; domestic violence and, 98–100, 104; global feminist norms and, 69; "good victim" stipulation for trafficking, 124; postcommunist theories, 31; prostitution/trafficking as individual vs. gender issue, 34, 133, 135; sexual assault prosecution and, 91–92; sexual harassment and, 78; Soviet class theories and, 25, 29
women's rights: George W. Bush use of, x–xi; human rights alignment with, 20–22, 54, 69, 77, 95; legal rights of victims of violence, 115; marriage rights, 94, 117; responsibility and, 157; right to sexual autonomy, 152–53; in Russia, xii; U.S. Supreme Court on, 151. *See also* human rights movement
Women's Rights Project (Human Rights Watch), 88–89, 125
World Health Organization, 23
World Organisation against Torture, 91, 110
World Trade Center attack, 60

Yaroslavl, 144
Yaroslavna Crisis Center, 53, 66
Yekaterinburg, *51*
Yeltsin, Boris, 27, 36, 40–41

Zavadskaia, Liudmila, 86
Zhirinovsky, Vladimir, x, 39
Zimbabwe, 21

**JANET ELISE JOHNSON**

is Associate Professor
of Political Science and Women's Studies
at Brooklyn College, City University of New York,
and editor, with Jean C. Robinson,
of *Living Gender after Communism*
(Indiana University Press, 2007).

Printed and bound by CPI Group (UK) Ltd, Croydon, CR0 4YY

13/04/2025

14656543-0003